AF654392

HANDBOOK
OF
AERIAL PHOTOGRAPHY AND INTERPRETATION

About the Author

Dr. K.K Rampal received his M.S. and Ph. D. from Ohio State University (USA) and M.Sc. and B.Sc. (Hons.) from University of Delhi. He was graduated with B.Sc. in Photogrammetric Engineering degree from the Institute of Aerial Survey and Earth Sciences, Delft, The Netherlands, with a Diploma in Photo-interpretation from the same Institute. He has several publications in national and international journals on the subject of Advanced Surveying, Photogrammetry and Remote Sensing and has supervised several sponsored and Consultancy Projects with the Government and industry houses. He has supervised several master degree thesis on the above-mentioned subjects and has attended national and international seminars. He served as Survey Officer with Survey of India from 1954 to 1963 and since then had been teaching Surveying, Photogrammetry and Remote Sensing where he was Head of Survey Division as a Professor. He was the author of three published books on Surveying and Photogrammetry mapping. He was a Visiting Professor at California State University, Fresno, U.S.A. and Asian Institute of Technology, Bangkok, Thailand. He was a fellow of the Institute of Engineers, Member of American Society of Photogrammetry and Remote Sensing, Member of Indian Society of Remote Sensing and Life Member of the Indian National Cartographic Association and Institute of Surveying (India). He was Visiting Professor at the Indian Institute of Remote Sensing, Dehra Dun for one year during 1991-92. He was a registered consultant with the Central Water Commission Govt. of India in Remote Sensing and a registered Photogrammetrist with RITES Government of India Undertaking.

HANDBOOK OF AERIAL PHOTOGRAPHY AND INTERPRETATION

K.K. RAMPAL
Ex-Professor
Indian Institute of Technology
Kanpur

CONCEPT PUBLISHING COMPANY, NEW DELHI-110059

© **Kunwar Krishan Rampal** (*b.* 1930-1996)

All rights reserved. No part of this work may be reproduced, stored, adapted, or transmitted in any form or by any means, electronic, mechanical, photocopying, micro-filming recording or otherwise, or translated in any language, without the prior written permission of the copyright owner and the publisher. The book is sold subject to the condition that it shall not, by way of trade or otherwise, be lent, resold, hired out, or otherwise circulated without the prior publisher's written consent in any form of binding or cover other than that in which it is published.

The views and opinions expressed in this book are author(s) own and the facts reported by him/her have been verified to the extent possible, and the publishers are not in anyway liable for the same.

ISBN-13: 978-81-7022-541-6 (HB)

First Published 1999

Published and Printed by

Concept
Since 1974

Concept Publishing Company Pvt. Ltd.
A/15-16, Commercial Block, Mohan Garden
New Delhi-110059 (India)
T: 25351460, 25351794, *F*: 091-11-25357109
E: publishing@conceptpub.com, W: www.conceptpub.com
Editorial Office: H-13, Bali Nagar, New Delhi-110 015, India.

PREFACE

The science of Aerial Photo Interpretation is one of the modern techniques of obtaining information about the features of the surface of the earth, both man made and natural by use of aerial photo taken by a camera placed in an aircraft at a pre-determined altitude. It forms part of one of the more wider subjects of Remote Sensing whereby information is obtained about objects at a distance through the information carrying media, that is, the electromagnetic energy as reflected or scattered by the object.

The objective of this book is to present the principles and application of black and white aerial photographs for interpretation of imagery as recorded by the aerial camera. However, before the interpreter starts using the photos, he must know about the geometry of the photos, the manner in which they are obtained and the camera characteristics.

Chapter 1 of the book deals with all about the photos and their geometry, the well known photo distortion and manner of flight design for obtaining the aerial photos with required overlapping.

Chapter 2 deals with the Aerial cameras, their types and calibration and information about the development of film and other related information.

Chapter 3 deals with Stereoscopy which is the art and science of viewing the objects in three dimensions using a pair of adjacent photos. It also discusses the simple instruments like stereoscopes and their uses.

Chapter 4 deals with Image interpretation and the techniques associated with interpretation together with the various discipline of application.

Chapter 5 describes helpful keys for interpreting certain specific objects both man made and natural. At the end of the Chapter follows a series of photos together with the description of the imagery and the nature of the objects as interpreted based on experience and the scientific principle of photo-interpretation. The imageries are from various disciplines and from various parts of the world.

Chapter 6 deals with the Satellite photography or rather imagery because the term 'photography' is restricted to lens type system. In the case of satellite imagery the picture is obtained using electro-optics based on scanning system, the ground scene being scanned bit by bit by sensors high above, generally 400 to 1000 km. or more. This chapter deals with those type of satellites which have been and are being used for taking pictures of the earth's surface. The LANDSAT system, the French SPOT system and Indian Satellite System IRS-IA and IB have been described alongwith some of the pictures taken by Space probes such as Appolo and Gemini Missions.

The author would like to acknowledge thanks to :

(i) Prof U.R. Rao Chairman ISRO and Secretary, Department of Space, Government of India (ii) Prof. B.L. Deekshatulu, Director NRSA for one year's visiting Professorship at I.I.R.S., Dehradun where the manuscript of this book was prepared.

(ii) Prof. S.K. Bhan, Head, I.I.R.S. Dehradun for the excellent library facilities of I.I.R.S.

(iv) Shri K.S. Bisht for drafting work, and

(iv) Mrs. Asha for the typing work.

Dehradun **K.K. RAMPAL**

CONTENTS

LIST OF FIGURES

LIST OF PLATES

(*Note* : See Description of Plates on Page 170)

1

INTRODUCTION

1.1 Definition

The word 'Photogrammetry' is derived from Greek words *photos, gramma* and *metron* meaning 'light' 'that which is drawn or written' and 'to measure' respectively. The word 'Photogrammetry' therefore, literally means measuring from a photograph. The universally accepted definition is 'the science of obtaining reliable measurements by means of photography in order to primarily determine geometric characteristic such as size, form and position of the photographed object.' When the measurements are of such a nature so as to give descriptive information about the photographed object the term *photo-interpretation* is used such as in geology, forestry and soil science, etc. In the earlier days, the terms photogrammetry and photo-interpretation were often used for any kind of information from an air photograph. However, in view of the vast development made in modern times, the two terms are strictly used for two different types of work. Whereas a photogrammetrist stands on his individual capacity as the one who is primarily interested in making precise measurements, a photo interpreter has to associate himself with either geology, soil science, forestry, geography or planning, etc.*

The object of photogrammetric measurements is primarily to prepare a map or a plan. This may be used for engineering purposes or for serving as a base map for the photo-interpreter. Since the aim is to make precise measurements, the instruments and techniques used by the photogrammetrist are quite refined and of a high order of precision. On the other hand a photo-interpreter needs most of the time a descriptive information unlike the photogrammetrist who is looking for metric information from the air photos. This outlook for information divides the field into two different compartments altogether. Whereas photogrammetry involves very costly equipment and considerable time to achieve a very high order of accuracy, the act of photo-interpretation requires simple and less expensive equipment and the results are obtained in a much shorter time. Due to recent developments in astronautics and 'Moon-mapping' both the fields have received considerable attention and interest.

1.2 Classification

Depending upon the position of the camera in space, photogrammetry can be divided into three classes: (i) Aerial (ii) Terrestrial and (iii) Satellite. In aerial photogrammetry the camera for taking the photographs is placed inside the aircraft which flies over the area to be mapped. When the

* The expression "Aerial survey" can be used to cover both photogrammetry and photo-interpretation. Photogrammetry is pure geometry (in space) whereas photo-interpretation is the task of drawing inferences from the qualities of photographed objects, namely, different tones of grey and black or different shades or colours in colour photography.

camera is placed on the ground and exposures made at more than one station we refer to it as terrestrial photogrammetry. The third class has come up only recently due to advances made in the science of rocketry and satellite orbiting. Photographs have been taken at great altitudes of the large portions of the earth and also that of the whole earth in which the American astronauts circled round the moon.

1.3 Aerial Photograph

The basis of all aerial mapping is the set of photographs taken by the camera placed in the aircraft. The manner in which the photographs are taken is discussed in Para 1.9. The first feature that strikes the observer when looking into an aerial photograph is that it gives a bird's eye view of the terrain as the photo has been taken from a certain height. There are three important parameters which govern the classification of aerial photographs. These are (1) the size of the photo (called the format) (2) the focal length of the camera taking the photographs, and (3) the inclination of the camera axis in space. Of these the last one is the most important. The first two are of importance in the actual act of photography and can be chosen or selected depending upon the requirement of the photogrammetric project. The inclination of the optical axis of the camera for the same values of the format and focal length can produce two types of photo, namely:

(1) Vertical Photos
(2) Tilted Photos

In the vertical photos the optical axis of the camera is in the truly vertical or very nearly vertical (within 3°) plane. As a result the plane of the negative plate or film is horizontal or very nearly horizontal. In the tilted photo the camera axis is tilted to the vertical plane. We call it a 'low oblique' when the axis is tilted appreciably and if in addition the horizon also appears in the photo, then we call it high oblique. Plate No. 1, 2, 3 and Fig. 5.2 and 5.15 these types of photos. A pair of low obliques taken in sequence along a fight in such manner that both photographs cover essentially the same area as shown in Fig. 1.1 are called 'convergent photographs'.

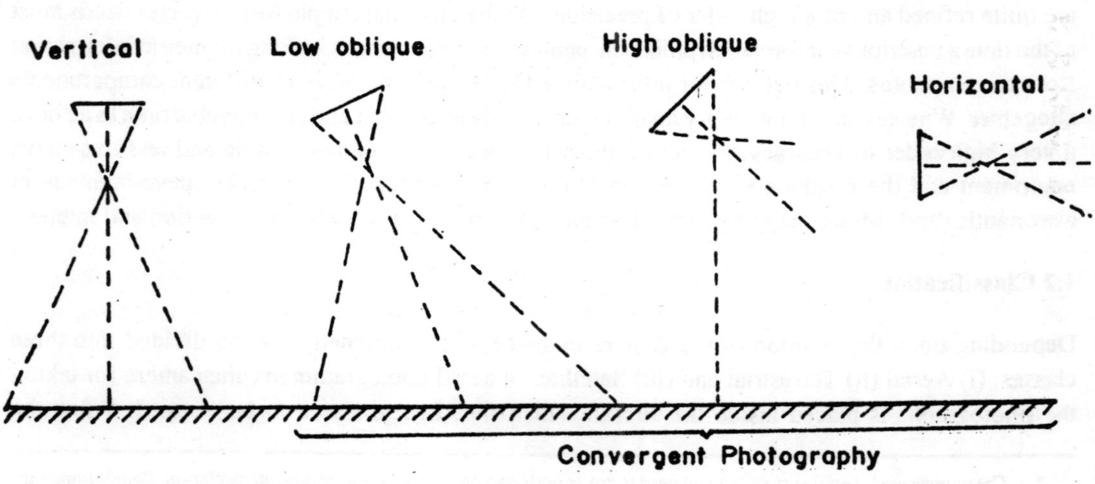

Fig 1.1 : Types of Aerial Photography

The first two parameters, namely the format and focal length which go together with the selection of a particular camera to be used, are combined to give a second category or classifications of photos. The angle subtended at the optical centre of the camera lens by the diagonal of the negative plate of the camera held at a distance equal to the focal length is a measure for classification. If this angle of the cone of the optical rays entering the lens is about 60°, we call it Normal Angle photography and 'Wide Angle' when this angle is 90° and 'Super Wide Angle' when the angle extends up to 120°. These are illustrated by means of Fig. 1.2. Table 1.1 shows the various types of lenses used, their focal length (strictly speaking 'principle distance' which will be discussed later) and the accompanying format of the negative plates or films used with the camera lens.

1.4 Difference between Map and Aerial Photograph

Since it is the object of photogrammetry to make a map out of an aerial photograph it is interesting to first find out in what way an aerial photo is different from a map. The two differ in the following ways:

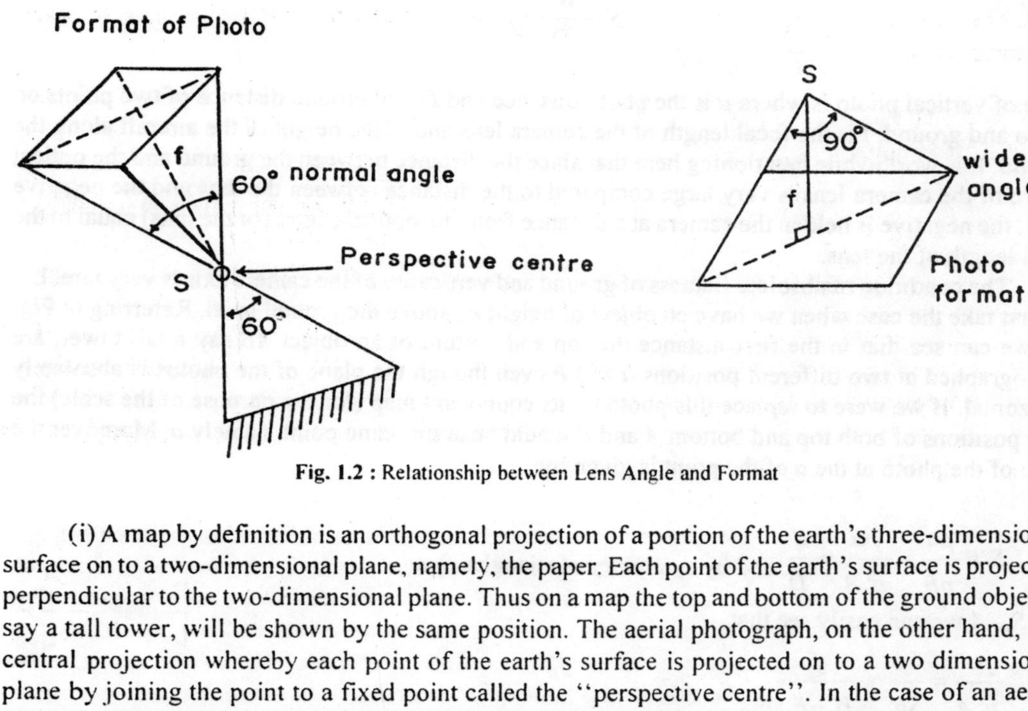

Fig. 1.2 : Relationship between Lens Angle and Format

(i) A map by definition is an orthogonal projection of a portion of the earth's three-dimensional surface on to a two-dimensional plane, namely, the paper. Each point of the earth's surface is projected perpendicular to the two-dimensional plane. Thus on a map the top and bottom of the ground objects, say a tall tower, will be shown by the same position. The aerial photograph, on the other hand, is a central projection whereby each point of the earth's surface is projected on to a two dimensional plane by joining the point to a fixed point called the "perspective centre". In the case of an aerial photo the perspective centre is the optical centre of the camera lens. The map and the air photo have one similarity that in both there is one to one correspondence of the points on the earth's surface and the map or photo position.

(ii) The usefulness of a map lies in its having a constant scale (except for maps of large areas of earth's surfaces such as in geographical maps). A map such as a project map or a topographical map is of immense help in planning and execution of an engineering project because the measured distances on a map will agree with the ground dista..ces. This is only partly true in the case of an aerial photo. Only when the ground is completely flat and level and the camera axis is truly vertical then the photo scale is constant all over the photo plane. Referring to Fig. 1.3, We can say that the

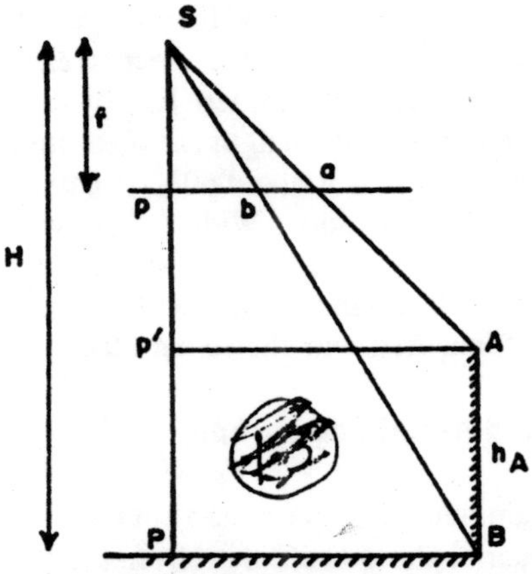

Fig 1.3 : Image Formation in Perspective Projection

$$S = \frac{d}{D} = f/H$$

scale of vertical photo is where d is the photo distance and D, the ground distance of two points on photo and ground, f is the focal length of the camera lens and H the height of the aircraft along the ground. It is worthwhile mentioning here that since the distance between the ground and the optical centre of the camera lens is very large compared to the distance between the lens and the negative plate, the negative is held in the camera at a distance from the optical centre (or the lens) equal to the focal length of the lens.

The condition of absolute flatness of ground and verticality of the camera axis is very rare. Let us first take the case when we have an object of height h_A above the ground level. Referring to Fig. 1.3 we can see that in the first instance the top and bottom of an object AB say a tall tower, are photographed at two different positions a and b even though the plane of the photos is absolutely horizontal. If we were to replace this photo by its equivalant map (for the purpose of the scale) the map positions of both top and bottom A and B would be at the same point, namely a. Moreover the scale of the photo at the a of the point is given by:

$$S = \frac{pa}{pB} = \frac{pa}{p'A} = \frac{d}{D}$$ and by symmetry of triangles Spa

and $S_{P'}A$ we can easily see that

$$\frac{pa}{p'A} = \frac{Sp}{Sp'} = \frac{f}{H - h_A}$$

Thus $S = \dfrac{f}{H - h_A}$

The scale, therefore, in a truly vertical photo, will vary according to the height of the object which is not the case in a map. In addition, if the photo is taken with a tilted camera axis even the shapes are not maintained on an aerial photo. It can be shown that a square on the ground will appear as trapezium in a photo. The displacement of point from its *true* position (map position) on a photo is known as a 'height distortion' and that due to a tilt of the camera axis, a 'tilt distortion'.

(iii) Another important factor which distinguishes a map from a photo is the amount of detail. A map shows only a selective detail, i.e. the information like roads, buildings, streams, contours, etc. which are required by the map user and that which can be depicted on that scale. In the case of an aerial photo, there is a wealth of detail. In fact whatever exists on the ground at the moment of exposure appears on the photo. The photo may, therefore, show unnecessary detail not wanted by the user. A lot of heavy detail may even render important points to be obscured and making identification more difficult.

(iv) On account of the symbolic representation there is a greater clarity of detail on a map than on a photo. On an aerial photo the objects appear in their natural form and combined with the immensity of detail can make the reading of a photo more difficult than a map.

TABLE 1.1 Type Lense Angle and Format

Name of camera	Angle of cone	Principal distance in mm	Format in mm	Remarks	Manufacturer
Russar	135°	55	180 × 180	Superwide angle	Russinow, USSR; Bertele
Supper	120°	88.5	230 × 230		Switzerland
Aviogon A Universal	90°	152	230 × 230	wide angle	-do-
Aviogon Topax	60°	210	180 × 180	normal angle	Ritcher & Kock, W. Germany
Aviotor	60°	210	180 × 180		
Pinatar	60°	210	180 × 180		Bertele, Switzerland
Lamegon	90°	115	180 × 180	wide angle	Zeiss, W. Germany

1.5 Making a Map from Air Photos

The process of making a map from an aerial photo essentially consists of elimination of the two major distortions, i.e. (i) height and (ii) tilt. In addition a few more distortions which are of second order have to be removed. These are : (iii) Lens Distortions; (iv) Film Shrinkage, and (v) Curvature and Refraction Errors.

The camera lens in practice is not a single lens but an assembly of several components to remove the lens distortions like spherical aberration, chromatic aberration, and astigmatism coma, etc. However, there are always some residual errors and these are to some extent compensated by applying corrections to the photo portions with the help of the calibration charts. The photographic emulsion also undergoes changes in dimensions by shrinking due to expansion and as a result the true position of the imaged point is displaced slightly.

Since the air has a definite coefficient of refraction (and is slightly greater than unity) a ray of light while travelling from the object space to the negative plate of the camera does not travel straight but has a curvature (the radius of curvature being almost 7 times the radius of earth). As a result the image on the negative plane is formed at a slightly different position than if the light had travelled in straight line. The linear displacement can be theoretically calculated and a correction accordingly applied.

Like all other ground survey methods transforming a photo into a map also requires ground control. However, in photogrammetry we have the advantage of supplementing additional control for air survey mapping by what is known as "Aerial Triangulation" and thus cutting down the cost of field work. However, a certain minimum ground control with a particular distribution is a must for aerial mapping.

Using the ground control and the supplementary aerial control it is the function of the photogrammetrists to correct for the defects and distortion in the aerial photo, mentioned above, select the detail which is to be shown and make a map out of it. There are several ways of achieving this and the existing methods are best illustrated by Fig. 1.4.

The detailed procedures are discussed under their respective chapters.

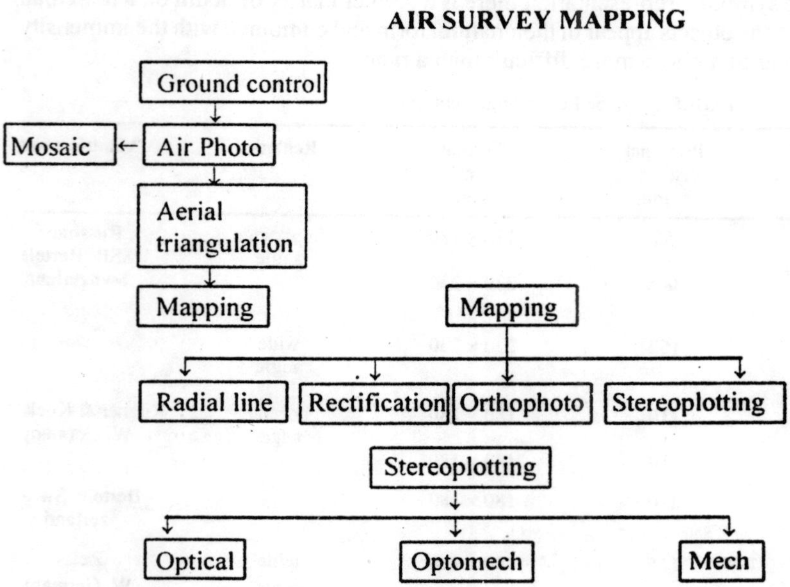

Fig. 1.4 : Air Survey Mapping Procedure

1.6 Air Survey (Photogrammetric) and Ground Surveys

Although aerial photos have to be properly combined and interpreted before a map can be made out of them, they possess distinct advantages over the conventional ground survey methods in the following ways:

(1) The cost and time are the major factors in any engineering project. From the cost point of view the aerial survey saves quite a lot of time especially when weather conditions do not permit a long duration of field work. Photographs can be taken in the few days of clear weather and mapped in the office later on.

(2) Another useful factor which saves lot of ground work is in the control density. The number of control points required for photogrammetric mapping is much less as compared to that required for ground survey. From the few ground controls available, more supplementary control can be generated by aerial triangulation techniques which are of very high accuracy. With the modern photogrammetric techniques even the ground control points can be checked for their accuracy.

(3) When the area is inaccessible such as in big desert, high mountain ranges, thickly wooded areas or enemy held positions, the photogrammetric mapping gives the only answer to the difficulties if not impossibility of ground surveys.

(4) For built up areas like big crowded cities, with heavy traffic, aerial mapping is found to be of extreme help.

(5) For revision surveys (where large changes have occurred since the last survey) it is much easier to insert or delete the detail rather than visit the ground and carry out the necessary changes.

(6) When an old survey exists and it is required to have map on a larger scale it is easier to do so from aerial photographs by direct enlargement from the negative (provided the photography is of good quality) rather than from existing ground survey maps. The change of scale, consistent with the amount of detail to be filled in is not possible in existing ground survey maps. For such large scale maps a totally new survey is required with additional great cost.

1.7 Fields of Application of Photogrammetry

Photogrammetry has been applied to the study of numerous phenomenon and is finding its applications in many fields. Some of the important fields are:

(a) Topographical Mapping: This is the field in which photogrammetry is now replacing the traditional and classical methods of ground surveys. In fact in the developed countries, the ground survey methods like plane tabling, technometric survey etc. have already become obsolete. All topographical mapping on scales 1:10,000, 1:25,000, 1,50,000, 1:100,000 and 1:250,000 are being done photogrammetrically.

(b) Geological Mapping : Air photos have been extensively used to carry out geologic interpretation and preparation of base maps. The science of photogrammetry is playing a great role in production of base maps from simple instruments, thus avoiding long field trips. Now it is possible to make a complete geological map of the area using interpretation and stereoplotting techniques. The field trip is now necessary only where information is doubtful or has to be verified.

(c) Forest Evaluation : The evaluation of forest wealth, such as for tree height, forest area, tree density combined with photo-interpretation studies such as types and classification of trees, areas of diseased and disease-free are a great help in preparing forest inventory by the photogrammetric techniques.

(d) Three-dimensional Studies: For studies of three-dimensional x-ray, architecture, structures very rapid and very slow moving phenomenon like the thermo-nuclear reaction or flight of jet and slow creep or expansion of solids are now being investigated in greater detail under the new branch of science, `Stereo-optics'. Here terrestrial photogrammetry is the major field for such investigations rather than aerial photogrammetry.

(e) Civil Works: Aerial photos are now a must for a highway engineer for the planning, alignment and execution of highway project. Similarly for telephone, telegraph, power transmission, drainage and sewerage and irrigation canals the use of aerial photos and subsequent mapping for engineering and civil project is of immense help in cutting down cost and time. The same can be said for determination of areas and volumes. The terrestrial photogrammetry (for small areas) can replace aerial photogrammetry in such cases.

(f) War-Time Studies: The whole field of photogrammetry and photo interpretation may be said to have originated with war time necessities. The aerial photographs are great spies having their eyes in the air and watching all enemy locations, movements and supply lines etc. The Second World War gave a big boost to the use of aerial photos for mapping enemy positions. Even now and for future, the aerial photography (combined with satellite photography and remote sensing) will remain the most powerful tool for strategic studies.

1.8 Geometry of Air Photos

Since an aerial photograph is a perspective view of the ground, the laws of perspective projection can be used to get the relationships between the various parameters involved in the perspective geometry. There are two cases, one when only a single photograph is involved and second, when we have a pair of consecutive photographs.

1.8.1 *Single Photo*

Figure 1.5 shows the position of a negative photo plane at the time of exposure, *S* is the perspective centre for the perspective projection which, for all geometrical considerations, is taken to be coincident with the optical centre of the camera lens. In the actual case there is no single optical centre as the camera lens consists of an assembly of lenses. However, the geometry of perspective rays is not altered so long as we assume one point for the bundle of rays to converge or emerge. If we draw a perpendicular from *S* on to the negative plane the point where this perpendicular meets the negative is called *principal point.* Similarly, if we draw a vertical line (as indicated by the direction of gravity) through *S* it will meet the photo negative, at a point called the *plumb point* (or nadir point). The bisector of the angle formed by these two lines, i.e. the vertical line and the perpendicular from the perspective centre meets the negative plane at a point called *isocentre.* It is found that three points lie on a line called the *principal line.* The plane containing the principal line and the perspective centre is called *principal plane.* It will be seen that the geometry is not changed if we hold a positive plane at a distance equal to the principal distance. Therefore for further reference we shall consider this plane called the 'positive' for geometrical considerations. It can be seen that if there is no enlargement or reduction of the photo negative then the principal distance equals the focal length of the taking camera as we know in the lens formula:

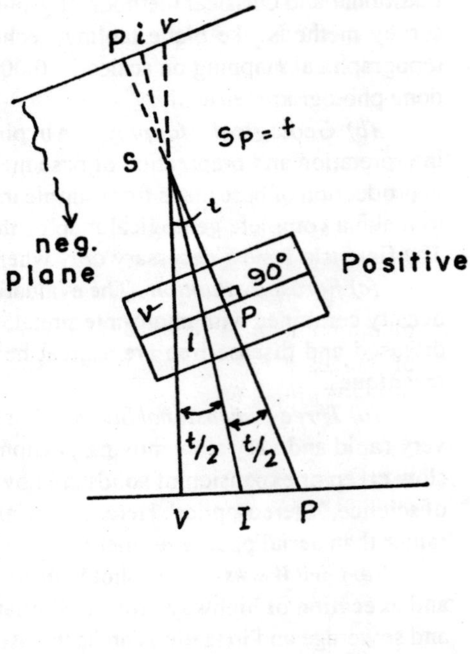

Fig. 1.5. Geometry of a Single Photo

$$\frac{1}{v}+\frac{1}{u}=1/f$$

as the distance between the lens system and the negative plane is much smaller compared to that between the ground and the camera so that $v = f$. This means we consider the ground rays to be a parallel bundle of rays as far as the image formation is considered. This, however, is not to be confused with the perspective image formulation so far as the geometry of the air photo is considered.

Figure 1.6 shows the case when there is enlargement or reduction, the principal distance is a multiple (or fraction) of the focal length. The inclination angle of the plane of the photo to the horizontal is called *tilt.*

From Fig. 1.5 we see that the following relationships hold :

$Sp = f$
$vp = f \tan t$
$ip = f \tan t/2$
$vi = f(\tan t - \tan t/2)$

The three points, namely the *principal paint*, the *isocentre* and the *plumb point* have their respective points on the ground which are obtained by extending these bundle of rays from *S* to the ground. Since corresponding to each photo point there is a ground point we call such points *homologous points.* These four points (*S, p, i. v*) constitute the most important part of the geometry of aerial photo. The plumb point owes its importance due to the fact that the height distortion increases radially from this point and the isocentre is the only point in the photo where angles measured between image points equal to those measured at the ground *isocentre* from the corresponding ground points.

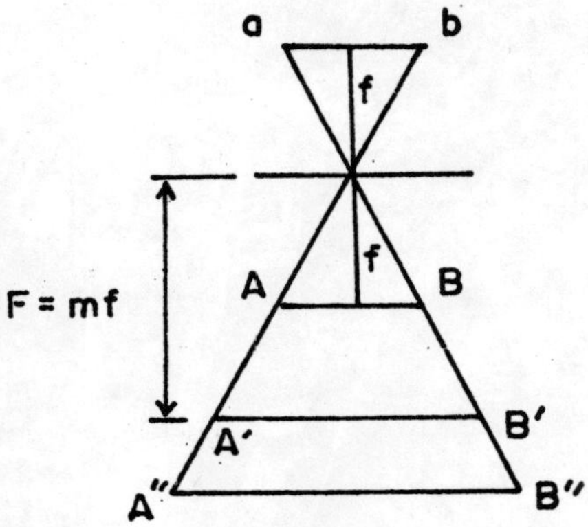

Fig. 1.6 : Principal Distance and Focal Length Relation

The principal point can be located on a photo as it is nearly the central point of the photo by joining four marks, called *Fiducial marks* at the four corners of the photograph. These marks are obtained by means of a pressure glass plate and these marks are developed on the negative during the process of photographic development. There are various kinds of marks as shown in Fig. 1.7 but those most commonly used are four cross ticks.

The other two points, namely the isocentre and the plumb point are difficult to locate. The plumb point can be located if there are tall buildings appearing in the photo. By producing the lines of images of the top and bottom it is possible to locate it (see Fig. 1.6.1). The isocentre is more difficult to locate because of the uncertainty of tilt at the time of photography. It is because of the ease of location of the principal point that it is used so much in aerial mapping by the radial line method. Joining of the four Fiducial marks does not always give the principal point and a certain amount of correction has to be applied. This is given in the calibration charts of the camera lens.

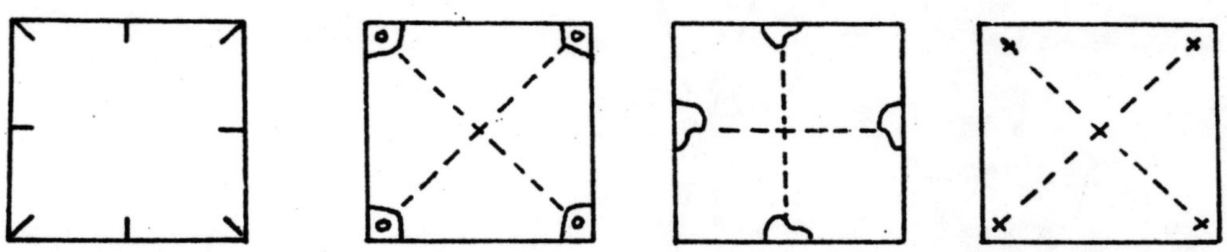

Fig. 1.7 : Fiducial Marks of an Aerial Photo

Mathematically speaking the principal point is connected by the equation for its principal distance (Fig. 1.8)

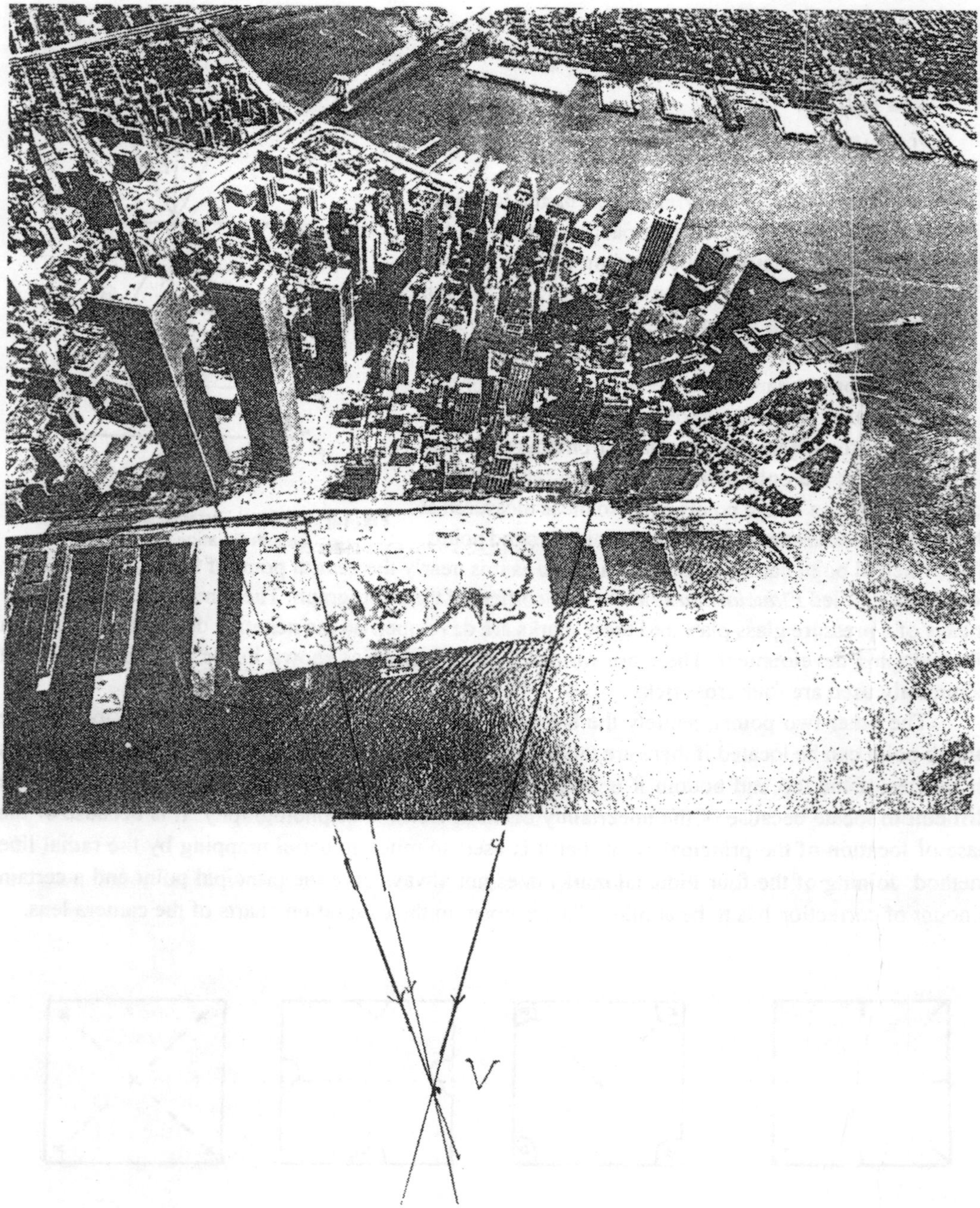

The Plumb point 'V' is obtained by intersection of lines joining the top and ground position of Tall Towns.

Fig. 1.6.1: Low-oblique Showing the Financial District of New York. (Photograph *Courtesy* of Air Photographics Inc.)

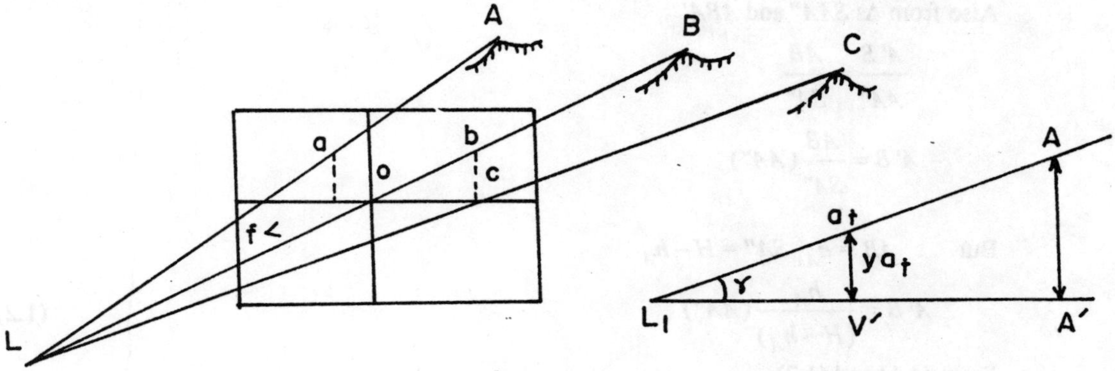

Fig. 1.8: Geometry of Terrestrial Photo

$$r = f \tan \theta$$

where r is the distance measured from the principal point to the image and θ the angle subtended by the image at the perspective centre.

1.8.2 *Height Distortion*

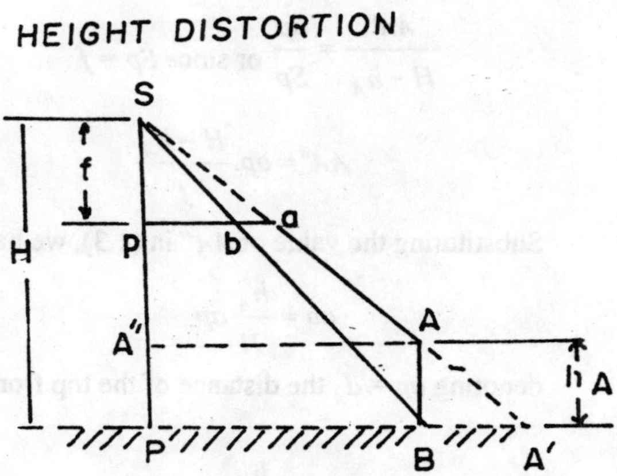

Fig. 1.9: Geometry of Height Distortion

Figure 1.9 shows how the images of a top and bottom of a ground object, say a power transmission tower or a tree, are photographed. It will be seen that the top and bottom are photographed at different places whereas a map would show them at the same position. If, similarly, high buildings are photographed the top and bottom lines will be seen to be converging to a single point in the photo. It is found that this point is the plumb point as defined earlier. This displacement of the image due to the height of the object is known as height distortion. This distortion is radial from the plumb point. By this is meant that the amount of distortion increases uniformly with the distance from the plumb points. The amount can be calculated for a photo plane which is truly horizontal as follows: Let us consider a ground object AB of height h_A. For the sake of simplicity, let us take a datum plane for this height h_A to be at the base B of the object. Referring to Fig. 1.9 we see that the images of A and B are obtained by joining these points to the perspective centre S.

Now ab = height distortion. From triangles aSB and $A'SB$

$$\frac{ab}{A'B} = \frac{Sp}{SP} = \frac{f}{H}$$

where H = height of aircraft above datum

$$\therefore \quad ab = \frac{f}{H}.A'B \tag{1.1}$$

Also from Δs *SAA"* and *ABA'*

$$\frac{A'B}{AA"} = \frac{AB}{SA"}$$

$$\therefore A'B = \frac{AB}{SA"}(AA")$$

But $\quad AB = h_A,\ SA" = H - h_A$

$$\therefore A'B = \frac{h_A}{(H - h_A)}(AA") \tag{1.2}$$

From (1.1) and (1.2)

$$ab = \frac{f}{H}\frac{h_A}{H - h_A}AA" = \frac{h_A}{H}\frac{f}{H - h_A}AA" \tag{1.3}$$

Now from Δs *SAA"* and *Sap*

$$\frac{Sp}{SA"} = \frac{ap}{AA"} \text{ or } \frac{Sp}{ap} = \frac{SA"}{AA"} = \frac{H - h_A}{AA"}$$

$$\therefore \quad \frac{AA"}{H - h_A} = \frac{ap}{Sp} \text{ or since } Sp = f$$

$$AA" = ap.\frac{H - h_A}{f}$$

Substituting the value of *AA"* in (1.3), we have

$$ab = \frac{h_A}{H}ap$$

denoting $ap = d_A$ the distance of the top from the plumb point we notice that

$$ab = \frac{h_A}{H}d_A$$

Hence, generalising this equation for any point of height on above the datum, the height distortion is given by

$$\text{Height distortion} = \frac{h}{H}.d$$

It can obviously be seen that for a point vertically below the perspective centre there is no height distortion, however high it may be. Now as we go away from the plumb point the distortion will increase, especially so near the edge of the photo. Moreover, since it is the ratio *h/H,* it will be seen that to keep distortion low, this ratio should be kept as low as possible. In practical case this is about 1/10. In this connection, we also see that if there is any object between *B* and *A* it will not be shown on the photo as it is covered by the object *AB.* The photograph may contain such areas, called "dead areas" which cannot be mapped due to their being falling in what we call 'perspective shadow zone' or 'dead' areas. This becomes quite pronounced in areas of very steep hills and valleys and very tall buildings, etc.

1.8.3 *Tilt Distortion*

When the camera axis is truly vertical so that the plane of the photo is horizontal, the images are displaced from the map position on account of the height of the objects. However, if the plane is not horizontal, but tilted, there is an additional displacement causing photographic distortion. Referring to Fig. 1.10 we see that if we have, for simplicity's sake, a flat ground then any ground point *A* is photographed at *a* in a tilted photo whereas in a vertical photo it would have been at *a'*, the horizontal plane passing through *i.* The reason of choosing *i* for this is based on the fact that *i* is the point where the tilt axis passes, tilt axis being the line perpendicular to the principal plane about which tilt takes place. This also is the only point where the angle property is true. To prove this, imagine the plane of the tilted photo to have been extended to meet the ground plane along a line *MN.*

TILT DISTORTION

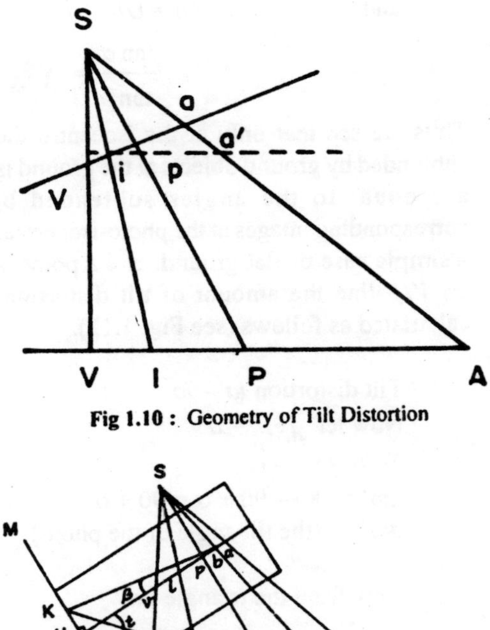

Fig 1.10 : Geometry of Tilt Distortion

Let us take a line *AB* on the ground making angle α with *VIP* line (see Fig. 1.11). Let *ab* be the photographed line and let β be the angle which *ab* makes with *vip* line. Now we shall show that the two angles α and β are equal at *I* then in the photo the same angle will be measured at *i* i.e., the shape of the ground object will be preserved at the isocentre. When two planes (photo and ground) in space intersect in line (*MN*) and a third plane cuts each of them (the principal plane) it is the fundamental property of planes in space that the traces of this third plane (*UA* and *US*) on to the two planes of projection must meet in a point of their line of intersection.

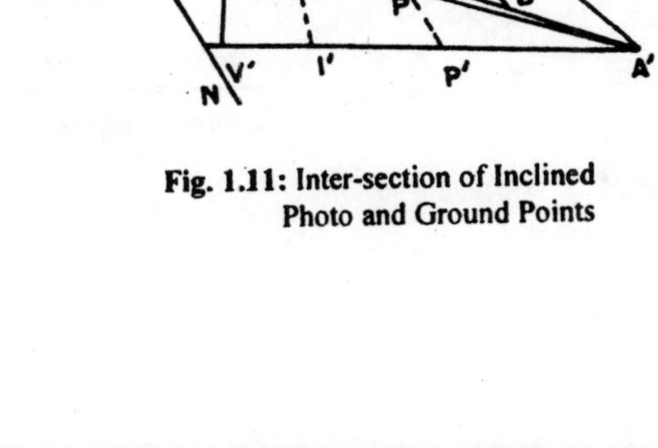

Fig. 1.11: Inter-section of Inclined Photo and Ground Points

Therefore $KUa = 90°$, $KUA = 90°$

Now $$\tan\alpha = \frac{KU}{UA}, \tan\beta = \frac{KU}{Ua}$$

$$\frac{\tan\alpha}{\tan\beta} = \frac{Ua}{UA}$$

Case (1) : Let us assume that A is coincident with P so that a is coincident with p, then

$$\frac{\tan\alpha}{\tan\beta} = \frac{Up}{UP} \quad \text{but} \quad \frac{Up}{UP} = \cos t$$

and therefore unless $t = 0$, $\alpha \neq \beta$

Case (2) : When A is coincident with V, a is coincident with p so that

$$\frac{\tan\alpha}{\tan\beta} = \frac{Uv}{UV} = \sec t$$

which again gives $\alpha \neq \beta$ unless $t = 0$

Case (3) : When A is coincident with I and `$a$' with `i' then

$$\frac{\tan\alpha}{\tan\beta} = \frac{Ui}{UI}$$

but

$$UiI = 90 - t/2$$

$$iUI = 180 - (90 - t/2) - t$$

$$= 90 - t/2$$

$$\therefore \quad UiI = UIi$$

and

$$Ui = UI$$

$$\therefore \quad \frac{\tan\alpha}{\tan\beta} = 1 \quad \therefore \alpha = \beta$$

Thus we see that only at the isocentre the angles subtended by ground objects at the ground isocentre are equal to the angles subtended by their corresponding images at the photo-isocentre. Taking a simple case of flat ground, and a point 'A' lying on VIP line the amount of tilt distortion can be calculated as follows (see Fig. 1.12).

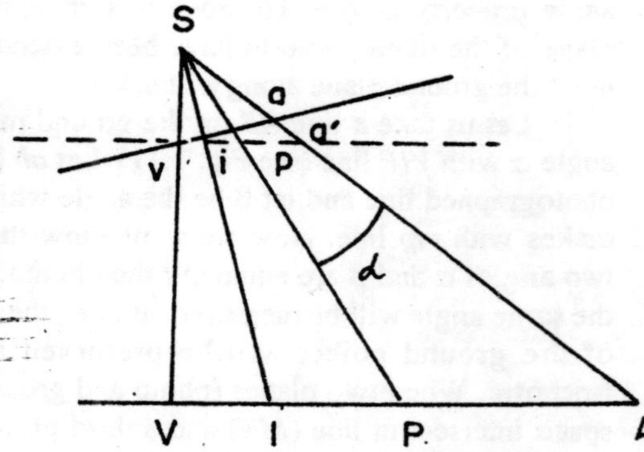

Fig. 1.12 : Tilt Distortion Illustration

Tilt distortion $ia' - ia$

Now let $A\hat{S}P = \alpha$

$Sa'p = 90 - \alpha$

$iaa' = 180 - 90 + \alpha = 90 + \alpha$

$aia' = t$ (the tilt angle of the photo)

Now from the triangle iaa'

$$\frac{ia'}{\sin(90+\alpha)} = \frac{ia}{\sin(180 - 90 + \alpha + t)}$$

$$\therefore \quad \frac{ia'}{\cos\alpha} = \frac{ia}{\cos(\alpha + t)}$$

here $$\tan\alpha = \frac{ap}{sp}$$

$$= \frac{ia - ip}{Sp}$$

but $Sp = f$ and $ip = Sp\tan(t/2)$ because $p\hat{S}i = t/2$

$$\therefore \quad \tan\alpha = \frac{ia - f\tan(t/2)}{f}$$

$$\therefore \quad ia' = \frac{ia'f}{f\cos t - ia\sin t + f\tan t/2}.\sin t$$

On further simplification this reduces to

$$\frac{ia'f}{f - ia\sin t}$$

or $$= \frac{ia'}{ia} = \frac{f}{f - ia\sin t}$$

$$\therefore \quad \frac{ia' - ia}{ia} = \frac{ia.\sin t}{f - ia\sin t}$$

$$\therefore \quad ia' - ia = \frac{(ia)^2.\sin t}{f - ia\sin t}$$

Therefore $$ia' - ia = \frac{(ia)^2\sin t}{f - ia\sin t}$$

It is easy to show that for a point *B* to the left of the ground isocentre *I*, the tilt distortion will be,

$$\frac{(ia)^2\sin t}{f + ia\sin t}$$

Hence we get that tilt distortion (T.D.)

$$T.D. = \frac{d^2\sin t}{f \pm d\sin t}$$

where *d* is the distance of the image from the isocentre. So far we have considered the point *a* on the *vip* line. For any point off the *vip* line tilt distortion can be obtained as follows: Let θ be the angle that line *ib* makes with *vip* line. Then the projection of *ib* on *vip* line is *ib* cos θ.

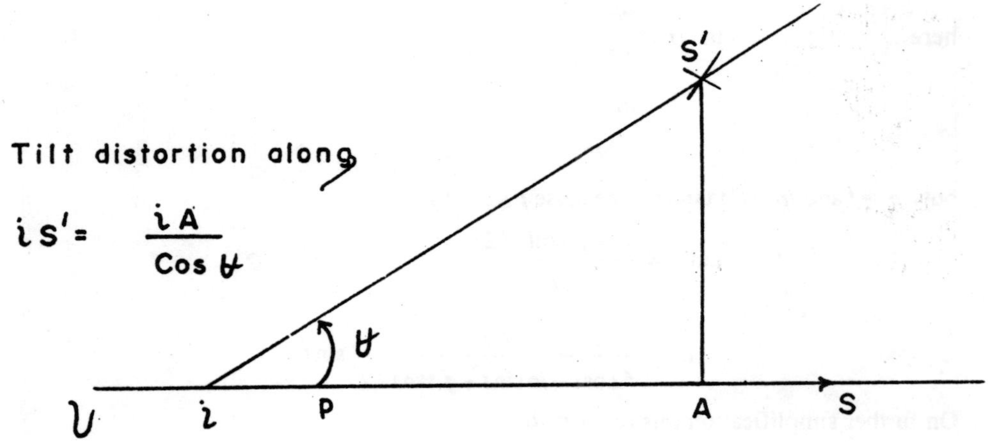

Fig. 1.13 : Components of Tilt Distortion Along Actual Line (a) and Along Axis (b)

Hence tilt distortion for the projection of this line (substituting this in equation for tilt distortion)

$$\text{T.D.} = \frac{(ib)^2 \cos^2\theta \sin}{f \pm (ib\cos\theta)\sin t} \text{ along } ia$$

To get the tilt distortion along the *ib* line we notice that $\frac{TD}{\cos\theta}$ is the required value (see Fig. 1.13)

$$\text{Hence for the line } ib \text{ T.D.} = \frac{(ib)^2 \cos\theta \sin t}{f \pm (ib\cos\theta)\sin t}$$

again if we put $ib = d$

$ib \cos\theta = ia$

$$\text{T.D.} = \frac{d^2 \sin t}{f \pm ia \sin t} \cos\theta$$

Therefore T.D. is maximum when $\theta = 0$ and zero when $\theta = 90°$. Thus for any image point which lies on a line perpendicular to *vip* line through *i*, there is no effect of tilt. For all points lying on *vip* line the effect of tilt is maximum. This line where the effect of tilt is zero is called Isoline and lines parallel to isoline called Isometric parallel or plate parallels.

A flat square *ABCD* (see Fig. 1.14) of side *d* will be photographed as a square *abcd* of side say *d* on a truly vertical photograph. But on a tilted photo only the line directly under the Isoline will be photographed true to scale of side *d*. But that portion of square say *BC* which is to the right will have smaller tilt distortion (because $d^2 \sin t/f + d \sin t$) and the other side *AD* will have larger distortion because of $d^2 \cdot \sin t/f - d \sin t$ on the negative and therefore on the positive the reverse of it.

The net result will be that due to tilt alone a square will appear as a trapezium on the photo causing distortion of shapes of ground objects. One way to remove this distortion is to rectify the tilted photo so as to get back the original square. The distortion of a square into a trapezium can also

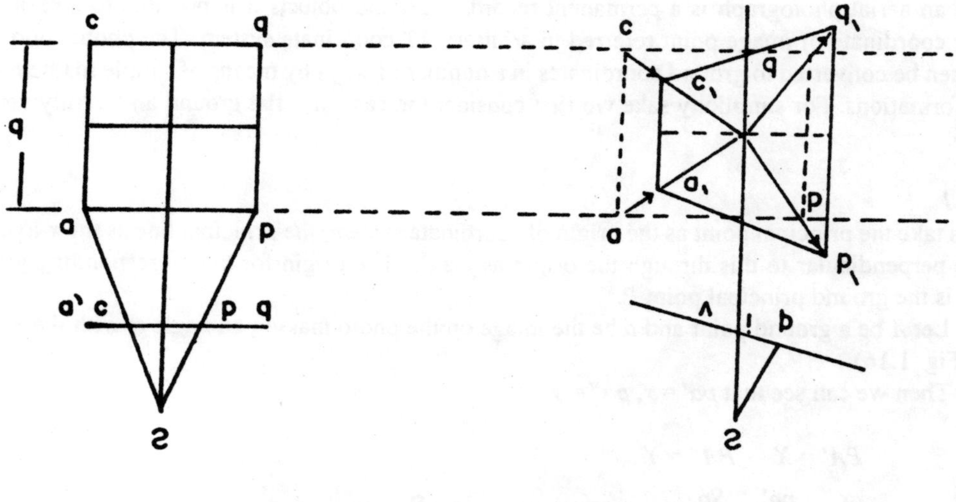

Fig. 1.14 : Distortion of a Square Into Trapezoid by Tilt

be seen by examining the tilted photo scales along the plate parallel.

For the scale along the isometric parallels we notice that (see Fig. 1.15):

$$\text{Scale} = \frac{Sp}{SP} = \frac{f}{H \sec t} = \frac{f}{H} \cos t$$

along an isometric parallel through the principal point.

$$\text{Scale} = \frac{Sv}{SV} = \frac{f \sec t}{H}$$

for an isometric parallel through the plumb point and similarly

$$\text{Scale} = \frac{Si}{SI} = \frac{f \sec t/2}{H \sec t/2} = f/H$$

Scale = f/H is scale through the isocentre and is constant.

Thus the scale along the plate parallel through the isocentre of a tilted photograph is the same as that over the whole surface of a vertical photograph if the ground surface is plane. For any other plate parallel not passing through *i* the scale variation will depend upon the angle of tilt *t*.

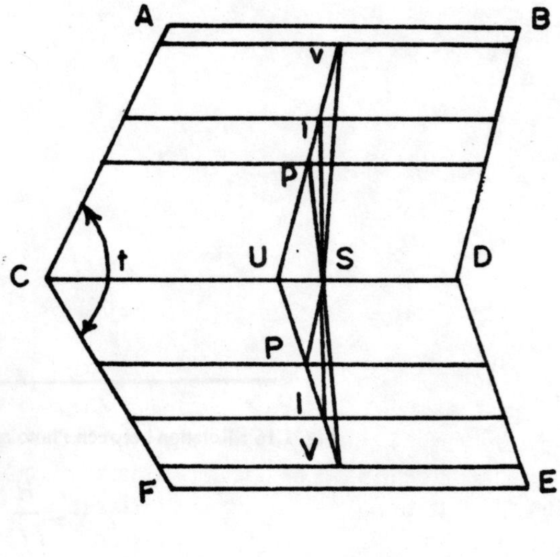

Fig. 1.15 : Illustrating Photo and Ground Points

1.8.4 *Relationship between Ground and Photo Coordinates*

Since an aerial photograph is a permanent record of ground objects it is possible to measure the linear coordinate of image point referred to arbitrary *XY* coordinate system. The photo coordinate can then be converted to ground coordinates in a number of ways by means of simple mathematical transformations. For simplicity sake we first consider the case of a flat ground and a truly vertical photo.

Case 1

Let us take the principal point as the origin of coordinate system, the principal line as the *x*-axis and a line perpendicular to this through the origin as *y*-axis. The origin for the corresponding ground point is the ground principal point *P*.

Let *A* be a ground point and *a* be the image on the photo making an angle α with the *X* axis. (See Fig. 1.16)

Then we can see that $pa' = x,\ pa'' = y$

$$PA' = X \qquad PA'' = Y$$

and $$\frac{x}{X} = \frac{pa'}{PA} = \frac{Sp}{SP} = f/H$$

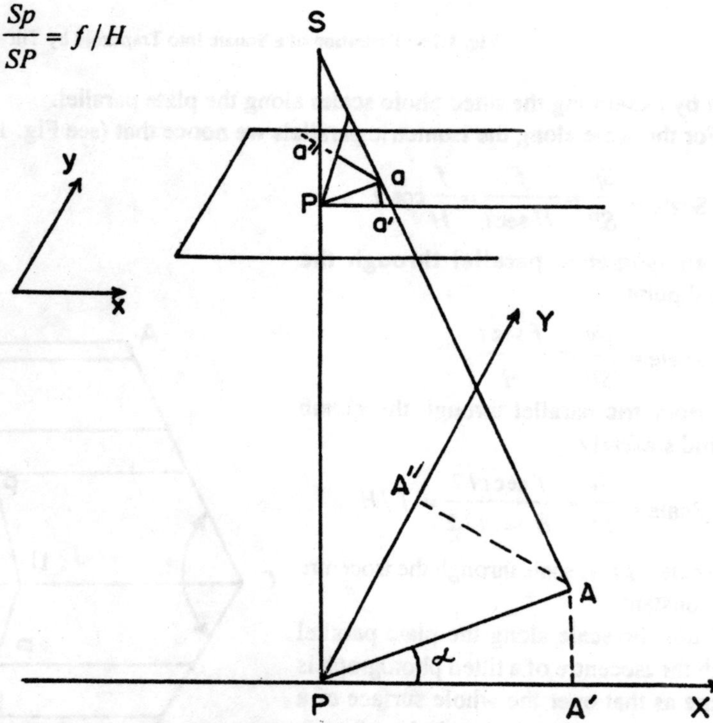

Fig. 1.16 : Relation between Photo and Ground Coordinated Axis

$$X = \frac{H}{f}.x$$

But $\frac{H}{f} = \frac{I}{S}$ where *S* is the scale of a truly flat area photo. Therefore $X_A = x_a/S$

$$\text{Similarly } Y_A = \frac{y_a}{S'} \text{ and for a point } B, = X_B = \frac{X_b}{S}$$

$$Y_B = \frac{Y_b}{S}$$

$$\text{Distance on the ground } D = \sqrt{(X_A - X_B)^2 + (Y_A - Y_B)^2}$$

$$\text{Distance on the photo} = \sqrt{(x_a - x_b)^2 + (y_a - y_b)^2}$$

$$\text{Therefore scale of photo} = \sqrt{\frac{(x_a - x_b)^2 + (y_a - y_b)^2}{(X_A - Y_B)^2 + (Y_A - Y_B)^2}}$$

Case II

When the photo is tilted and the principal point is the origin and ground considered flat.

Let *a* be the image of ground point *A* (see Fig. 1.17). From *A* draw *AA'* perpendicular to *VP* line so that—

$$PA' = X$$
$$aa' = y$$
$$AA' = Y$$

Let $PSA' = \alpha$

Now $x = pa = Sp \tan\alpha \because Sp$ is perpendicular to $vpa' = f\tan\alpha$

$$\text{and } \frac{y}{Y} = \frac{aa'}{AA'} = \frac{Sa'}{SA'} = \frac{sp\sec\alpha}{SV\sec(t+\alpha)} = \frac{f\sec\alpha}{H\sec(\alpha+t)}$$

$$\text{and } \tan(\alpha+t)\frac{VA'}{SV} = \frac{VP+PA'}{SV} = \frac{H\tan t + X}{H}$$

$$\text{Thus we have } \tan\alpha = \frac{x}{f}$$

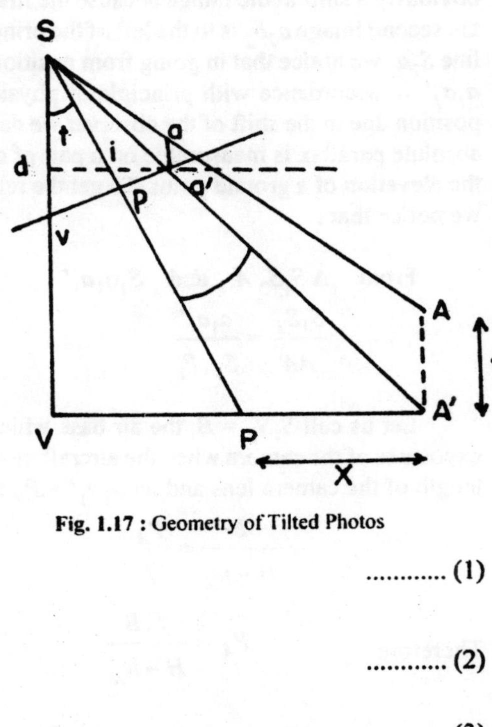

Fig. 1.17 : Geometry of Tilted Photos

or
$$\alpha = \tan^{-1}\frac{x}{f} \qquad \text{.........(1)}$$

$$X = H\tan(\alpha + t) - H\tan t$$
$$= H\{\tan(\alpha + t) - \tan t\} \qquad \text{.........(2)}$$

$$Y = \frac{H\sec(\alpha + t)}{f\sec\alpha}.y \qquad \text{.........(3)}$$

These are the required relations between the photo coordinates and ground coordinates. When the ground is not flat the relations become more complicated as the scale varies according to the height of the point.

1.8.5 *Geometry of Two Overlapping Photographs*

1.8.5.1 *Height Difference*

Though a single photograph is a complete record of the ground covered and can be used for measurement of coordinates of the ground object it is not sufficient to record the third dimension, i.e. the height of the object. For this we need a second photograph in which the same ground has been photographed but from a different angle or viewpoint. Referring to Fig. 1.18 we notice that an object—

AA' of height h_A above ground appears photographed as a_1b_1 in the left photo with S_1 as the perspective centre.

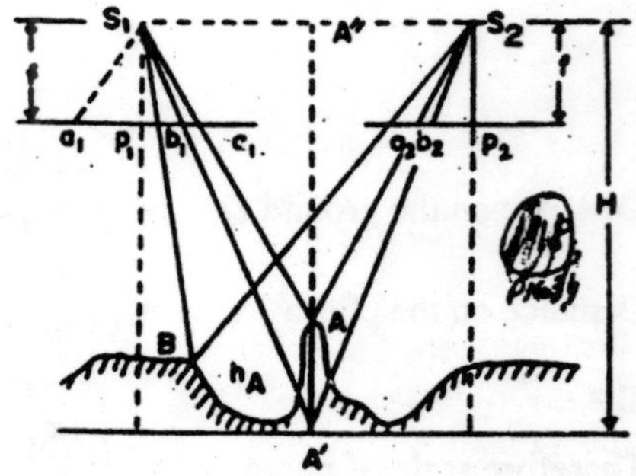

Fig. 1.18 : Geometry of Two Photos

But when the aircraft flies to a position S_2 the same object AA' appears as a_2b_2. There is obviously a shift in the image because the first image a_1b_1 is to the right of the principal point p_1 and the second image a_2b_2 is to the left of the principal point p_2. Thus if we draw a line S_1a' parallel to the line S_2a_2 we notice that in going from position S_1 to S_2 the image of A has been shifted by an amount a_1a_1'. In accordance with principle of physics where parallax is defined as the shift in the image position due to the shift of the observer we define a_1a_1' as the *Absolute Photographic Parallax*. This absolute parallax is measurable on a pair of consecutive photographs and can be used to determine the elevation of a ground point. To get the relationship between the absolute parallax and the height we notice that :

From ΔS_1S_2A and $S_1a_1a_1'$

$$\frac{S_1S_2}{AA'} = \frac{a_1a_1'}{S_1, P_1}$$

Let us call $S_1S_2 = B$, the air base which is the distance in space between the two successive exposures of the camera when the aircraft moves from 1st to 2nd exposure station, $S_1P_1 = f$, the focal length of the camera lens and let $a_1a_1' = P_A$ the absolute parallax of the point A then

$$\frac{B}{H-h_A} = \frac{P_A}{f}$$

Therefore $$P_A = \frac{f.B}{H-h_A}$$

Similarly for a point B, we have $P_B = \dfrac{f_B}{H-h_B}$

Since we are generally interested in the difference of heights we define a similar term as *Parallax difference* which is the difference of parallax of a fixed or reference point and any other point. In the above example if we take B as the fixed or reference point as the datum for measurement of height, then

$$P_A - P_B = \Delta p$$

is the parallax difference and accordingly.

$$\Delta p = P_A - P_B = fB\left(\frac{1}{H-h_A} - \frac{1}{H-h_B}\right)$$

This is the basic equation connecting the parallax difference and the height of two points *A* and *B*. If the height of one of the points is known, the height of the second point can be determined from the above equation when the other parameters like *f*, *H* and *B* are known.

In deriving the above expression we have assumed that the height of the aircraft *H* above the ground does not change and also that there is no tilt, i.e. two consecutive photographs are in horizontal positions. Under such circumstances the line joining the two image positions, that is, $a_1\,a_2$ will be parallel to the direction of flight p_1p_2. However, in practical case this is seldom the case. Due to tilt and the inclination of the air base (due to change of aircraft height) the line a_1a_2 will be found slightly inclined to the air base. For calculating the height of the object we have to ensure that we take only the component parallel to the direction of flight. The component of parallax perpendicular to the direction of flight is known as *Y*-parallax

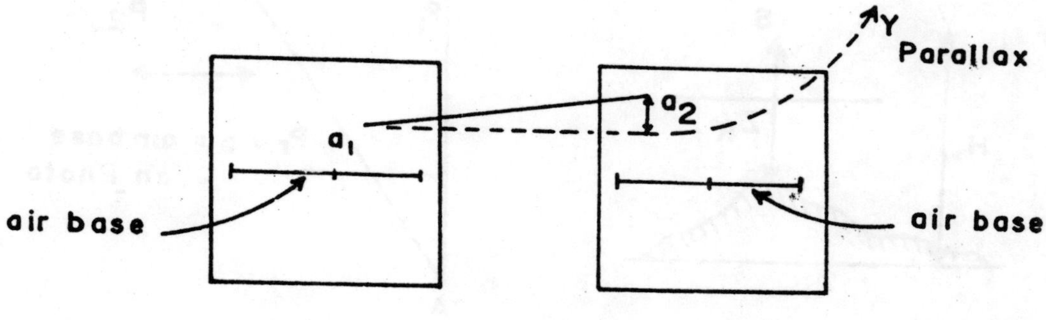

Fig. 1.19: Parallax in Two Overlapping Photos

Equation for Δp can also be written in the following way:

Let $\Delta h = h_A - h_B$

$\Delta p = p_A - p_B$

$$\Delta p = fB\left[\frac{1}{H-h_A} - \frac{1}{H-h_B}\right] = \frac{fB(h_A - h_B)}{(H-h_A)(H-h_B)}$$

but

$$p_B = \frac{fB}{H-h_B}$$

$$\Delta p = \frac{p_B(\Delta h)}{(H-h_A)}$$

$$\Delta h = (H - h_A)\frac{\Delta p}{P_B}, P_B = p_A + \Delta p$$

$$\Delta h = \frac{(H - h_A)\Delta p}{p_A + \Delta p}$$

If we take A as the reference point for measurement of parallax as well as for height, then $(H - h_A)$ is the height of the aircraft above the reference point. Let $H - h_A = Z$ so that

$$h_{AB} = \frac{Z.\Delta p}{p_A + \Delta p}$$

Normally it is the practice to use the left hand principal point p_1 as the reference point and in that case it is easy to show for the diagram (See Figs. 1.19, 1.20 and 1.21) that $P_A = P_R = b$ the air base as measured on the right hand photo.

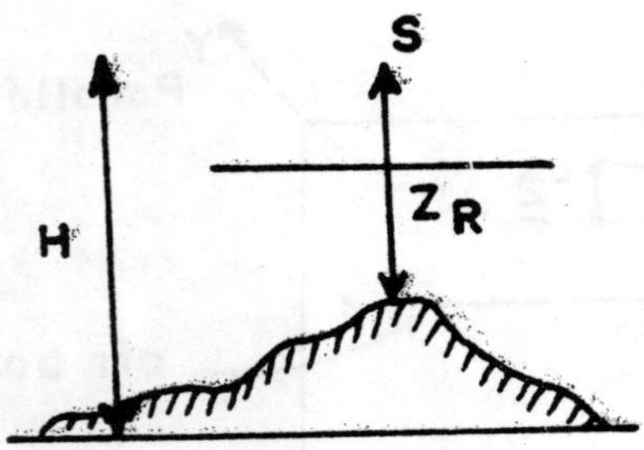

Fig. 1.20 : Reference Point for Height

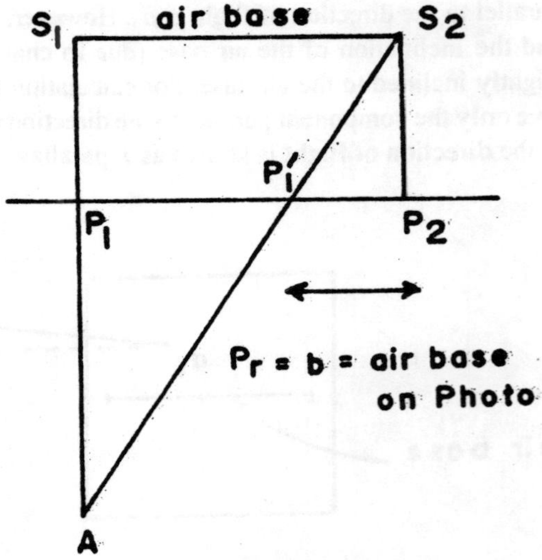

Fig. 1.21 : Ground Distance

$$\Delta h = \frac{Z_R.\Delta p}{P_R + \Delta p}$$

or $$\Delta h = \frac{Z_R.\Delta p}{P_R + \Delta p}$$

This is the exact expression for the determination of height of any point B above the reference point which is the left hand principle point of the photo.

1.8.5.2 *Determination of Height*

The parallax difference is obtained by a simple instrument called *Parallax Bar*. It consists of two small glass plates attached to a bar. The glass plates carry two small dots marked on them. The

distance between these two dots can be changed by means of a micrometer and the changes read in terms of millimeters. The bar has one scale for direct reading in millimeters and a circular vernier in the form of micrometer head to read fraction of a millimeter (see Fig. 1.22).

The two black dots are also known as `floating marks' for the simple reason that when these two dots are seen under a stereoscope so as to be fused into one, they appear to be floating in space. To measure the height of an unknown point from a pair of photos the principal points of the two photos are transferred to the corresponding photo and then joined by lines. A line is then drawn on flat surface, say a drawing sheet on a table, and the pair of photos so placed as to have their principal points on this line.

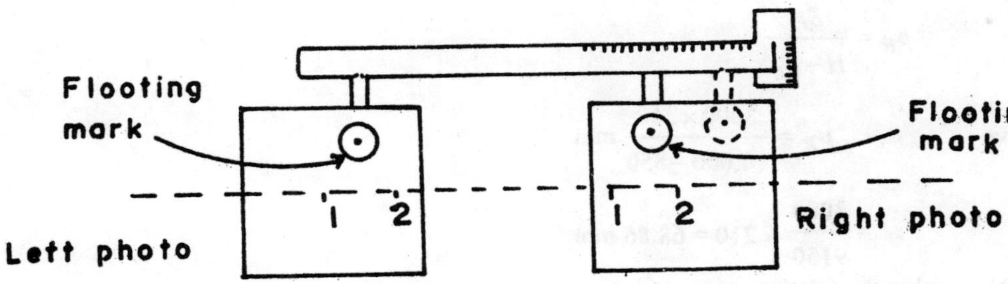

Fig. 1.22: Micrometer Parallax Bar

The photos are then moved along these lines so as to have stereoscopic fusion (see chapter on Stereoscopy) of the two images of the known points or the reference point whose ground height is known. The parallax bar is next so placed that the left black dot or the floating mark is on the detail say a 'road junction' whose ground height is known and the right hand floating mark on the corresponding image in the right hand photo (see Fig. 1.22). To measure the component of parallax parallel to the flight direction, the parallax bar is so placed that it is parallel to the line joining the principal points of the two photos. Moreover the placing of the two floating marks on the corresponding image points must be done stereoscopically. It will be seen that when one of the floating marks, say the right one, is not exactly over the right image but slightly away from it, the two floating marks, when seen through a stereoscope as `one' floating mark, will appear to be at a different elevation than that of the ground point either higher or below. Only when the two floating marks are exactly over the corresponding identical image points that the floating mark will appear at the same elevation as the image point of the stereoscopic three-dimensional model. Before any readings are taken it is ensured that the two photos are not disturbed while moving the micrometer to change the distance between the two floating marks for getting stereoscopic fusion. The photos should be giving firmly held down by weights or adhesive tapes. The readings of the parallax bar are noted for the point of known height and also for those whose heights are required.

There are two ways by which the height can be computed. In some cases the air bases B is given directly and in some cases the air base b is measured on the photographs. Either way the same results are obtained. This is clear from the following examples.

Example 1

From the following data and observations compute the height of two points 1 and 2:

$B = 3000$ ft., $H = 10{,}000$ ft., $f = 210$ mm

Point	*Ground elevation*	*Micrometer reading*
B.M.	850 ft	15.48 mm
1.	Required?	16.03 mm
2.	Required?	13.22 mm

For point 1 we see that

$$\Delta p = 16.03 - 15.48 = 0.55 \text{ mm}$$

Using the relation

$$p_R = \frac{Bf}{H - h_R}$$

we have

$$p_R = \frac{3000 \times 210}{10{,}000 - 850} \text{ mm}$$

$$= \frac{3000}{9150} \times 210 = 68.86 \text{ mm}$$

Now using the relation

$$\Delta h = \frac{Z_R \times \Delta p}{p_R + \Delta p}$$

Since $Z_R = 10{,}000 - 850 = 9150$ ft

$\Delta p = +\,0.55$ mm

$p_R = 68.86$ mm

$$\therefore \quad \Delta h = 9150 \times \frac{0.55}{68.86 + 0.55} = \frac{9150 \times 0.55}{69.41} = +\,72.5 \text{ ft}$$

Hence height of point no. 1 = 850 + 72.5 = 922.5 ft.

For point 2 is$\Delta p = 13.22 - 15.48 = -\,2.26$ mm

$$\therefore \quad \Delta h = -\,9150 \times \frac{2.26}{68.86 - 2.26} = 9150 \times \frac{2.26}{66.60} = -310.5$$

$$= -\,310.5 \text{ ft.}$$

Therefore height of point '2' = 850 – 310.5 = 539.5 ft.

Example 2

The following are the observations and data for height determination :

Air base = 90 mm

Focal length = 12"

H = 10,000 ft above mean sea level

Level of C point = 327 ft above mean sea level

Parallax reading for $C = 10.71$ mm
Parallax reading for $A = 12.47$ mm
Find the length of A above mean sea level.
For solution of the problem we note that:

$$\Delta p = 12.47 - 10.71 = +1.76 \text{ mm}$$
$$Z_R = 10{,}000 - 327 = 9673 \text{ ft}$$
$$\therefore \quad \Delta h = 9673 \times \frac{1.76}{90 + 1.76} = 9673 \times \frac{1.76}{91.76}$$
$$= 185.5 \text{ ft}$$

$\therefore$ Height of A above mean sea level
$= 327 + 185.5 = 512.5$ ft

Sometimes a different instrument called 'stereocomparator' is used to determine the x parallax. The instrument consists of two carriages, the left and right one over which the left and right photos are placed. A stereoscope is also fitted over them and the photographs can be moved by the carriages along the direction of flight which is termed as x axis. As usual there are two floating marks attached to the two carriages. Here instead of reading the parallax the x and y coordinate of image points for the left and right photograph can be determined with reference to the principal points as the origins or some other arbitrary origin. Thus each point will have $x_L\, y_L$ (left photo) and $x_R'\, y_R$ (right photo). Sometimes we may use a 'mono comparator' where a single photo is used for recording coordinates. This system of using the mono or stereocomparator can enable us to determine the absolute parallax as the sum (with proper signs) of the x parallaxes. For determination of the sign of x, readings to the right of the principal point are taken as positive (+ve) and those to the left as negative (–ve). This will be clear from the following example where a mono comparator has been used.

	Photo left	*Photo Right*
x-coordinate from principal point to the top of tower,	= + 89.5 mm	= + 37.2 mm
x-coordinate of bottom of tower from P.P.	= + 84.1 mm	= + 35.0 mm

Focal length = 507 mm; Air base = 780 ft.

H above datum = 8100

Base of the tower is at datum level.

Solution :

Here Absolute parallax p for the top = 89.5–37.2 (See Fig. 1.23)
= 52.3 mm

Absolute parallax p for bottom = 84.1–35.0 = 49.1 mm

Now $p_R = \dfrac{B.f}{H-h_A}$ (since $h_A = 0$)

$$p_R = \frac{B.f}{H} = \frac{780}{8100} \times 507 = 48.82\,mm \text{ since } h_A = 0$$

$$Z_R = H$$

$$\therefore \quad h_R = h_A = \frac{8100 \times 3.2}{48.82 + 3.2} = 8100 \times \frac{3.2}{52.02}\text{ ft} = 495.6 \text{ ft.}$$

Hence the height of the top of the tower above datum=495.6 ft.

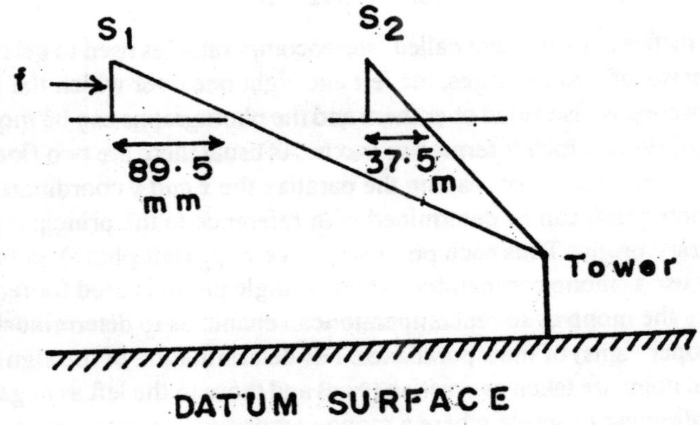

Fig. 1.23 : Height Determination of a Tower

1.9 Flight Planning and Design

1.9.1 *Introduction*

In order to compare the cost of ground surveys and that of aerial surveys it is necessary to estimate the cost of flying and aerial mapping. The estimates can be obtained if we know:

(i) Total number of photographs required to cover the area
(ii) Total flight time
(iii) Scale of photography
(iv) Type of photographs
(v) External factors like weather, etc.

1.9.2 *Number of Photographs*

In the first instance this depends upon the manner of flight. It also depends upon the forward overlap, lateral overlap and the external shape of the area. For a rectangular area it is easy to plan the direction of flight, flying being parallel to the longer sides. However, for hilly areas and irregular shape, planning is much more difficult. Let us take a simple case of an area, say *L* miles in length and *W* miles in width which is to be covered by flying parallel to L side, say from West to East. Referring to Fig. 1.24 we notice that in order to have overlaps in the two adjacent photographs the two exposures of the camera at the two instants in space at S_1 and S_2 (called exposure station) must be properly timed. This depends upon a number of factors, namely the percentage overlap, the speed of the aircraft, etc.

It can be seen from the Fig. 1.25 that the total number N, required to cover the area is given by N = Number of exposures in one strip × number of strips = $n \times m$.

Let us first work out the number of exposures (i.e., the number of photos in one strip).

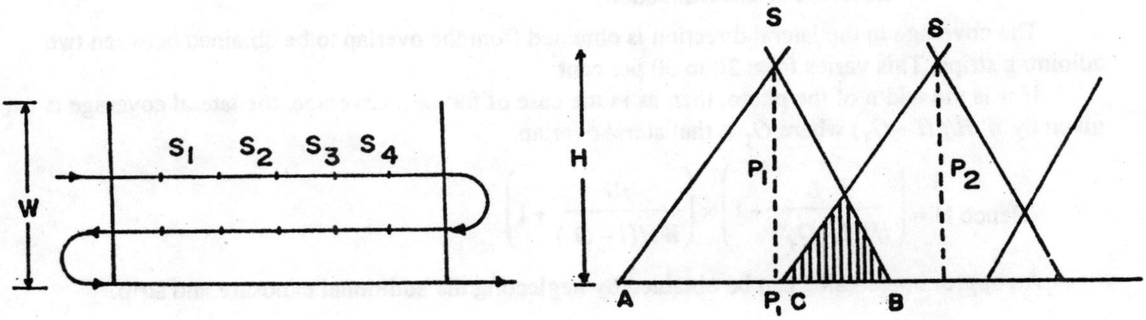

Fig 1.24: Flight lines East–West

Now $n = \dfrac{L}{S_1 S_2}$ assuming the exposure interval to be equal through the strip.

$S_1S_2 = AC$ $\quad S_2 C$ is parallel to S_1A in Fig. 1.24

$= AB - BC$

Now $BC = O_f \times AB$ where O_f is a fraction indicating the forward overlap, i.e. length common to two photographs.

and if f = the principal distance of the camera lens

$= S_1p_1$ = focal length of the camera lens.

Then we can see that if l is the length of the photographic plate on film, then

$$\frac{ab}{AB} = \frac{S_1 p_1}{S_1 P_1} \quad \text{or} \quad \frac{l}{AB} = \frac{f}{H}$$

$$AB = \frac{lH}{f}$$

Substituting the value of AB above, we get

$$S_1S_2 = AB - BC = AB - AB.O_f$$

$$= AB\,(l - O_f)$$

$$= \frac{lH}{f}(l - O_f)$$

Therefore $n = \frac{Lf}{S_1S_2} = \frac{Lf}{lH(l - O_f)}$

However to ensure complete coverage over the edge at least one more exposure is made for the photo and one extra strip is flown.

So that $N = (n + 1)(m + 1)$.

To calculate m, we notice that

$$m = \frac{W}{\text{Coverage in lateral direction}}$$

The coverage in the lateral direction is obtained from the overlap to be obtained between two adjoining strips. This varies from 20 to 30 per cent.

If w is the width of the photo, then as in the case of forward coverage, the lateral coverage is given by $W\,H/f\,(l - O_1)$ where O_1 is the lateral overlap.

$$\text{Hence N} = \left(\frac{f.L}{lH(l - O_f)} + 1\right) \times \left(\frac{fW}{WH(l - O_1)} + 1\right)$$

An approximate value can be obtained by neglecting the additional exposure and strip.

$$\therefore N_{\text{app}} = \frac{f^{-} LW}{lwH^{-}(l - Of)(1 - Ol)}$$

If we write $LW = A$, area on ground to be covered

$l_w = a$, area of photographic plate (called photo format)

then $S = f/H$ the scale of photographs

$$N = S^2 \frac{A}{a(l - O_f)(l - O_l)}$$

with $O_f = 0.6$

$O_l = 0.3$

$$N = 3.5.S^2.\frac{A}{a}$$

Example

An area 10 × 20 square miles is to be photographed with a 6" focal length camera. Given forward overlap to be 60 per cent and lateral overlap 30 per cent, and format of the photo 9" × 9", calculate the number of photographs on scale 1 :20,000.

Here, the scale $= \frac{1}{20,000}$

$f = 6"$

Therefore H, the height at which the aircraft is to fly is calculated from $S = f/H$ or (1/20,000)

$$= \frac{6}{12H}$$

$$\frac{1}{20{,}000} = \frac{1}{2.H}$$

$$H = 10{,}000 \text{ ft}$$

Now $N = 3.5\,(S^2)\,A/a$ (See Fig. 1.25)

$$N = 3.5(1/20{,}000)^2 \times \frac{(10 \times 5280 \times 12) \times (20 \times 5280 \times 12)}{9 \times 9}$$

$$= 87$$

To get a still better value and taking into account the coverage for edges.

$$\text{Total No. of strips} = \frac{10 \times 5280 \times 6}{9 \times 0.7 \times 10{,}000} + 1$$

$$= 6$$

$$\text{No. of photos in one strip} = \frac{20 \times 5280 \times 6}{9 \times 0.4 \times 10{,}000} +$$

$$= 19$$

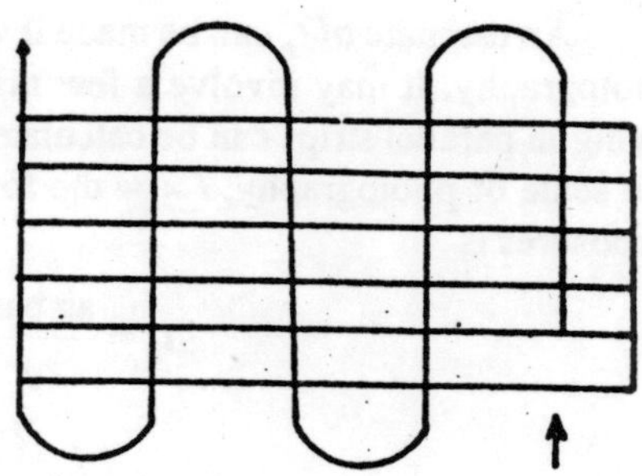

Fig. 1.25 : Flight lines North–South

Hence the total number of photographs = 19 × 6 = 114.

It will be seen here that the number of photographs will differ if flight is not made parallel to the longer side but parallel to the short side. In working the above number of photographs, it has been assumed that the flight direction was parallel to the longer side, namely, 20 miles. If we take the flight parallel to the shorter side of 10 miles, then we see that number of strips

$$= \frac{20 \times 5280 \times 6}{9 \times 0.7 \times 10{,}000} + 1$$

= 12 (rounding to full number for a fraction)

$$\text{No. of photos per strip} = \frac{10 \times 5280 \times 6}{9 \times 0.4 \times 10{,}000} + 1$$

$$= 9 + 1 = 10$$

No. of photographs = 12 × 10 = 120

Thus it will be seen that the number of photographs required to cover a given area for a given forward and lateral overlap depends on the flight directions, i.e. east-west or north-south or any other direction.

1.9.3 *Flight Time*

To decide whether any given area can be covered in one flight or more it is necessary to calculate or estimate beforehand the total flight time. This may include time required to fly from the base, where the aircraft is stationed, to the area of photography. The total flight time T can be written as

$$T = t_b + t_c + t_s$$

Where t_b = the time taken to fly from the base to the area of photography including the trial flight time over the area for aligning purposes;
t_c = time spent in circling from one strip to the next;
t_s = time spent in photographing the strips.

An estimate of t_b can be made if we know the distance between the base station and the area of photography. It may involve a few minutes to several hours. The time for photographing area by flying in parallel strips can be calculated knowing the speed of the aircraft. If v is the speed and S is the scale of photography, $l \times w$ the format of the photograph, then the time interval between two exposures is

$$t_s = \frac{\text{air base}}{v} \text{(single photo)}$$

$$= \frac{l}{S} \frac{(1-O_f)}{v} \text{ or } \frac{lH}{f} \frac{(1-O_f)}{v}$$

If there are N exposures which is the same as the total number of photographs, then

$$t_s = \frac{Hl(1-O_f)}{f\,v}.N$$

Referring to the earlier problem with $N = 114$, $O_f = 0.6$

$$l = 9", S = \frac{1}{20{,}000}$$

and taking $v = 200$ miles per hour, we have

$$t_s = \frac{114 \times 9 \times 0.4 \times 20{,}000}{200 \times 5280 \times 12} \text{ hours}$$
$$= 38.86 \text{ minutes}$$

The time for going from one strip to the next can be estimated from the number of loops in between the strips.

Taking each loop as a semi-circle, the time in completing one semi-circle is—

$$t_{loop} = \frac{\pi r}{v} \text{ where } r \text{ is the radius of the loop.}$$

now r = half the distance between the strips

$$= \frac{1}{2} \frac{wH(1-O_l)}{f}.$$

$$t_{loop} = \frac{H(1-O_l)}{2f.v} \pi \varpi$$

If m is the no. of strips then the no. of loops is m–1.

$$t_c = t_{loop} \times (m-1)$$

$$= \pi\varpi \frac{H(1-O_l)}{2vf}(m-1)$$

where, as shown earlier, $m = \dfrac{fW}{wH(1-O_l)} + 1$

Taking the above example with $m = 6$

$v = 200$ miles/hour

and $S = \dfrac{f}{H} = (1/20{,}000), O_l = 0.3, w = 9"$

$$\frac{1}{tc} = \frac{2 \times 200 \times 5280 \times 12}{9 \times 0.7 \times 20{,}000} \times (6-1)$$

$$\frac{1}{t_c} = \frac{2 \times 200 \times 5280 \times 12 \times 5}{\pi \times 9 \times 0.7 \times 20{,}000 \times 5}$$

$$t_c = \left(\frac{9.36}{2}\right) \text{ minutes } 4.68$$

1.9.4 *Scale of Photographs*

The scale at any point of the photograph is given by $S=f/(H-h_a)$ where h_a is the elevation of the ground point above the datum and H, the height of the aircraft above the same datum. This scale, therefore, varies from point to point. However for flight planning we can take an average elevation of the ground. For flat or slightly undulating ground this gives no problem. However, in a steep and rugged mountainous country. lots of problems arise as it is not possible to assume an average elevation. The scale of photographs over the mountain peaks will be much larger as compared to those on steep mountain slopes and valleys. This also calls for a greater value of lateral overlap between the adjoining airstrips so that at no time the lateral overlap between any two adjoining strips falls below a certain minimum. This will increase the number of strips and thus the cost. Sometimes it may be possible to have separate flight missions for valleys and mountain peaks and slopes. Flight planning in a highly mountainous area becomes a real tough job. On the selection of a scale for a particular job depends the type of camera and the height at which the aircraft will fly. Since there is a ceiling for each type of aircraft, it will be seen that flying for a very small scale photography introduces many problems.

1.9.5 *Type of Photographs*

The ground coverage on aerial photograph depends upon the tilt of the aerial camera. By increasing the tilt to a point when the horizon appears, the coverage can be very much increased. This method is used for very difficult and inaccessible areas. Large portions of North Canada were mapped by high oblique aerial photographs. A special mounting is provided for the camera with one camera pointing directly back under the tail of the aircraft, the second pointing out of one window at 45° to the other and the third similarly in a position to the left. All pictures are taken simultaneously. The ground coverage is shown in the Fig. 1.26. Even though the ground coverage is much large compared to vertical air photography this method has not found much use due to difficulties in mapping. The vertical photography with tilt within ± 3° remains the most widely used method of air mapping.

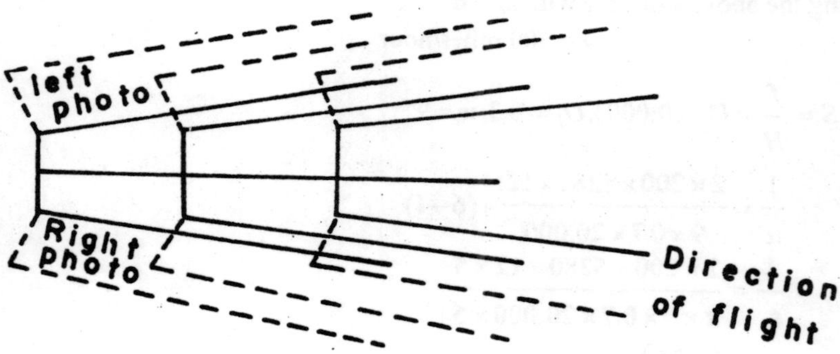

Fig.1.26 : Ground Coverage Loss

1.9.6 *External Factors*

(1) *Meteorological conditions* (a) *Wind effects* : While calculating the number of photographs required to cover a given area it was assumed that the aircraft flies in parallel straight strips. This assumes no wind and navigational flight being strictly along the proposed straight and parallel strips, i.e. the nose of the aircraft being in the line of the proposed flight direction and the body of the camera also aligned in the direction of the nose. However, if there is wind, the aircraft will move bodily and fly in a course inclined at angle θ to the proposed course where $\tan\theta = (u/v)$, u being the wind velocity and v the velocity of the aircraft. (See Fig. 1.27 and 1.28)

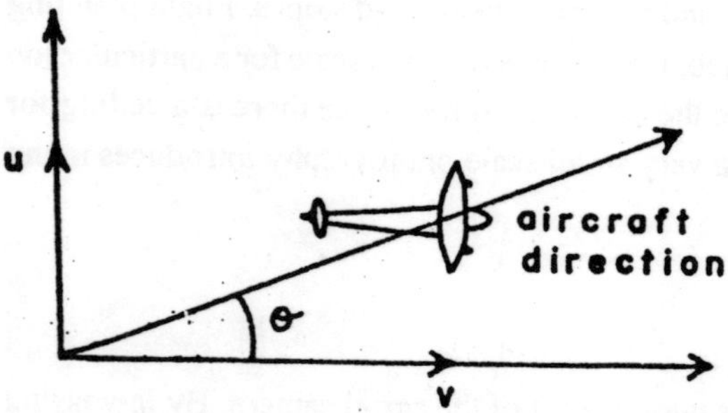

Aircraft in direction of proposed fly
θ = Drift angle

Fig. 1.27: Effect of Wind and Crabbing

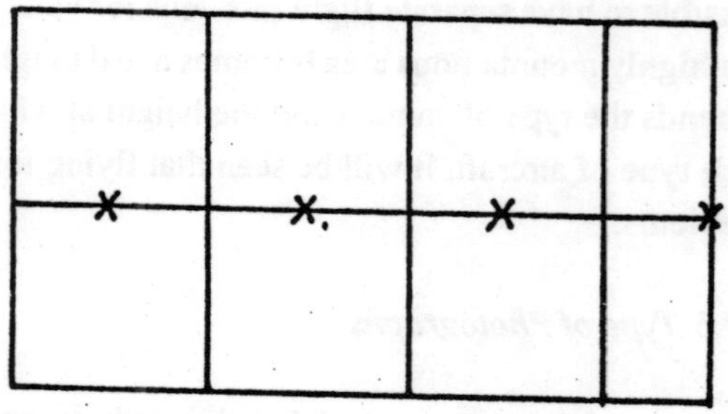

No wind. All *pps* lie on a straight line in the direction of the proposed flight

Fig. 1.28: Improvement in Overlapping with Correction for Crabbing

This angle θ is called the *Drift Angle.* On account of the drift of the aircraft, the principal points of the individual photographs do not lie on the proposed course but an angle θ to it. This reduces the effective forward and lateral overlap and thus creating the possibility of 'gaps' in air photography. To avoid this the aircraft should fly in a direction θ away from the proposed course as shown in the Fig. 1.29.

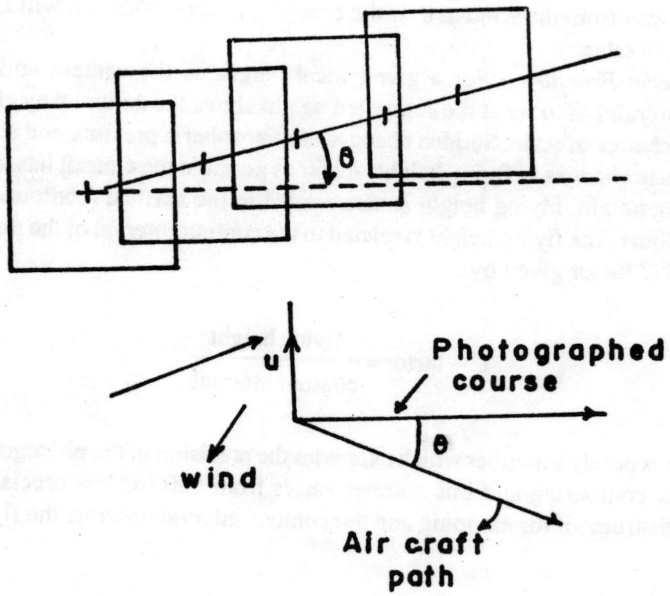

Fig. 1.29 : Effect of Drift

This however creates another problem. Since the nose of the aircraft is inclined at an angle θ to the proposed course to avoid 'drift' the camera having been aligned in the direction of the nose will take photographs as shown in Fig. 1.30.

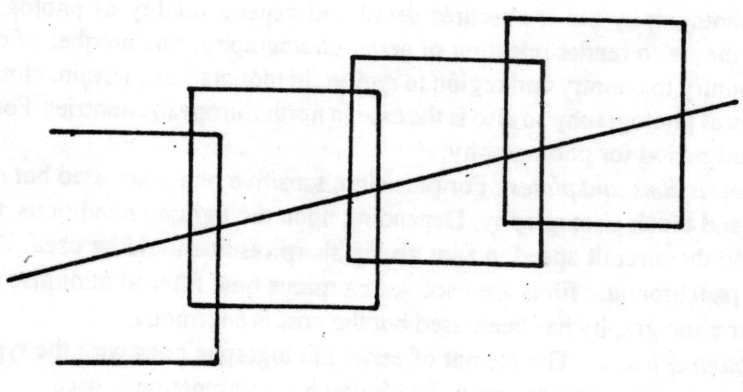

Fig. 1.30 : Overlapping Loss Due to Drift

The edges of the photographs will be now at an angle to the proposed flight direction. This angle formed between the flight line (True) and the edges of the photographs is called 'crab angle'. It is caused by not having the focal plane of the camera squared with the direction of flight at the instant of exposure. It is, therefore, clear that in trying to avoid 'draft' we introduce 'crabbing'. The solution lies in flying at an angle θ (the drift angle) which can be computed beforehand from the known wind and aircraft velocities and turning or rotating the camera about the vertical axis of the camera mounting away from the wind at θ. If the crabbing is not avoided, it will again cause loss of forward and lateral overlap.

(b) *Atmospheric Pressure* : For a given focal length of the camera and desired scale of photography, the aircraft has to fly at the computed height above the datum. Any change of height of flight will result in change of scale. Sudden changes of atmospheric pressure and eddy currents in the atmosphere will cause changes in flying height. As far as possible the aircraft has to be maintained at the computed flying height. Flying height is also related to the vertical (contouring) accuracy of a map from the air photos. The flying height is related to the contour interval of the map by an empirical relationship, called *C*-factor given by :

$$C - \text{factor} = \frac{\text{flying height}}{\text{contour interval}}$$

This *C*-factor is purely a number which expresses the precision of the photogrammetric mapping instrument used for contouring and this number varies from 500 (of low precision instrument) to 2000. For a given instrument for mapping and the contour interval possible the flying height is then fixed.

1.9.7. *General Factors*

(i) Time of photographs: Photographs should be taken at a time when the shadows of the object are neither too long nor totally absent. Too long shadows obscure detail and absence of shadow creates difficulty in recognition of detail and formation of a good three dimensional effect. The photography should be restricted to when the sun is at least 30° above the horizon, normally between 10 to 11.30 a.m. and 1.30 to 3.30 p.m. in tropical countries.

(ii) Visibility : Good visibility and clear weather is essential for good photography. Haze may not obstruct photography but it obscures detail and general quality of photography. Presence of cloud patches may also render rejection of aerial photography. The number of clear days in a year varies from country to country and region to region. In mountainous terrain, cloud cover may allow only a few days of photography so also is the case in north European countries. For tropical countries, winter is a good period for photography.

(iii) Camera films and plates : For precision, sensitive plates are used but normally the film is used for strip and block photography. Depending upon the lighting conditions, the type of camera, photo scale and the aircraft speed, a film giving sharp result should be used. For black and white photography, panchromatic films are used with a minus blue filter to minimise scattering and haze effects. Colour photography has been used but the cost is enormous.

(iv) Photograph size : The format of aerial photographs goes with the type of lens used, i.e. normal, wide angle or superwide angle. The following combination is used:

	Focal length	*Format*
Normal angle	300 mm	15 × 15 cm
Wide angle	152 mm	18 × 18 cm
Superwide angle	89 mm	23 × 23 cm

(v) Cost of Aerial Photography: The cost of the aerial photography increases sharply with an increase in scale. The cost of certain subsequent operations for map reproduction depends upon the number of photographs involved, and increases therefore proportionally to the square of the scale factor. On the other hand, the amount of field work for identification and completion of photo-interpretation increases with a decreasing photo scale. The following table gives a rough indication of aerial photography and the number of photographs required for coverage of a unit area 1000 km^2.

Scale	No. of photos	Cost of photography (in US Dollars)
1 : 6,000	1640	10,000
1 : 10,000	600	6,000
1 : 15,000	260	3,800
1 : 20,000	150	2,700
1 : 30,000	66	1,600
1 : 40,000	37	1,100
1 : 50,000	24	750

1.9.8 *Flying Mission*

It will be seen from the above table of costs that in enlarging the scale of photography from 1/20,000 to 1/10,000 the cost of aerial photography also becomes almost double. Thus it appears that to reduce the cost of aerial photography we should go for small scale photos. But this reduction in cost is offset by loss of resolution. This can be seen as follow :

The minimum distance that the human eye can resolve is about 1/100 of an inch or 0–254 mm. On the scale of 1:10,000 of the photo, the corresponding ground distance is 25.4 cm whereas with scale 1:20,000 it will be 50.8 cm and thus the ground resolution is pcwered. The scale of air photography is also governed by the ground resolution. For example for maps for engineering purposes the minimum distance, as for road alignment may be of the order of 10 cm. In that case the scale must not be smaller than to 1:4000. Assuming no enlargement or reduction of the photos is done and that we must have the scale of air photo to be 1:4000 and with a camera of focal length 6" the height of aircraft has to be 8000 feet above the ground level. As there is a ceiling on the lower height of aircraft (no less than 500 ft) the flight planning has to be carefully done with aspect to cost and scale of air photography.

1.9.9 *Contract for Air Photography*

Aerial photography is obtained by placing a contract with agencies capable of taking air photos processing and delivery as per specifications. The specifications should be prepared very carefully as the process of air photography is expensive and any reflight for photography can be still more expensive. While preparing specifications the following have to be very clearly stated in the contract:

(i) Forward and Lateral overlaps.
(ii) Area to be photographed, its geographical location and its shape.
(iii) Photographic format.
(iv) Type of photographic paper, that be glossy or matt.
(v) Nature of prints that is negatives on films or diapositives on glass.
(vi) Quality of photography, that is the allowable tone or darkness with respect to clarity or detail.
(vii) Type of lens to be used: Whether superwide, wide or normal angle lens (consistent with format).
(viii) Percentage of cloud cover allowed.
(ix) Allowable tilt i.e. for vertical photography it should not exceed ± 3°.
(x) Average scale of air photography so that the contractor decide about the type of camera and flying height.
(xi) Likely period of completion of air mission.
(xii) Estimated number of photos, strips and extra photos (beyond the area of interest) generally one or two photos per strip and one or two extra strips beyond the boundary of area so as to ensure continuity of photography for later work.

Incidentally in India, all air photography is done by Indian Air Force as air photography is classified except for one private agency such as Air Survey Company of India, Dum Dum, Calcutta. In most of the countries, such as U.S.A. and U.K. air photography is open to all private contractors and agencies.

Before the actual flying is done a photo Index Map is prepared by the agency responsible for air photography. The Index is made on any available map and it shows all the flight lines, the position of exposure station, the spacing between flight lines and the turning direction, important land marks for the guidance of the pilot. Generally one trial run is made to ensure the photography as per specifications. The film is loaded into the magazine and as far as possible kept at constant temperature to avoid any excess expansion or contraction of the film.

After the photography is over the film is developed by the standard procedure and contact prints on paper obtained. The prints are then laid matching detail from photo to photo and line by line what is called "Mosaicing". This is essential to ensure that the specified forward and lateral overlaps in determining if there is any gap in photography. If the aircraft did not follow the required directions or no wind corrections applied there may be 'gaps' in photography for which a rephotography has to be done to cover up the gaps. Once air photography is completed and gaps again checked by temporary mosaic the photographs are supplied with correct aerial numbering, sortie number and strip number. Each photo also has information about the focal length flying height etc. A view of the 'level' is also printed to indicate the time of exposure of the photo. The photo also carries the impression of the four more fiducial marks such as crosses or short ticks. If the camera was calibrated by the air company a copy of the calibration paramenter such as the co-ordinates of the principal points, the calibrated focal length and coefficient of lens distortion such as K_1, K_2, K_3 are also supplied to the indentor.

Fig. 1.31 shows the equipment for developing of aerial negatives. Fig 1.32 shows the Drier for drying the film negatives and Fig 1.33 shows the film making Kit. Fig 1.34 shows the film identification stamping machine and Fig. 1.35 shows the contact printer with prematic plate, and Fig. 1.36 shows the whole setup of determining the gaps, if any, in the aerial photography by photo layouts and temporary mosaics.

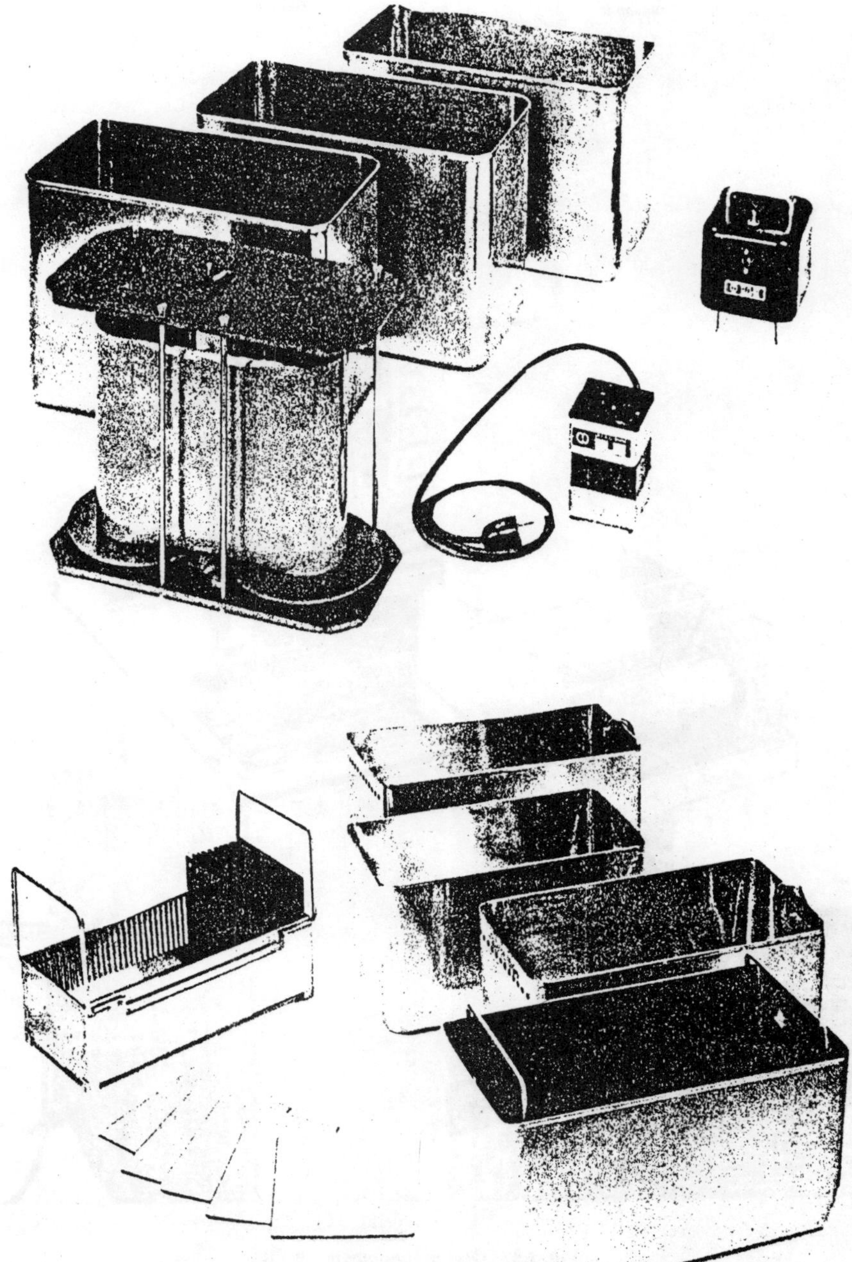

Fig. 1.31: Developing Equipment for film (top) and for plates (bottom)
(*Courtesy* of Wild Heerbrugg Instruments, Inc.)

Fig. 1.32: Drying Equipment for Film
(*Courtesy* of Wild Heerbrugg Instruments, Inc.)

Fig. 1.33: Film Marking Kit (Photo from Files of Gordon Enterprises)

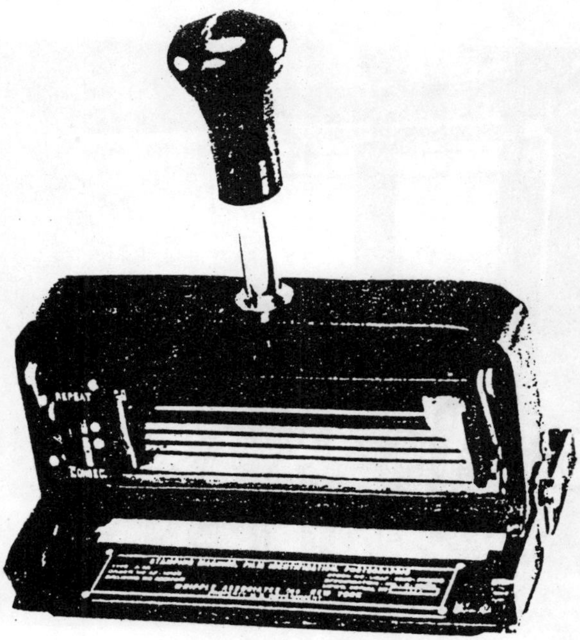

Fig. 1.34: Film Identification Stamping Machine (Photo from Files of Gordon Enterprises)

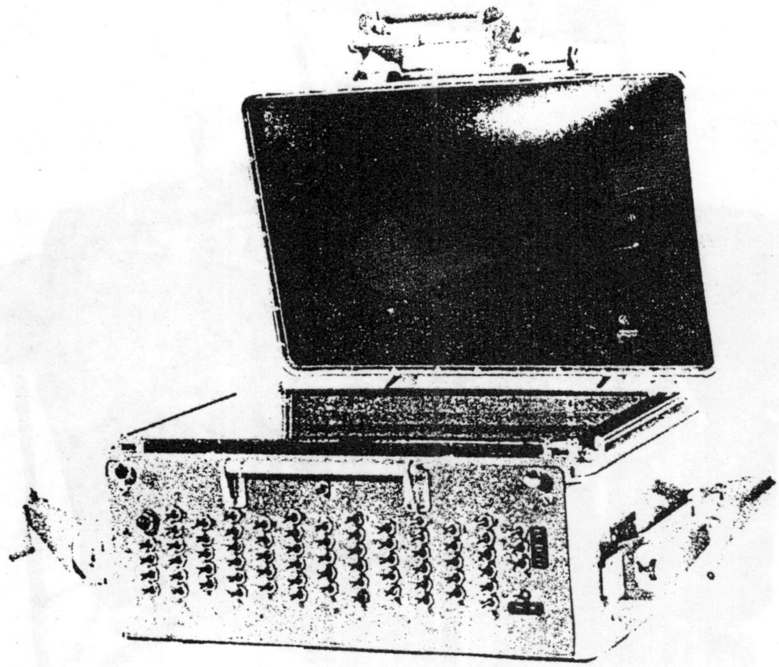

Fig. 1.35: Contact Printer with Pneumatic Plate
(Photo from Files of Gordon Enterprises)

Fig. 1.36: Construction of Photo. (*Courtesy* of Jack Ammann Photo-grammetric Engineers, Inc.)

1.10 Mosaic

A mosaic is a combination of vertical air photographs, cut and fitted in proper layout and sequence forming one single composite picture (a bird's eye view) of the terrain with continuity of detail. Mosaics are prepared for qualitative study of the terrain before any work is started on the project. For all kinds of preliminary studies, without rigorous maps mosaics are found to be of great help both from speed and cost point of view.

An essential difference between a photo mosaic and a photo index is that the latter is only a trace showing the principal points, photo numbers and strip numbers and their direction of flight. A photo index may consist of air photos in proper sequence without any cut or pasting. In a mosaic all the overlap areas are cut out and the photo is thus pasted together without any gaps to show the continuity of the detail.

A mosaic differs from a map in the following ways:

(i) In a map the scale is uniform throughout and ground objects appear in their azimuth or directions while in a mosaic this is not so because of distortions by tilt and relief;
(ii) A mosaic is more useful to a layman who is not conversant with the map symbols and interpretations as the detail in a mosaic appears in its natural form;
(iii) Spot height, coordinates, and other information like names are not there in a mosaic and hence not suitable for quantitative studies whereas in a map measurements can be made;
(iv) A mosaic can be prepared in a much shorter time as compared to map making which is a long and costly affair; and
(v) A mosaic can be prepared only of flat terrain and of vertical photos. It is extremely difficult to make a mosaic of an oblique photo or a vertical photo of highly mountainous terrain because of large scale difference.

1.10.1 *Type of Mosaics*

Broadly speaking mosaics can be of two types :

(i) Controlled mosaics
(ii) Uncontrolled mosaics

In an uncontrolled mosaic no ground control point appears. Photos are laid and joined for the sake of continuity of detail only. Such a mosaic serves the purpose of visual inspection of the terrain, no measurements possible for estimating ground distance between objects. In a controlled mosaic the ground control points are marked on the photos. These points are positioned into the plotted position on a drawing sheet. This enables the estimation or approximate measurement of ground distances and establishment of an approximate scale of photography.

1.10.2 *Preparation of a Mosaic*

The preparation of a mosaic needs great skill and practice especially if a change of scale occurs due to presence of small tilt, relief and change of photographic tone (black and white).

To start with, for an uncontrolled mosaic, all the photos are laid out on a masonite board stripwise, covering the overlap areas and matching the details as best as possible. The line of overlaps is carefully noted and marked because the cutting has to be made along this line. Fig. 1.37 shows the overlap of four photos with a common overlap. This common area has to be cut and removed from one of the photos and then while cutting along the boundary of common overlap attention is paid to special features, namely :

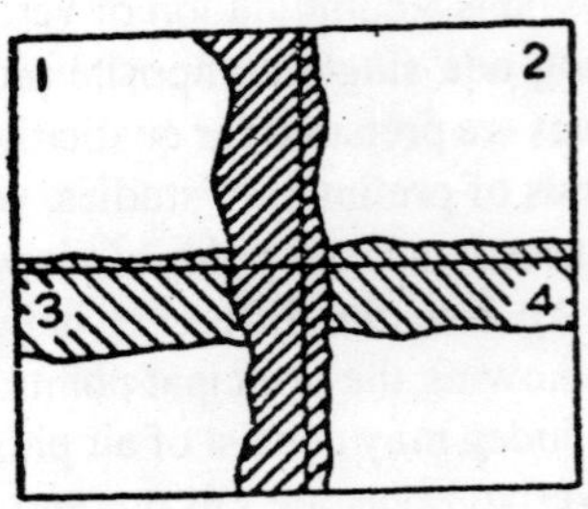

Fig. 1.37: Overlap Photo with Common Area.

(i) Cutting through important details like roads and buildings or single line stream is avoided. For such detail, cutting is done slightly away and parallel to them.

(ii) The cutting is done through a line involving least amount of detail.

(iii) For cutting in an undulating country, it follows a direction normal to the contours' line. Whether the mosaic is controlled or uncontrolled each photo after cutting has to be trimmed and feather edged. For this a single edge razor blade is used to just barely cut through the emulsion of the photo (see Fig.1.38) The photo is picked up and bent back along the cut to expose the paper backing. The photo is then placed with the emulsion side down and the discarded portion is turned back towards the portion to be used. This process gives the edge of the photograph a feathered appearance. Finally a sand paper is used to smoothen out the feather edge (see Fig. 1.39). The strokes of the sand paper being outward and perpendicular to the trimmed edge. The adhesive is then spread on to

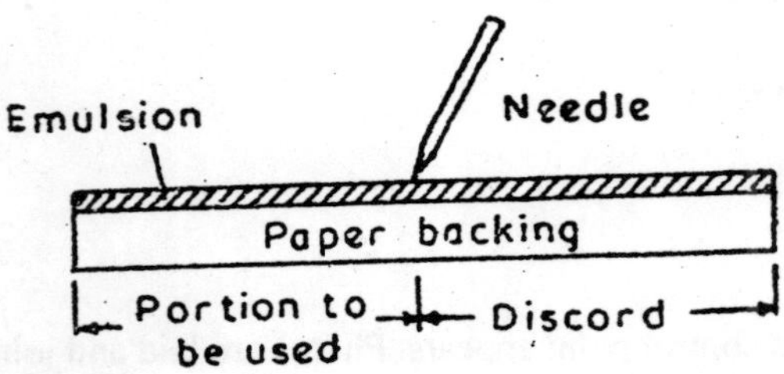

Fig. 1.38 : Photo of Emulson

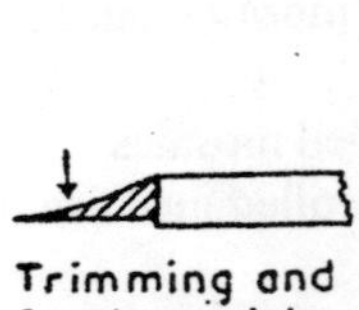

Fig. 1.39 : Smoothen out the Feather Edge

the back of the print and the print then placed in position on the mounting board. After the first photo has been laid out and fixed on the board the rest of the photos after trimming are joined with adhesive in proper positions forming a composite and complete picture. For a controlled plot, it is necessary that the scale of all the photos be the same as the scale of plotting. For this the photos have to be "rectified' first. Rectification is applicable where tilt is present but not excessive height distortion. Rectification removes the distortions due to tilt. Rectified prints are obtained and then trimmed and feather-

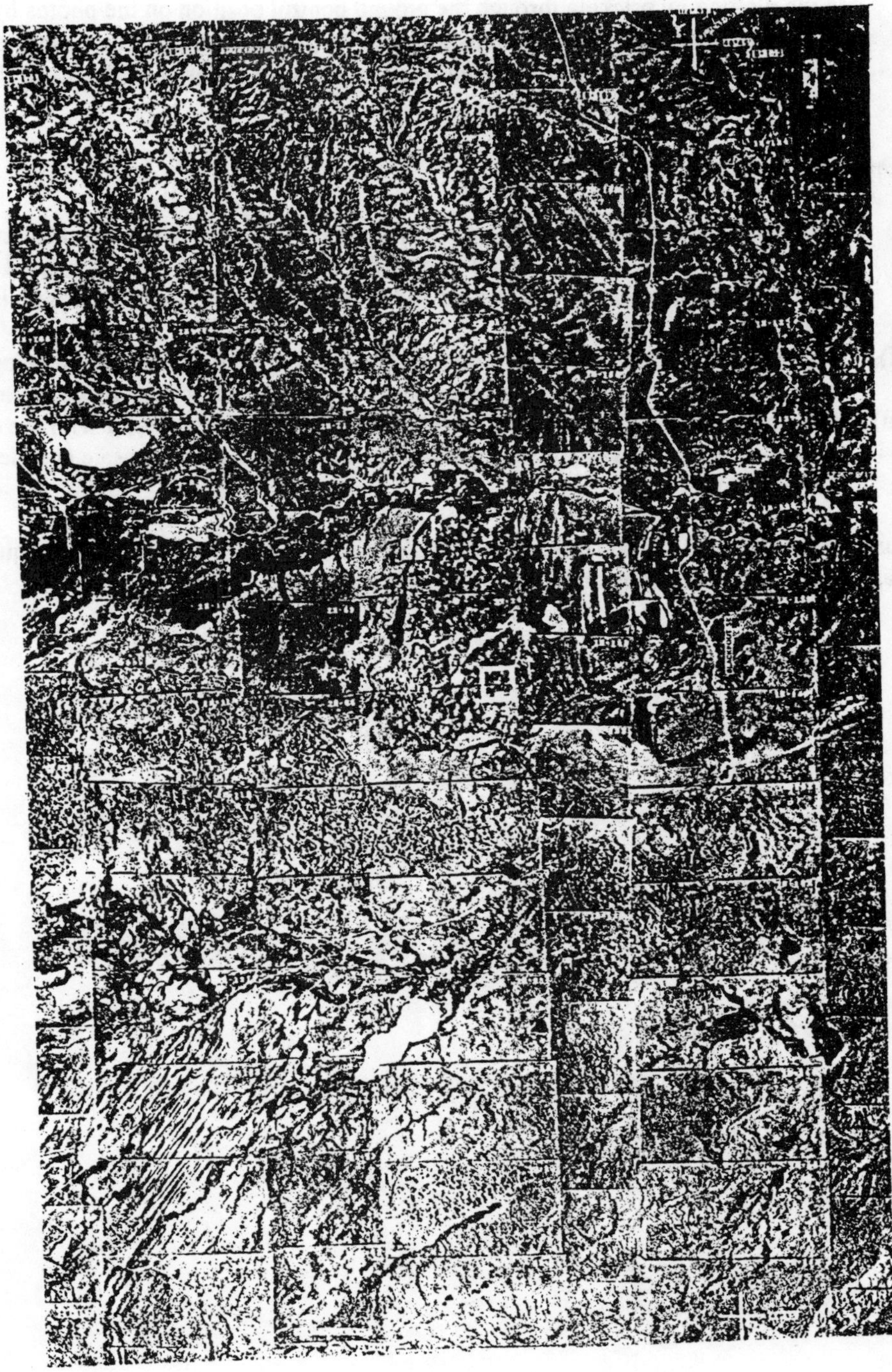

Fig. 1.40: Example of a Photo-masaic (*Courtesy* of Jack Ammann Photogrammetric Engineers, Inc.)

edged the same way as in uncontrolled mosaic. The photos are then properly aligned on to the plotting by pricking through the ground control position on the photos by means of needles. These pricked positions are then so placed that they fill exactly over the plotted positions. The photos are then fixed by adhesive material on the board. Fig 1.40 shows an example of a photo mosaic.

1.10.3 *Other kinds of mosaic*

(i) *Semi-controlled mosaic :* If rectified prints are not available but the ground control point as appearing on the original aerial photos are matched to the plotted ground control points so that directions and distances can be estimated, the resulting mosaic is called semi-controlled mosaic.

(ii) *Strip mosaic :* Mosaics prepared out of strip photography (photography being taken along one line) as for rai!, road and other line of communication are called strip mosaics.

(iii) *Wet mosaic :* If no glue is pasted but photos are in proper continuity with the overlap portion cut out so that the mosaic can last for a day or so such a mosaic is called a wet mosaic.

For any mosaic to be of good quality, we should have very low height relief good quality of photography, good flight planning and a skilled mosaic compiler.

2

AERIAL CAMERAS

2.1 Introduction

Figure 2.1 shows the situation for an ideal photographic system and the actual case at the time of aerial photography. In the ideal case we have a point source of radiation sending out spherical waves through a very clear (non-interacting) atmosphere so that the light waves travel without distortion as perfect spherical waves (without under going any refraction or bending). The lens collects these waves and forms, without any optical distortion, an image on a film which is also free of any deformation i.e. no film contraction or expansion. The image formation is under the true collinearity condition, i.e. the object point, the optical lens centre and the image point are all in one straight line. The image intensity also is in accordance with the diffraction principle (Airy's rings). It is assumed that there is no image motion due to the movement of the aerial camera in the direction of flight and the film is perfectly flat.

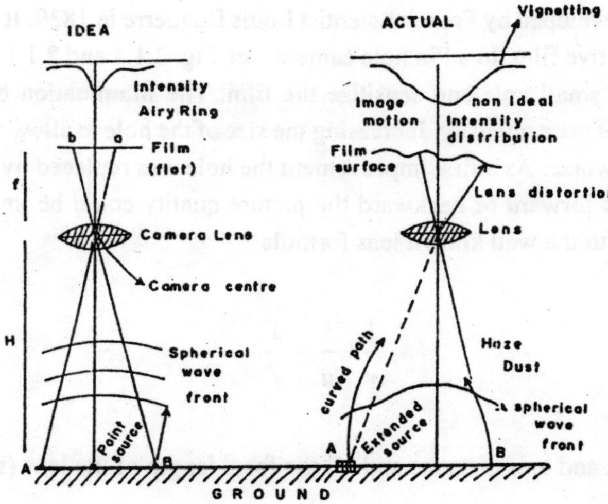

Fig. 2.1 : Ideal Versus Actual Air Photography

However in actual aerial photography none of these ideal conditions exist. In the first place we do not have point source but an extended one. Even if we were to have a point source, the spherical waves will become non-spherical due to varying refraction co-efficient of the air, the density of air decreasing exponentially as we go higher and higher. In addition there may be turbulence and haze in the air. In addition no lens is perfect and as a result the light ray will get bent due to lens distortion. The image will also be distorted due to film deformation (non-uniform surface of film emulsion) and image motion due to movement of the aircraft with respect to ground object. Because of the finite aperture of the lens, the intensity distribution on the film will follow $\cos^4\alpha$ law, causing 'Vignetting' effect whereby the intensity will decrease rapidly as we go toward the edges of the film. Here α the angle that the light ray makes with the optical axis of the lens as it enters the lens system. The image motion (displacement of the image from its true position) is given by $(f/H.\ v).\ t$ where f is the focal length of the lens, H is the flying height of the camera above the ground, v is the velocity of the aircraft relative to ground and t is the time during which the shutter of the lens is open during photography.

The lens distortion is due to the typical radial and tangential distortion whereby the image is displaced from its true position by an amount depending on its distance from the centre of the film and according its position on the film (for tangential distortion).

2.1.1 *Photographic System*

Photographic system can be of three types : Single Camera, Single Camera with Multilens for Multiband Photography and Multi Camera System.

2.1.2. *Photographic Development*

The first Camera was developed by French Scientist Louis Daguerre in 1839. It was really a Pin hole box camera with a sensitive film. In a Pin hole camera (see Fig. 2.1.1 and 2.1.1.1) light was allowed to pass through a very small hole and sensitize the film. The illumination being very small the developed picture was of poor intensity. Increasing the size of the hole to allow more light pass made the picture quality still worse. As a first improvement the hole was replaced by an optical glass lens and by moving the lens forward or backward the picture quality could be improved with a sharp image in accordance with the well known lens formula :

$$\frac{1}{v} + \frac{1}{u} = \frac{1}{f}$$

when u, v are the object and lens distance and 'f' the focal length of the lens (see. Fig. 2.1.2)

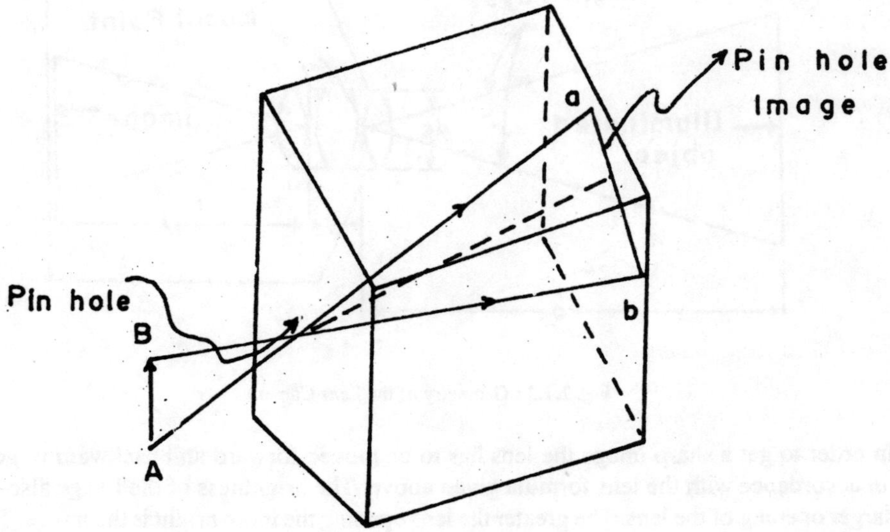

Fig. 2.1.1 : Pinhole Box Camera

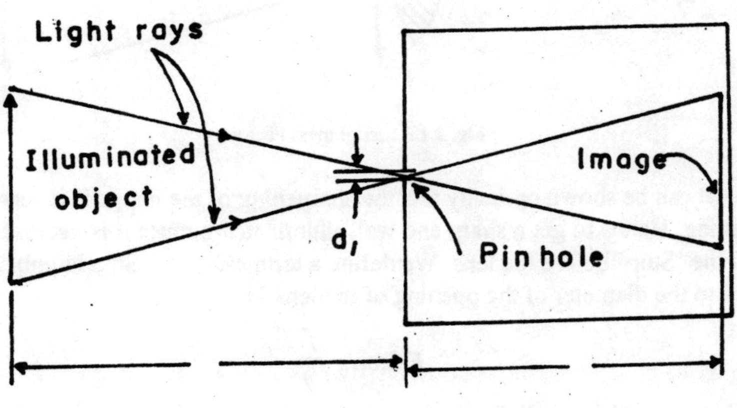

Fig. 2.1.1.1 : Pinhole Lens of the Pinhole Camera

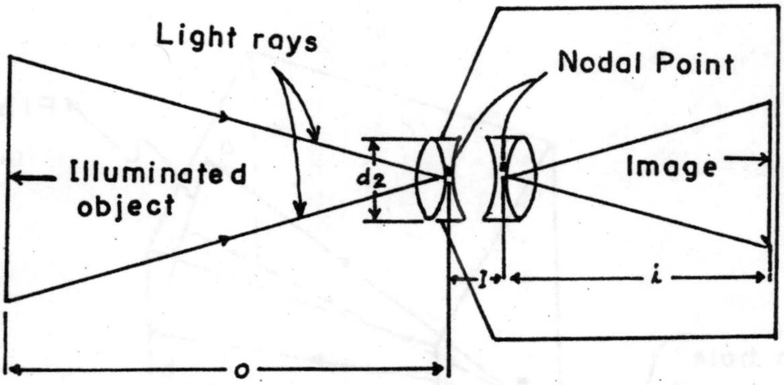

Fig. 2.1.2 : Geometry of the Lens Camera

In order to get a sharp image the lens has to be moved forward and backward to get a sharp image in accordance with the lens formula given above. The brightness of the image also improves due to larger opening of the lens. The greater the lens opening the more bright is the image. Therefore, we define 'Brightness Factor' as the ratio of lens diameter to the focal length of the lens i.e. Brightness factor $= \dfrac{d}{f}$

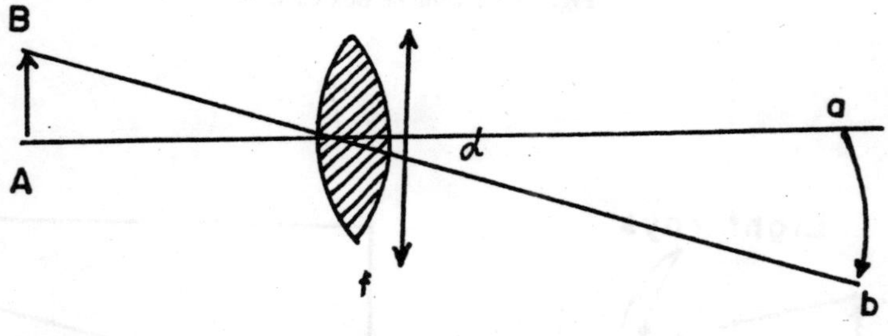

Fig. 2.1.3 : Brightness Factor

However, it can be shown optically that the sharpening of the image is inversely proportional to the lens opening. Hence to get a sharp and well illuminated picture it is necessary to provide an opening called the 'Stop' before the lens. We define a term called "*F* Stop Number" as the ratio of the focal length to the diameter of the opening of the lens i.e.

$$F \text{ Stop} = \frac{f}{d}$$

Thus a Camera with a small *F* Stop has large diameter of the opening and the Camera with large *F* Stop Number will have small opening. In modern Camera provision is made to adjust *F* Stop Number depending upon the lighting conditions and the speed of the film. By 'Speed' of the film is meant the capacity of the film emulsion to respond to poor or good lighting conditions.

2.1.3 *Photographic Film*

The Photographic film consists of parts (i) the sensitive chemicals i.e. the emulsion, and (ii) the base. The base may be paper, plastic film or glass. On this base is given a coating of the emulsion which is Silver Halide i.e. Silver Bromide in the form of fine crystals. When light falls over such a material the bond between silver atoms and the halide atoms is broken i.e. silver becomes free. When such a film is exposed to light in a Camera a kind of 'latent' or hidden image of the object is formed. Where the light intensity is more, there is more of silver in free state. When this exposed film is removed from the Camera body (in dark) and put in the 'Developer' (in dark or red light) the unexposed part is removed and the free silver turns black. Next the film is placed in a 'Fixer' solution which fixes the silver and removes the halide and the sensitive part of the film leaving the image and rest of the film as white or clean and this results in the "Negative Image". In the negative white parts of the image are seen dark and dark shades as white and hence the name 'Negative'. In order to get the 'positive' or correct picture, the negative is washed and dried. It is then developed by the method "Contact Printing" or 'Enlarge Printing' or "Projection Printing."

2.1.4 *Positive Picture*

The positive or the true photo is obtained by exposing the negative in contact with an another film (emulsion to emulsion) and then going through the usual process as for negative. The result is a photo where true shades and grey tones are seen just opposite of a negative. Sometimes it is required to get a larger size of the positive print from a small negative (usually 35 mm × 35 mm). For this use is made of an Enlarger as shown in Fig. 2.1.4. The negative is placed in the Projector and lens moved up or down so as to get the desired magnification (or reduction). The sensitive printing paper is placed on the Easel (in dark or red light) and exposure made. The development of the printing paper is done as described earlier to get the desired Positive Print (Enlarged or Reduced).

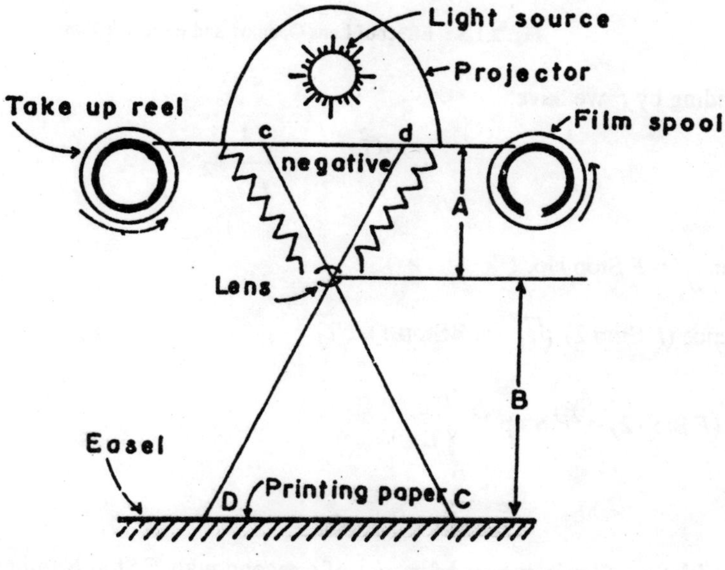

Fig. 2.1.4 : Geometry of Enlargement with a Projection Printer

2.1.5 *Change of F Stop Number*

Many times it is necessary to change the *F* Stop Number for exposure due to different lighting condition. For example if the picture is to be taken in sunny weather condition outside, we need to open the shutter smaller but when a picture is to be taken inside a room we may have to open the shutter more. Also it depends upon the speed of the film. If the film is fast it needs small time for exposure whereas a slow speed needs more time. There is a relationship between the *F* Stop Number and the time of exposure. Let d_1, be the lens opening and t_1 the exposure time for the first case. Suppose we change the lens opening to d_2 then the exposure time has to be changed to t_2. The amount of light being the same, it is equal to $\pi \frac{(d_1)^2}{4} t_1$ in the first case and $\pi \frac{(d_2)^2}{4} t_2$ in the second case, hence we have (See Fig. 2.1.5)

$$\frac{\pi(d_1)^2}{4} t_1 = \frac{\pi(d_2)^2}{4} t_2$$

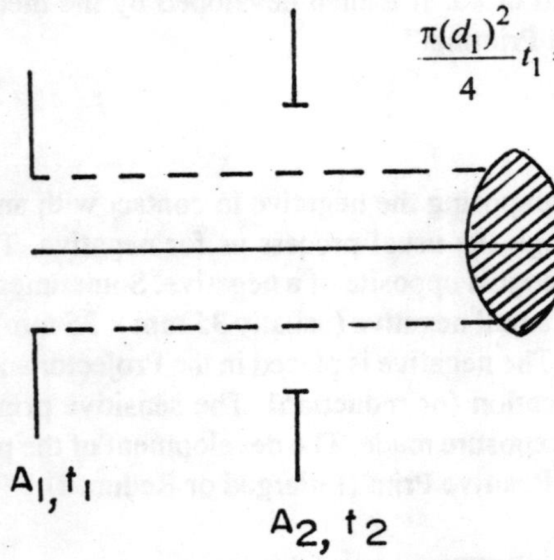

Fig. 2.1.5 : Effect of Lens Opening and Exposure Time

Dividing by f^2 we have:

$$\frac{d_1^2}{f^2} t_1 = \frac{d_2^2}{f^2} t_2$$

But $\frac{f}{d_1} = F$ Stop No. 1

Hence (F Stop 2) $\sqrt{t_1}$ = (F Stop 1). $\sqrt{t_2}$

or (F Stop 2) = (F Stop 1) $\sqrt{\frac{t_2}{t_1}}$

Example

Suppose initially a film is exposed for $\frac{1}{1000}$ of a second with F Stop Number 2.8. Now we want to

change it to the exposure of $\frac{1}{500}$ a second. The new *F* Stop Number is given by :

$$(F\text{ Stop}) = 2.8 \times \sqrt{\frac{\frac{1}{500}}{1/1000}} = 2.8\sqrt{2}$$

$$= 4.0$$

2.1.6 *Speed of Film*

The speed of film, as described earlier, is an indication of the property of the film to respond to incoming light on exposure. This characteristic property depends upon the grain size and number of the silver halide. When the film is exposed to light all the grains get sensitized. However, as the size of grains increase the (See Fig. 2.1.6) number of grain occupying the same surface area become less. In order to

Fig. 2.1.6 : Effect of Grain Size

give the same intensity of light as the image we need less light for exposure. In other words, as the grain size increases the total number of grains in the emulsion decreases and the amount of light required to properly expose it decreases. We call such a film 'Fast Film'. If the grain size is small we call it 'Slow Film'. In order to give some numerical value the American Standards Association (ASA) has prescribed the system of ASA numbers to describe the speed of the film. In this system the ASA number assigned to a film is roughly equal to the inverse of shutter speed in seconds which is required in sunlight (no clouds) of a lens *F* Stop No. of 16. Thus if the shutter speed is $\frac{1}{200}$ of a second the speed of the film is 200 ASA. The corresponding German Standard Association is DIN. Roughly 400 ASA is 21 DIN. A film 400 ASA is considered 'Fast' and that of 100 ASA as 'Slow'. For exposure in dark areas we need a Fast Film whereas recording objects in bright sunshine and moving objects we need Slow Film.

2.1.7 *Film Density*

If a film is exposed for a long time say one minute it will appear very dark on development. If the same film were to be exposed for a very little time, say $\frac{1}{500}$ of a second the film will appear very clear and transparent after development. The darker the film the less light it will allow to pass through it. In other words it will be opaque to light. Similarly it will be transparent with very little exposure and will transmit all the light energy passing through it. The 'Density' of a film is a measure of the

opaqueness or darkness of the developed film. Numerically we define the density 'D' of the film as:

$$D = Log_{10}\left(\frac{I_0}{I_t}\right)$$

Where I_0 is the intensity of the incident radiation and I_t of the transmitted radiation (see Fig. 2.1.7).

Thus when $I_t = I_o$ all the light passes through the film, the density being zero the film is transparent. When $I_t = 0$, no light is able to go through the film, the density is infinite and the film is perfectly black. If 10 per cent of the light is able to go through the film, then the density is $D = Log_{10}\frac{I_0}{I_0/10} = 1$. If $\frac{1}{100}$ of the original incident light is able to pass through the film the density is 2.0. Both the original and transmitted light can be measured by the instrument called 'Densitometer'.

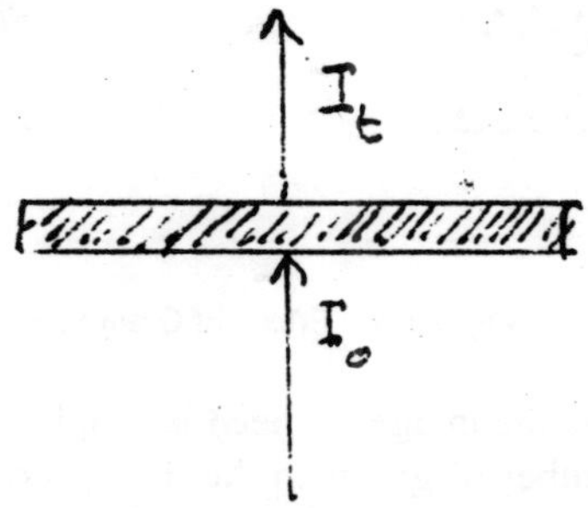

Fig. 2.1.7 : Incident and Transmitted Light

2.1.8 : *Characteristic Curve*

It we were to plot a graph between '*D*' and the logarithm of the Exposure the resulting curve is as shown in Fig 2.1.8. Such a plot is called the "Characteristic Curve" or the "H&D Curve". Here the *X* axis is the 'Log exposure' and *Y* axis is the density *'D'*. The upper part of the curve is called the 'Shoulder' and the lower part the 'Toe'. The angle that the straight line makes with '*X*' thin axis is called 'Gamma,' in fact is the slope of the straight part and is an indicator of the 'Contrast' of the film. It can be seen from the lower part of the curve that even when there is no exposure the film has a certain density. This is called the 'Fog Level'. The Fog level is an indicator of 'age' of the film. If the film has been stored for a long time it will have large Fog Level i.e. the film on development shows a milky or foggy appearance in the background of the image, thus reducing the contrast of the picture. A freshly prepared sensitive film will have very little Fog Level. The γ value also tells us about the 'speed' of the film. A very low value of 'γ' indicates a 'Slow Film' and large value a Fast Film. A 'γ'' value of the unity is an indicator of average film, i.e. neither Fast nor Slow. A film required to show good contrast must have 'γ' greater that 1.0 and a film of poor contrast i.e. just a uniform area of dark or grey levels will have and much less than a value of 1.0.

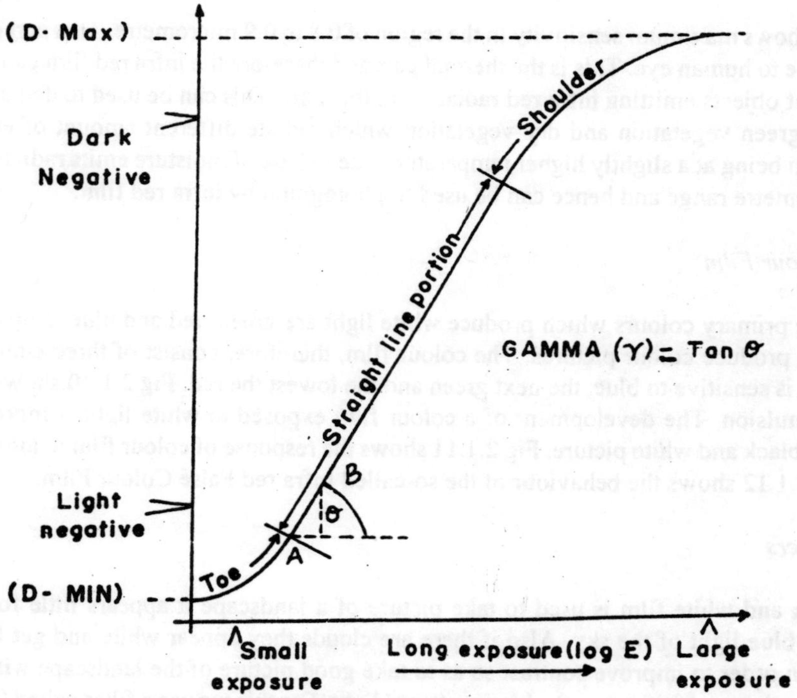

Fig. 2.1.8 : The Characteristic Curve of a Film

2.2. Sensitivity of Film Emulsion

By sensitivity of film emulsion is meant its capacity to respond to different wave lengths of the incoming light. The film emulsion which gives uniform exposure in the visible part of the spectrum, namely, from 0.4 micrometre to 0.7 micrometre is known as Panchromatic film. Fig 2.1.9 shows the Panchromatic infra red film and ordinary printing paper towards the different wave length. The infra

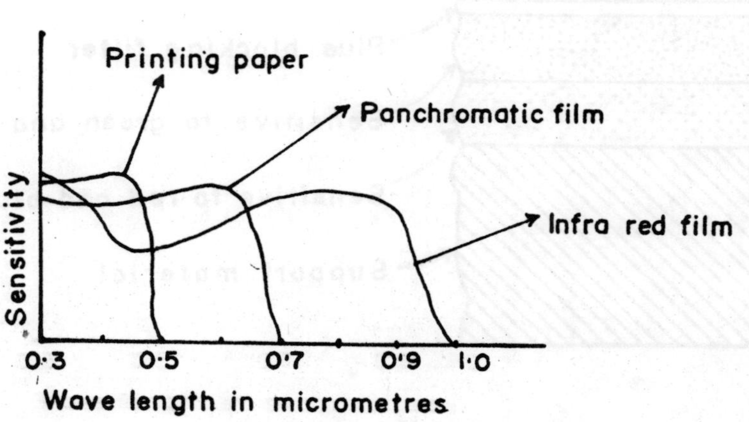

Fig. 2.1.9 : Sensitivity Versus Wavelength for Different Films and Printed Paper

red film shows maximum sensitivity in the region of 0.8 to 0.9 micrometre. This part of the spectrum is invisible to human eye. This is the thermal part and therefore the infra red film can be used to take pictures of objects emitting infra red radiation in this part. This can be used to detect the difference between green vegetation and dry vegetation which radiate different amount of energy. The dry vegetation being at a slightly higher temperature due to lack of moisture emits radiation in the 0.8 to 0.9 micrometre range and hence can be used to photograph by infra red film.

2.2.1 *Colour Film*

The three primary colours which produce white light are green, red and blue. Any combination of these can produce colour pictures. The colour film, therefore, consist of three emulsions. The top emulsion is sensitive to blue, the next green and the lowest the red. Fig 2.1.10 shows the set up of a colour emulsion. The development of a colour film exposed to white light is more complex than ordinary black and white picture. Fig 2.1.11 shows the response of colour film to incoming radiation and Fig 2.1.12 shows the behaviour of the so-called Infra red False Colour Film.

2.2.2 *Filters*

If a black and white film is used to take picture of a landscape it appears little foggy due to the scattered blue light of the sky. Also if there are clouds they appear white and get lost in the back ground. In order to improve contrast so as to take good picture of the landscape with clouds in the back ground we must remove the blue scattered light. For this we use a filter called 'Minus Blue' or yellow filter (it apears yellow) to cut off the blue part. A good camera has this filter in front of the camera lens. One disturbing factor of the filter is that it absorbs a part of the incoming light and hence reduces the light energy going through the optical len and decreasing the illumination of the image.

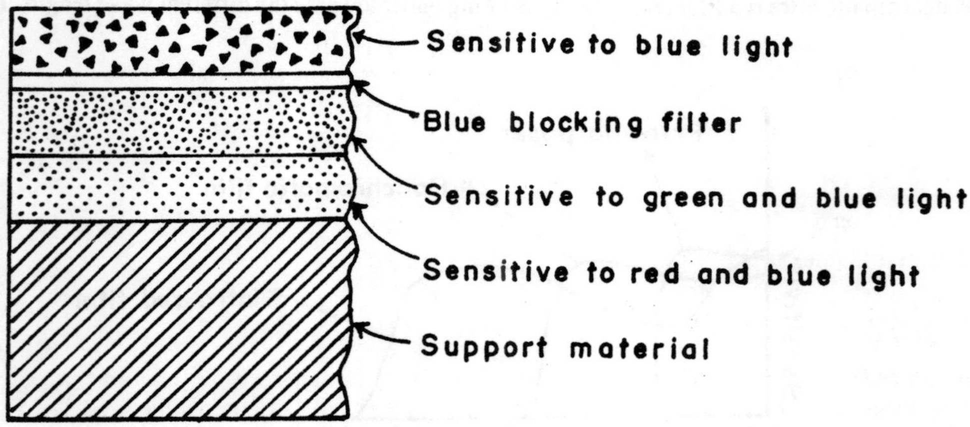

Fig. 2.1.10 : Cross-section of Normal Colour Film

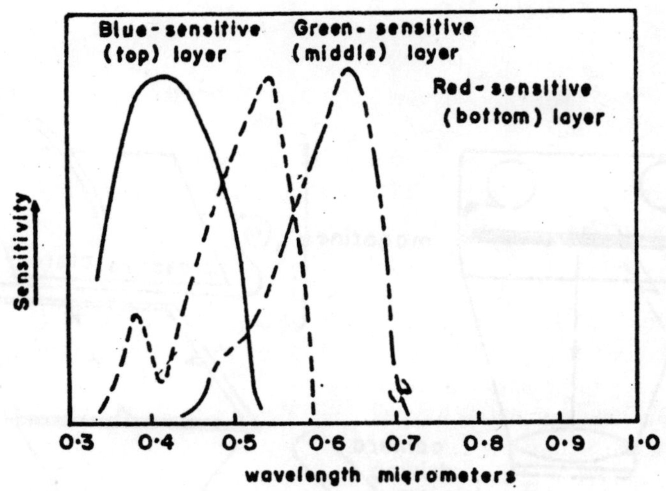

Fig. 2.1.11: Colour Sensitivity of the Three Layers of Normal Colour Film

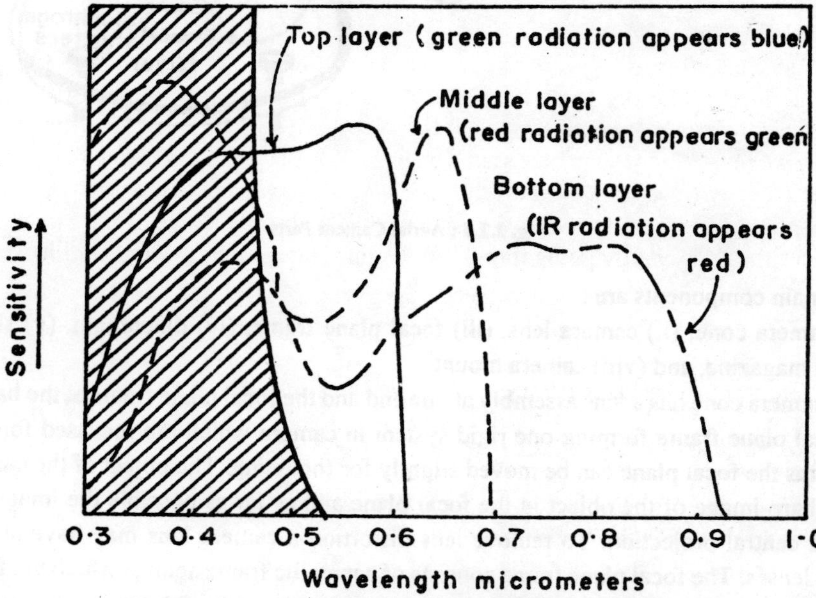

Fig. 2.1.12 : Sensitivity of Colour Infrared (false-colour) film

2.3 Aerial Cameras

2.3.1 *Aerial Cameras Types*

Several types of aerial cameras are available, the more important being manufactured by Wild (Switzerland), Zeiss (E. and W. Germany), Sopelem (France) Officine Galileo, (Italy), Fairchild (U.S.A.) and Williamson (U.K.) Fig 2.2.1 shows the set-up of a typical aerial camera.

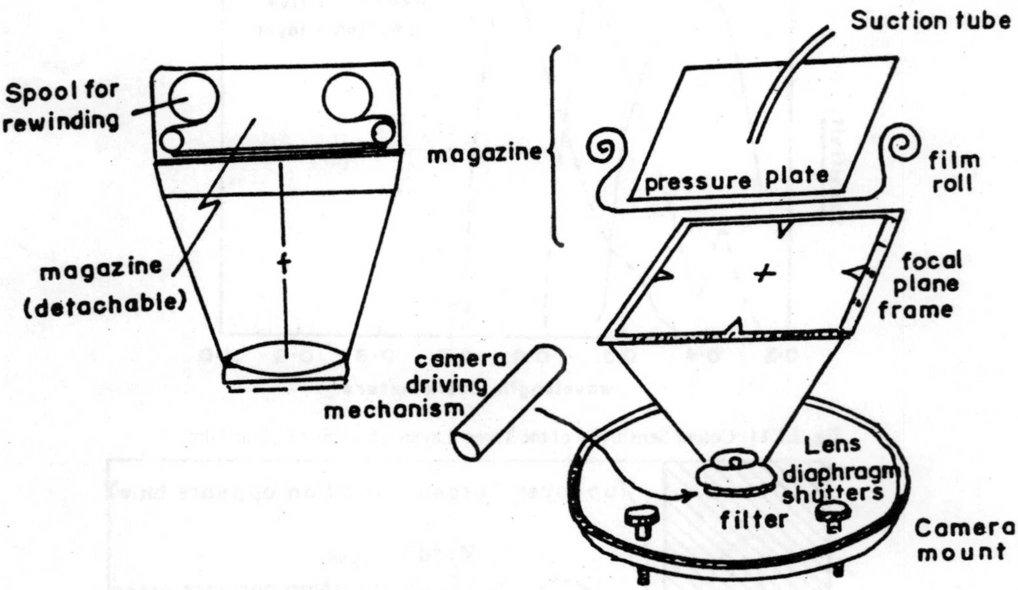

Fig. 2.2.1 : Aerial Camera Parts

The main components are :

(i) Camera cone, (ii) camera lens, (iii) focal plane frame, (iv) diaphragm, (v) shutters, (vi) filters, (vii) magazine, and (viii) camera mount.

The camera cone has a lens assembly at one end and the focal plane frame at the back, the lens and the focal plane frame forming one rigid system in camera which are focussed for infinity. In some cameras the focal plane can be moved slightly for focussing. The object of the camera lens is to form a sharp image of the object in the focal plane and as far as possible the image projection should be a central projection. To remove lens distortion a camera lens may have as many as 9 component lenses. The focal plane frame consists of a metallic frame against which the film or glass plate negative is placed before exposure takes place. Some times the fiducial marks are part of this frame. In some other cameras the fiducial marks are projected by small lenses on to the film negative in the same way as for other indications like watch dial for time of photography, altimeter reading for height of aircraft and counters for exposures. In some other type of cameras, instead of a metal plate there is a register plate which is a glass plate against which the film is pressed before exposure. In such cases, the fiducial marks are engraved on this glass plate.

The diaphragm regulates the amount of light passing through the camera lens, normally operated automatically and defined by its relative aperture = Focal length/Diameter of diaphragm.

Fig. 2.2.2 shows camera in flight.

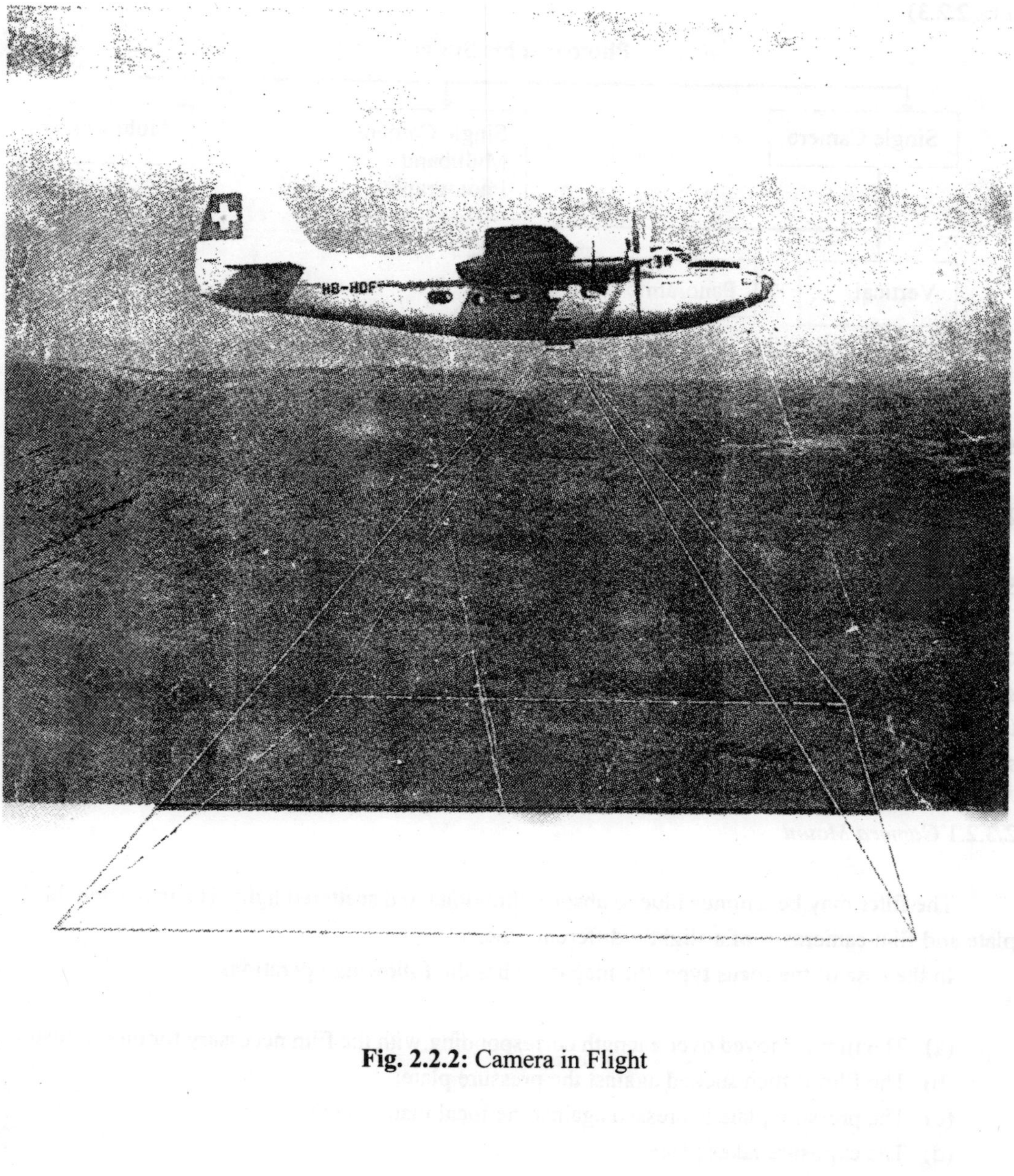

Fig. 2.2.2: Camera in Flight

The single camera can again be of three types, vertical frame, Panoramic and Strip film types. (Fig. 2.2.3)

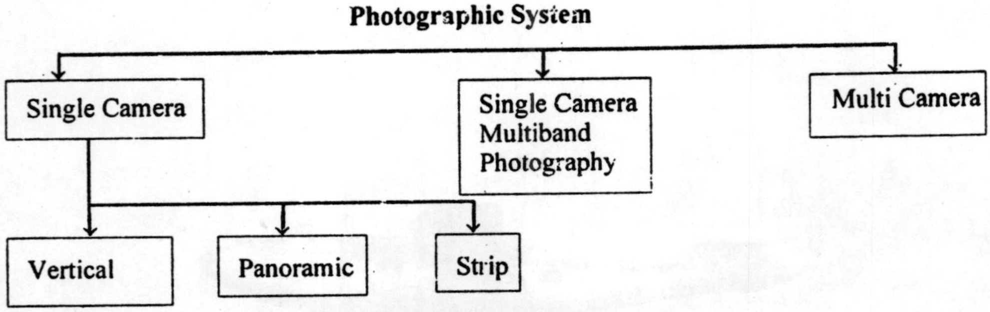

Fig. 2.2.3 : Aerial Photography System

Fig. 2.2.3 gives the description of the single aerial camera used for aerial photography (Black & White) and Fig. 2.2.3.1, 2.2.3.2 and Fig. 2.2.3.3. show the cut out of an aerial camera.

2.3.2 *Shutters*

Shutters are of two types : (i) Focal plane shutter, (ii) Between-the-lens shutter. (See Fig. 2.2.4.).

The first type is very rarely used in aerial cameras because it does not satisfy the requirement of maximum possible light in the shortest possible time to reduce image motion. Between-the-lens shutters are of two types: (i) Leaf shutters, (ii) Rotating disc shutters. In leaf shutters four or five leaves which are at rest move quickly to open the diaphragm and then shut it again. The rotating disc shutters have four small and one large disc which rotate continuously in the same directions.

2.3.2.1 *Camera Mount*

The filter may be a minus blue to absorb ultraviolet and scattered light. The magazine for the plate and film cameras is of a slightly different type.

In the case of the focus type, the magazine has the following operations :

(a) The film is moved over a length corresponding with the film necessary for one exposure.
(b) The film is then sucked against the pressure plate;
(c) The pressure plate is pressed against the focal plane frame;
(d) The exposure takes place;
(e) The pressure plate is lifted; and
(f) Air is blown through the suction tube to make the film free of the pressure plate.

Fig. 2.2.3.1: Automatic Plate Camera

(a)

(b)

Fig. 2.2.3.2 : Type T-11 Mapping Camera Disassembled
(a) Magazine holding 390 feet of film (b) data recording equipment in Camera body; (c) lens cone and shutter Fairchild Camera and Instrument Corporation

(e)

Fig. 2.2.3.2 : (*Contd.*) Lens Cone and Shutter Fairchild Camera and Instrument Corporation

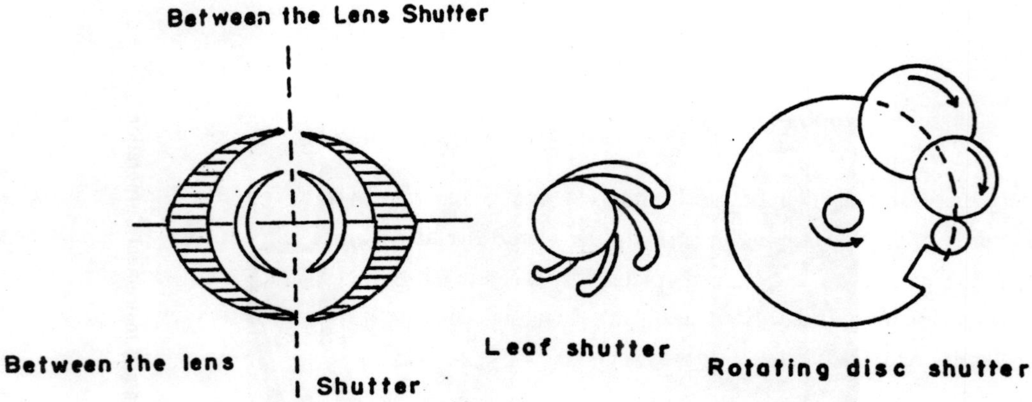

Fig. 2.2.4 : Shutter Types

The camera mount consists of a ring which is supported on three points and turned with levelling screws for levelling the aerial camera with the help of a level bubble. The camera cone is mounted on vibration dampers to stabilise the camera free of vibrations. Besides the aerial camera there are other auxiliary aids for navigation such as 'statoscope" and "horizon camera" for recording the height variations and tilts. Auxiliary 'sights' are also provided to make the edges of the aerial photos parallel to the flight direction. The time required for exposure to ensure the necessary overlap is obtained by an "intervalometer" whereby in the field of view of aerial cameras, lines appear moving across the field of view. These lines can be made to appear stationary with respect to the Ground. The speed of the lines in the field of view regulate the time interval between two exposures and hence the forward overlap. The aircraft, to house the aerial camera, has to be a special type in which there is an opening for ground view by the aerial camera. Survey flights for aerial mapping call for much greater accuracy than normal flights. The special requirements for such an aircraft are:

(i) Camera mounting ,
(ii) Camera protection,
(iii) Vacuum connections,
(iv) Power supply D.C.,
(v) Navigation sights,
(vi) Alternating power supplies for gyroscopes for camera stability,
(vii) Vibration damping,
(viii) Oxygen for crew at high altitudes,
(ix) Inter-communication equipment for crew,

(x) Facilities for spreading maps and charts, and

(xi) Camera control box for levelling of aircraft before taking photographs.

2.4 Panoramic Cameras

There are two types of Panoramic Cameras : Direct Scanning and Bar Type (Fig. 2.2.4.1). The chief advantage of the panoramic camera is the very large ground coverage (almost 180°) from horizon to horizon (Photo 2.2.4.2 shows such a picture of Manhatten, New York, U.S.A. for horizon to horizon). However, the biggest disadvantages is the changing scale and the distorted imagery, largely due to perspective and non-perspective distortion.

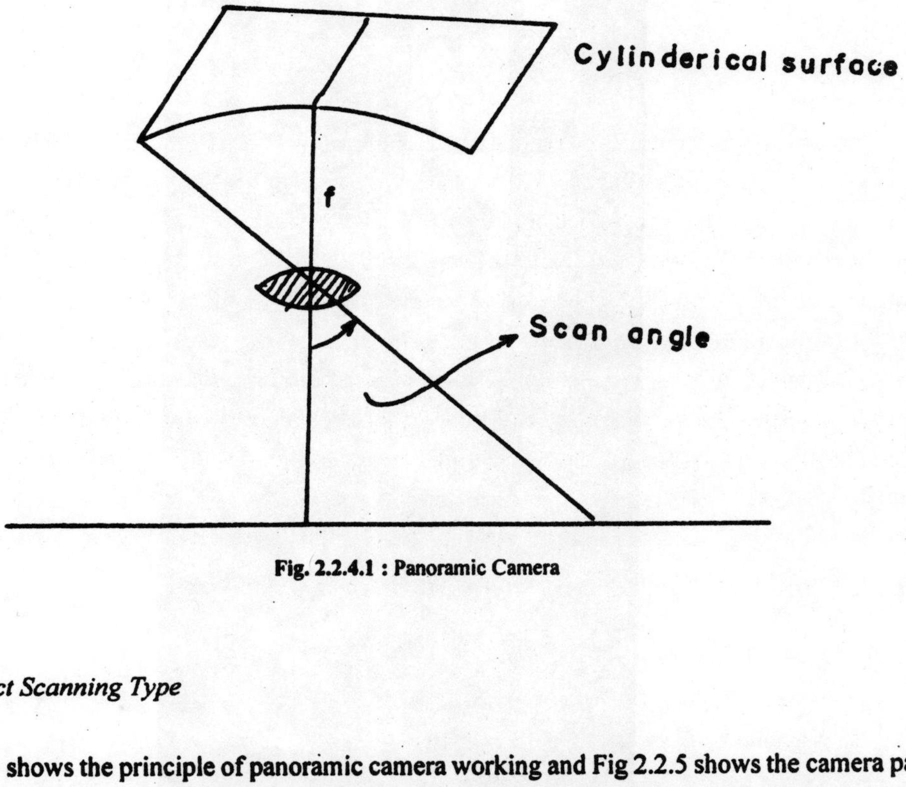

Fig. 2.2.4.1 : Panoramic Camera

2.4.1 *Direct Scanning Type*

Fig 2.2.4.1 shows the principle of panoramic camera working and Fig 2.2.5 shows the camera parts. A cylindrical surface carrying the film, is placed at a distance equal to the focal length of the camera lens. The lens with a slit opening rotates about horizontal axis. The Scan angle may very from 70° to 90°. The magazine section of the camera is similar to an ordinary aerial camera except that the lens, instead of being fixed, rotates and forms an image as the cylindrical surface. As seen from Fig. 2.2.6 the scale of the scanning or perspective distortion (see Fig 2.2.7). Superimposed on this is the so

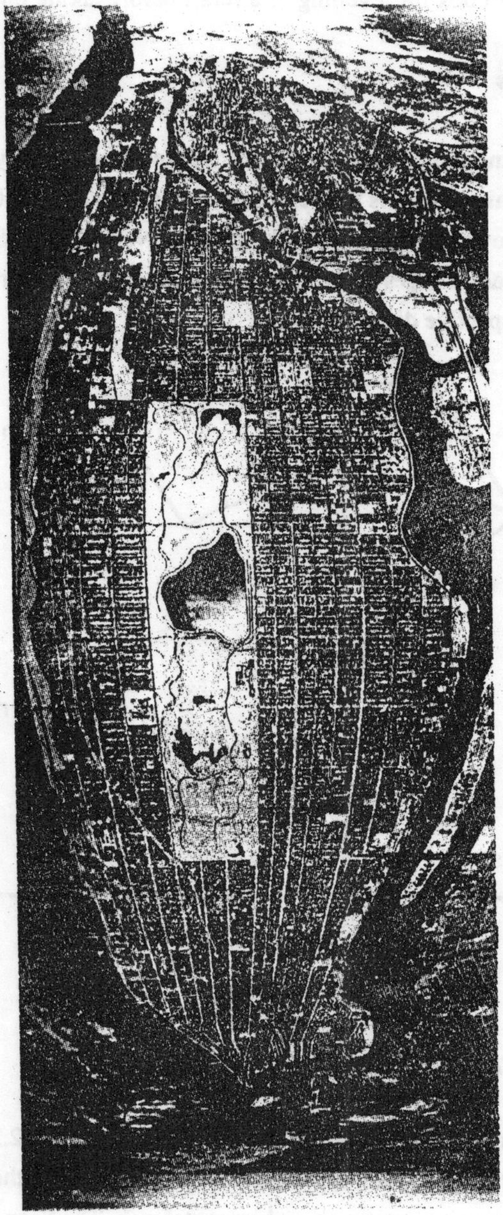

Fig. 2.2.4.2 : Panoramic Photograph of Manhattan from 10,000 feet (*Courtesy* of Itek Corp.)

called panoramic distortion due to displacement of image points from the true position due to curved nature of the image plane. Thus corresponding to a grid square on the ground will have the distorted grid on the imagery as shown in Fig. 2.2.8

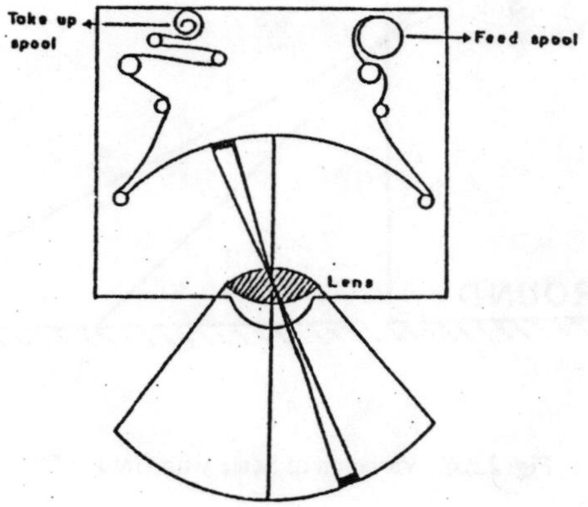

Fig. 2.2.5 : Direct Scanning Type

2.4.2 *Bar Type Camera*

Fig 2.2.9 shows the set up of a Bar type Camera. Here the film on a curved surface for a given scene is fixed but the image is formed by a series of strip images due to the rotation of a prism. However to compensate for the image motion (IMC) the film drum is moved along in the direction of the flight depending upon the aircraft velocity and the flying height. The chief advantages of such a camera are :

(a) very high resolution due to a very narrow strip and a small opening of the lens at the time of exposure and being close to optical axis,
(b) very large coverage,
(c) single exposure of the camera instead of multi exposures as on ordinary aerial camera,
(d) knowledge of exact flying height.

2.4.3 *Strip Camera*

The chief difference between the Strip camera and the Bar type camera lies in the fact that in the former case the lens is fixed and it is the film surface which moves at a constant (pre calculated speed) so as to have a continuous image formed by a series of strip images 2.2.10. The advantages are : (i) Simultaneous exposure of multiband of the same scene (area of the ground) at the same instant of exposure, (ii) High resolution and great geometric precision with proper lens filters combination), (iii) Film-filter combination being exposed simultaneously there are no illumination changes, that is, the imageries of all bands are of same intensity, (iv) possibility of several film filter combinations.

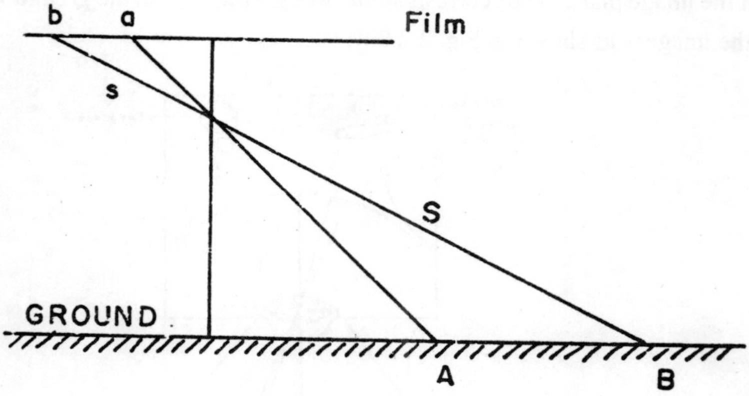

Fig. 2.2.6 : Variation of Scale with Ground Distance

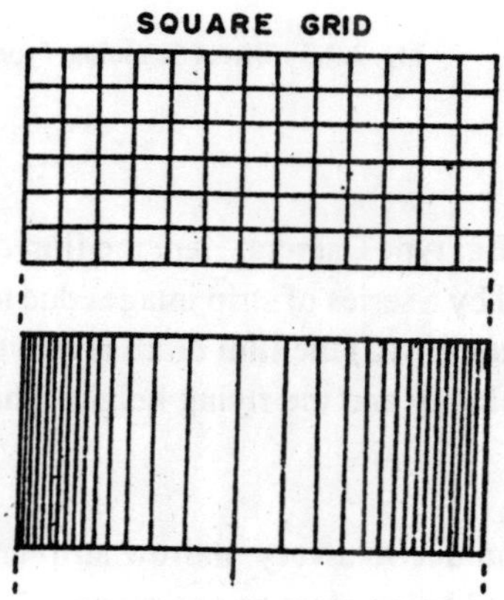

Fig. 2.2.7 : Scanning Distortion due to Changing scale in the Direction of Scan.

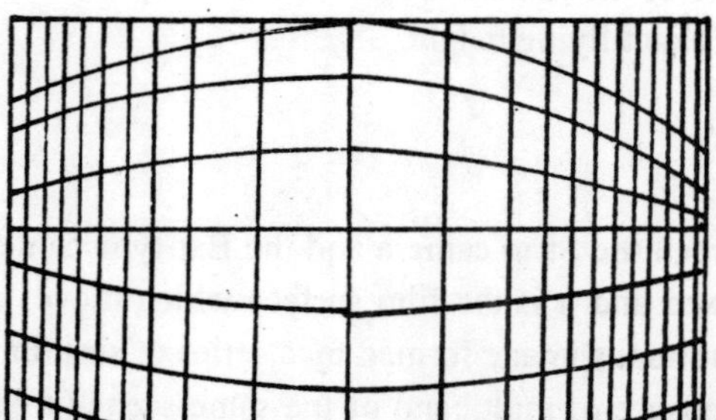

Fig. 2.2.8 : Panoramic Distortion

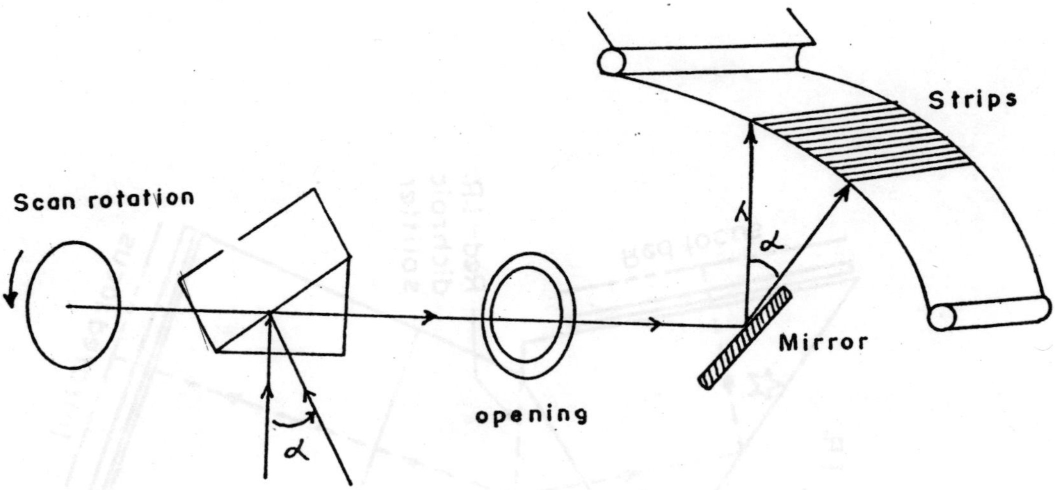

Fig. 2.2.9 : Bar Type Camera

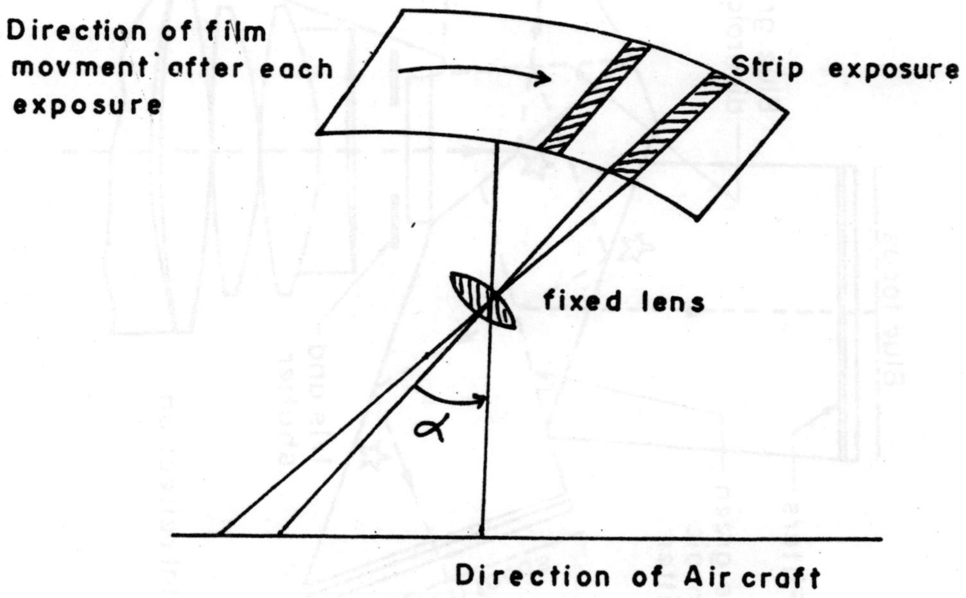

Fig. 2.2.10 : Strip Camera

An another example of the multiband camera is the Beam Splitter Prism Camera (See Fig 2.2.11), Using the principle or 'total internal reflection' the incident light as gathered by a single lens system is split into 4 bands. Using a 'dichrotic splitter' the original beam is split into Green, Blue, Red and Infra Red parts.

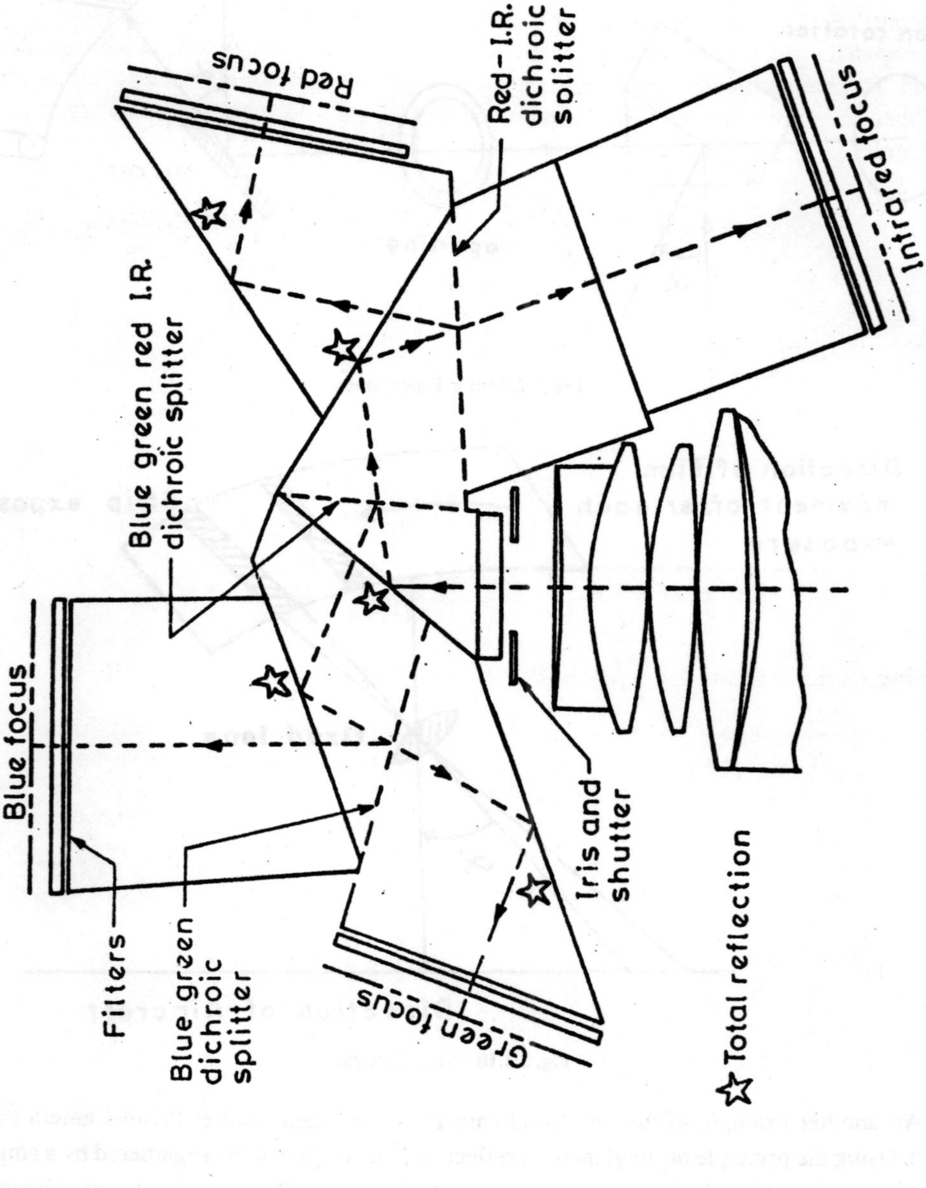

Fig 2.2.11 : Total Internal Reflection Type Camera

2.4.4 *Multi-Camera System*

The typical camera is a Trimetrogon Camera in which three cameras are placed in the aircraft with fixed angular relationship to each other. Fig 2.2.12 shows a typical Trimetrogon Camera working. Camera '1' has vertical optical axis. Camera '2' has camera axis inclined 60° to the vertical in the forward direction and Camera '3' in the backward direction with respect to the direction and motion of the aircraft. Thus three exposures of the ground with forward overlap are possible giving a large coverage of the ground. Such a system is obviously very useful for mapping of difficult and inaccessible terrain. The main difficulty lies in the changing scale of the Forward and Backward oblique imageries and, therefore, the mapping procedures are tedious and time consuming as compared to 'vertical' photography.

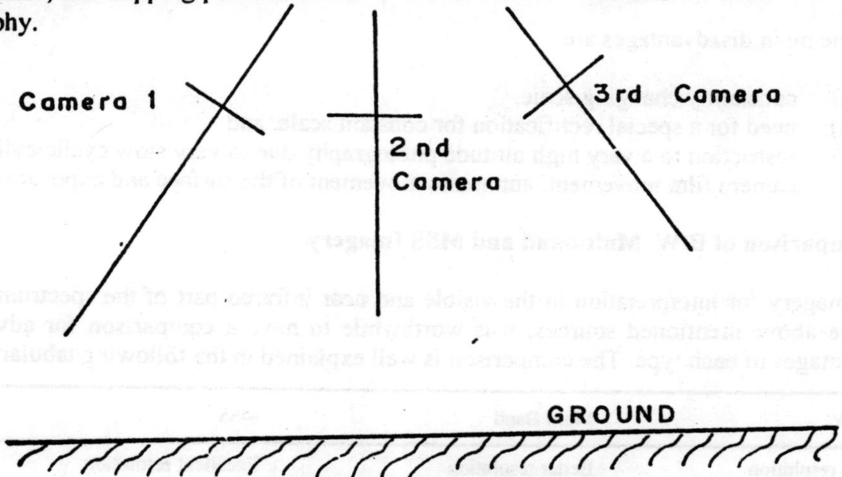

Fig. 2.2.12 : Set up of Trimetrogon Camera

2.5 Single Camera Multilens – Multi-Band Photography

The typical camera in this case is the one developed by Itek Corporation USA for 4 Band photography with 9 lens or 4 lens system. In the case of 9 lens camera (see Fig 2.2.13) six exposures (simultaneous and synchronized) are made in the visible part of the spectrum and 3 in the Infra–Red (IR) so that there are 9 exposures in all. Each exposure film size is 2/1/4" × 2/1/4". The imagery has Image

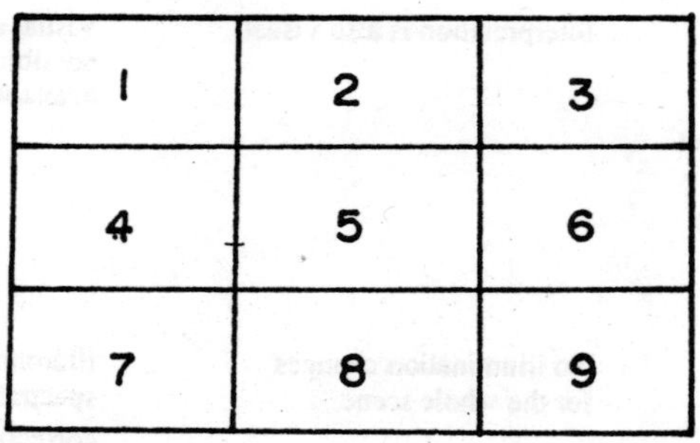

Fig. 2.2.13 : Multi-Band Camera Exposures

Motion Compensation (IMC). In the 4 lens camera developed by Fair- child Corporation USA, 4 rolls of 70 mm film are exposed to pre selected 4 bands of the spectrum. The advantages of the multiband of the camera are :

(a) photography need not be vertical i.e. the camera axis need not be along the direction of gravity;
(b) much less film length is required to have the same ground coverage as compared to classical vertical multi-exposure photography; and
(c) The whole scene of the ground covered is in one exposure, rather than number of exposures of film as in ordinary vertical photography (for lateral and forward overlap).

The main disadvantages are :

(a) constantly changing scale,
(b) need for a special rectification for constant scale, and
(c) restriction to a very high altitude photography due to very slow cyclic cylindric rate of camera film movement, automatic movement of the surface and exposure etc.

2.6 Comparison of B/W, Multiband and MSS Imagery

Since imagery for interpretation in the visible and near infrared part of the spectrum is available from the above mentioned sources, it is worthwhile to have a comparison for advantages and disadvantages of each type. The comparison is well explained in the following tabular form.

	B&W	Multi Band	MSS
1.	Poor resolution	Better resolution	Excellent resolution
2.	Vignetting Effect	Vignetting Effect	No Vignetting Effect
3.	Only two shades (Black & Grey) possible, no spectral differentiation possible	Differentiation in Grey tone possible	Differentiation possible, each wave band giving its characteristics grey tone.
4.	Information about shape and size of objects can be accurately determined by photogrammetric techniques due to large scale of imagery	Both shape and size and characteristic spectral information possible	Because of very small scale (1:1 million or so) size and shapes not possible to determine precisely
5.	Interpretation is visual and subjective based on the laws of converging evidence such as the result of tone, texture, pattern, association, shadows and scale of photo and the experience of the interpreter	Interpretation is also visual	Visual as well as Digital processing possible due to the additional information available on CCTs.
6.	There are no illum-ination changes for one scene.	No illumination changes for the whole scene.	Illumination change possible in different spectral bands, requiring sometimes correction for correct interpretation.

2.7 Comparison of Colour, IR and Panchromatic Film

2.7.1 *General*

Most procedures in photogrammetric mapping depend on the detection and recognition of objects and features, and therefore anything which contributes to mapping is of interest to the photogrammetrist.

The photograph, wherein is held most of the necessary information, is the basic tool of photogrammetry. Thus it is important to determine how meaningful are the differences in the object-detection capabilities of various types of emultion. It is of interest to determine whether the supposedly new dimensions of information, which the colour photography has revealed, could offset the cost, complexity and uncertainty of colour, when compared with the proven merits of panchromatic photography.

2.7.2 *Panchromatic (Pan) Film*

Panchromatic film has proven itself its utility over the years. Its technology is advanced, well known and widely practiced, and the equipment and materials which it needs are almost universally available. Among its well-known assests is its adequacy for general interpretation work, particularly where utmost definition and resolution of fine detail is desired. It is inexpensive compared to colour or false colour films, and widely considered to be best for identifying cultural features when large scale photography is used.

2.7.3 *Black and White Infrared Film*

Black and white infrared film is usually exposed only to light from the red and infrared parts of the spectrum. Its contrast is very high, but it suffers from a total loss of shadow detail. However, it facilitates the tracing of water features, and is comparable in cost with black and white film.

2.7.4 *Colour Film*

Colour film, sensitive to the whole visible spectrum attempts to reproduce, as far as practicable, the colour of objects as seen in nature, and this it very nearly succeeds in doing. A relatively new comer to photogrammetric uses, colour has made rapid progress during the past few years, but its procurement costs are higher than those of panchromatic or black and white infrared, while equipment and facilities for its exposure, processing, and photogrammetric usages are still limited. Also it is generally believed that there are quite a few technical problems connected with colour photography which today remain unsolved. However, the added dimension of colour appears to facilitate photo interpretation.

2.7.5 *Colour Infrared (False Colour) Film*

Colour Infrared Film makes no attempt to reproduce the natural colouring of objects and features, but sensitive to all visible light (except blue) and also to the infrared section of the spectrum, it produces unnatural colours (for instance live vegetation usually appears to be some shade of red in colour) accentuating the differences within specific bands of the spectrum. However, like colour the film is more expensive, needing special processing facilities.

2.8 Advantages and Disadvantages

The Panchromatic photography is adequate for most photo interpretation projects, but in general false colour is best for interpreting natural features, especially water and vegetation while colour is best for cultural detail.

In the context of identification and interpretation of those features which are usually depicted on a topographical map, colour is the best general tool, and it can be effectively used to cut down considerably on the ground checking and field completion of maps produced by aerial survey.

Colour could be used to advantage in identifying objects in shadow, and in difficult (e.g. remote mountanious, or forested, or swampy) terrain, especially where the land is not valuable and the features not particularly important. It would then enable a fairly realistic map to be drawn without the necessity of sending a field survey party into the district.

Colour could be used to advantage in identifying cultural features.

Colour photography, expensive as it is, would effect considerable saving here, since it is well known that photography is generally the cheapest major fact of the air survey, while the ground survey (aspect provision of control and field completion) is nearly always the most expensive.

It may not be possible to have a complete change over to colour in every respect. Apparently, besides the expense, there are still a few technical problems to be ironed out. It is suggested, however, that mapping photography could be taken in colour, and colour negative developed. Then, as much of the job as is possible would be done using black and white prints and diapositives, made from the afore mentioned negatives. Colour prints, transparencies, and/or diapositives would then only be made and used as needed for special interpretation, identification and even mapping tasks.

2.9 Camera Caliberation

2.9.1 *Introduction*

The objective of Camera calibration is to determine the numerical values of the Camera focal length (principal distance), the co-ordinates of the principal point with respect to fiducial axes and the coefficients of lens distortion elements K_1, K_2, K_3, etc. These values not only allow the camera setting for aerial photography but also enable to carry out analytical procedures, like analytical aerial triangulation etc.

2.9.2 *Methods*

Basically there are four methods for aerial camera calibration. They are :

(i) Stellar method,
(ii) Laboratory method,
(iii) Analytical or Dynamic method,
(iv) Field method.

2.9.3 *Stellar Method*

In this method the camera axis points towards the zenith and the negative plate is exposed to stars for a period of time so that star trails are recorded on the camera plate. The stars are identified and their directions (Right Ascension & Declination) recorded using a star Catalogue. The time of exposure is also recorded to convert the star co-ordinates in a rectangular earth frame co-ordinate system. The plate co-ordinates of the star images are measured precisely with respect to fiducial axes. Then a mathematical transformation between the measured plate co-ordinates of star images and their rectangular (projection) co-ordinates is carried out to determine the camera elements, namely the focal length 'C', the principal point co-ordinates X_0, Y_0, and the elements of lens (symmetrical) distortion K_1, K_2, K_3 etc.

Let α and δ be the stellar co-ordinates (Right Ascension and Declination) of an observed star. Consider a geocentric co-ordinate system *XYZ* (see Fig 2.2.14 and 2.2.15). Let the X axis point towards the First point of Aries.

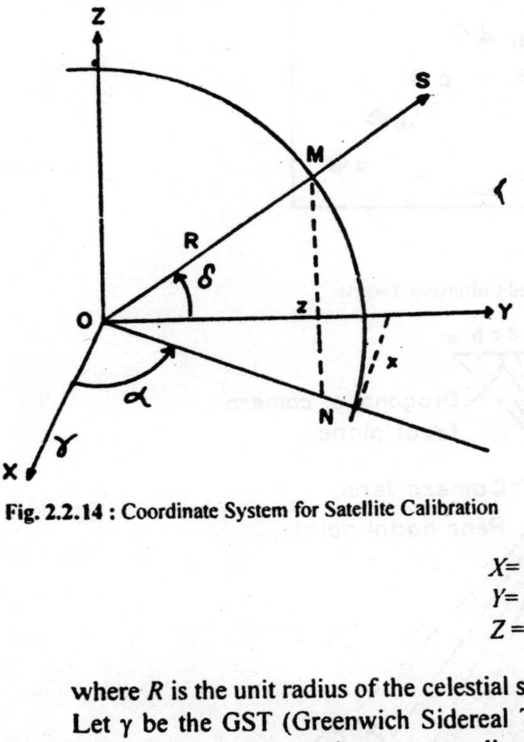

Fig. 2.2.14 : Coordinate System for Satellite Calibration

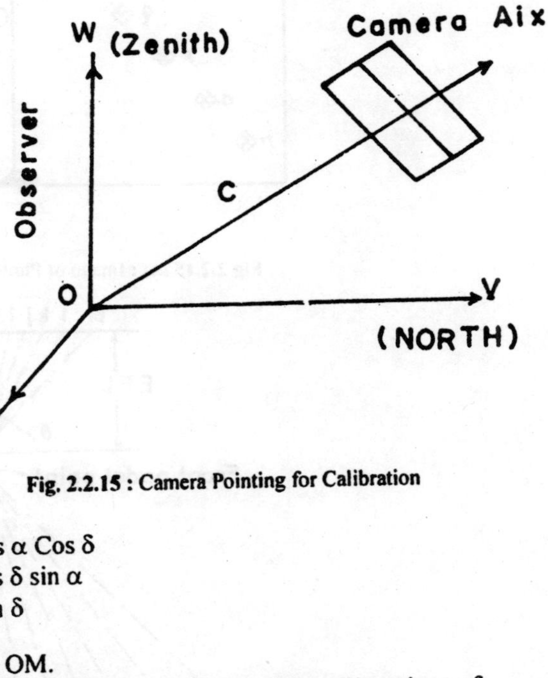

Fig. 2.2.15 : Camera Pointing for Calibration

$$X = R \cos \alpha \cos \delta$$
$$Y = R \cos \delta \sin \alpha$$
$$Z = R \sin \delta$$

where *R* is the unit radius of the celestial sphere OM.

Let γ be the GST (Greenwich Sidereal Time) according to the local observation time of photography. Then we rotate the *x,y.z* co-ordinates by γ to bring it into the topocentric co-ordinates and write.

$$\begin{bmatrix} u \\ v \\ w \end{bmatrix} = R_1(\gamma) \begin{bmatrix} x \\ y \\ z \end{bmatrix}$$

where R_1 (γ) is the rotation matrix.

Now let *R, Q, W* be the rotation elements of the camera system, x_0, y_0 the co-ordinates of the principal point and *x, y* the measured co-ordinates of the star image.

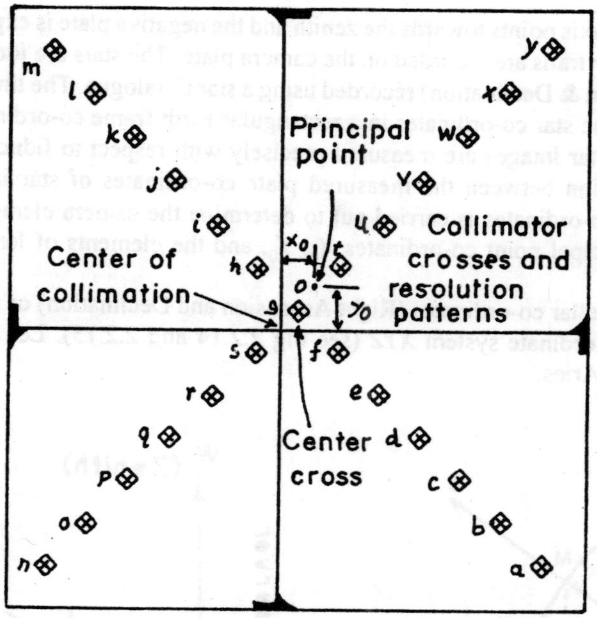

Fig 2.2.15 (a) : Image of Photographed Collimator Targets.

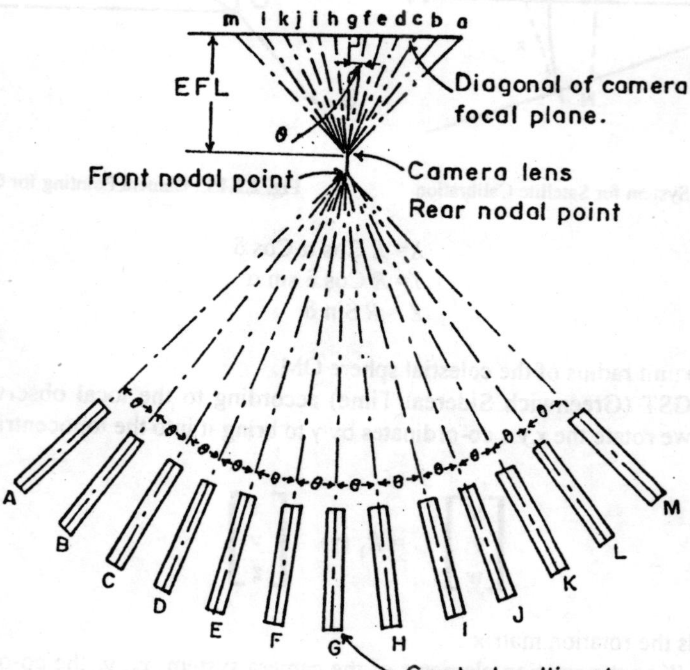

Fig 2.2.15 (b) : Band of Thirteen Collimators for Camera Calibration.

Now we have

$$\begin{bmatrix} x \\ y \\ c \end{bmatrix} = K R_1 (K) R_2 (Q) R_3 (W) \begin{bmatrix} u \\ v \\ w \end{bmatrix}$$

where $x' = x - dx$

$y' = y - dy$

K = scale factor and R_1, R_2, R_3 the rotation matrices

$dx = [K_1 r^3 + K_2 r^5 + K_3 r^7]$ x/r. $dy = [K_1 r^3 + K_2 r^5 ....] y/r$

$r = \sqrt{(x-x_0)^2 + (y-y_0)^2}$

Generally 30 to 40 stars may be observed and the solution from observation equations obtained by the method of least squares. Here the unknown are $C, x_0, y_0, K_1, K_2, K_3$ and the observation are the measured plate co-ordinates. The estimated value of x_0, y_0, are obtained from the mean value of x, y, that is–

$$x_0 = \Sigma x_i / n \quad i = 1 \text{ to } n$$

$$y_0 = \Sigma y_i / n \quad i = 1 \text{ to } n$$

where n is the number of stars images recorded.

2.9.4 *Laboratory Method*

This method, till recently, was the most commonly used technique of calibration. As the name suggests the calibration is done in laboratory using an instrument called 'Goniometer'. The instrument has basically a number of targets (crosses) marked along two diagonals, the angular direction of which can be measured using a telescope (see Figs. 2.2.15 (a) and 2.2.15 (b)). The camera to be calibrated is exposed to these targets and images recorded on the film. In principle, if 'f' is the focal length (the camera optical centre being at 'o' (see Fig 2.2.15) and Oc is the camera axis, θ the direction of the recorded image, the distance 'r' from O^1, then $r = f$. tan (θ).

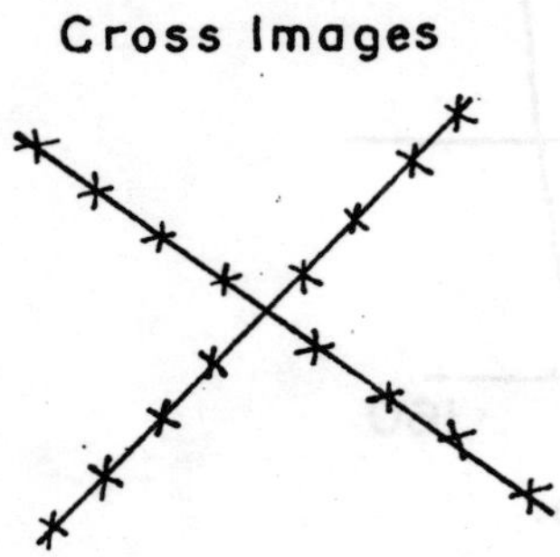

Fig. 2.2.16 (a) : Fiducial Marks for Camera Calibration

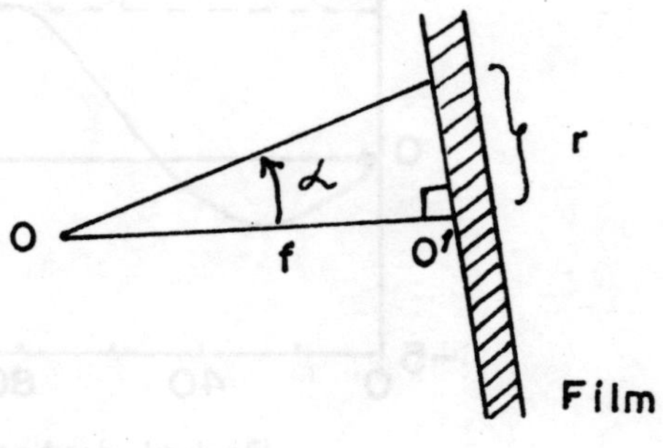

Fir. 2.2.16 (b) : Relation of Radial Distance and Focal length

The distance '*r*' can be computed from the observed co-ordinates *x, y* of the image i.e. $r = \sqrt{(x-x_0)^2 + (y-y_0)^2}$ and θ is measured by the collimating telescope. This then, enable *f* and x_0, y_0 to be computed easily. Because of optical distortion the computed distance '*r*' away from the centre of photograph will not agree with the observed or measured distance. In order to compute the distortion caused by the lens, we define a quantity called the equivalent focal length EFL which is given by = (See Fig 2.2.17).

$$EFL = \frac{on + ob + oc + od}{4}\left(\frac{1}{\tan\theta}\right)$$

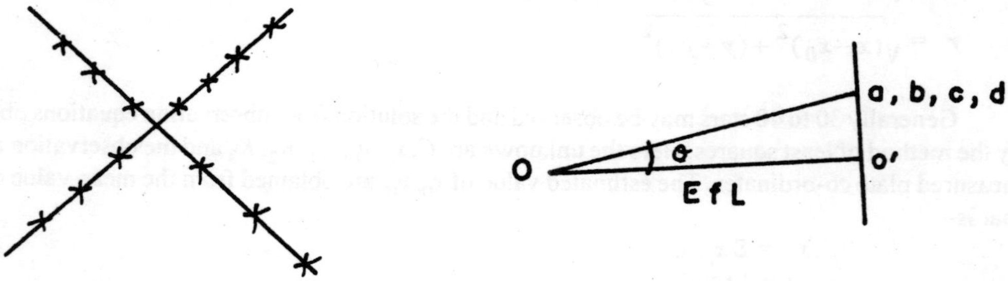

Fig. 2.2.17 : Equivalant Focal Length

where *a, b, c, d* are the first four cross images nearest to the centre and θ is the angle subtended by each of these at the optical centre of the lens and is measured directly.

We define the 'Radial Distortion' as the difference between the computed '*r*' and measured '*r*' from the cross images. Then a plot is made of Radial Distortion versus the radial distance along the diagonal from the centre of the photo. A typical Radial Distortion plot looks as shown in the Fig 2.2.18.

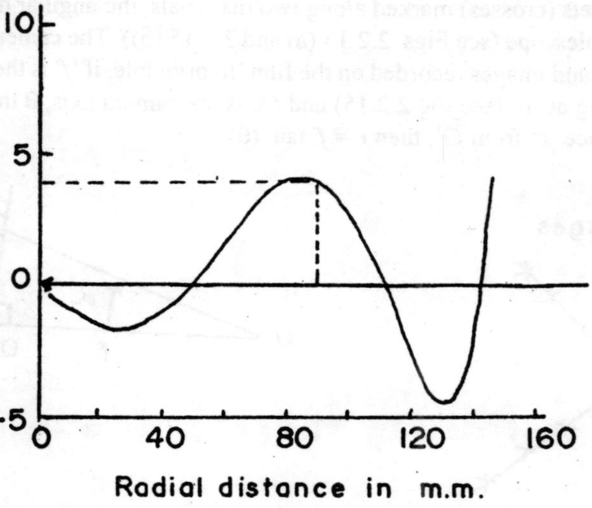

Fig. 2.2.18 : Radial–lens Distortion Curve for the Zeiss Aerial Camera Lens.

From the graph we can determine the balancing line such that the maximum positive radial distortion is equal to the maximum negative distortion. This distance shown as AB in Fig 2.2.19 is measured and then the Calibrated Focal Length (CFL) is calculated from the relation:

$$CFL = \frac{AB}{\tan\theta'}$$

where θ^1 is the angle corresponding to distance AB.
This θ^1 is again observed graphically by a plot of θ^1 versus 'd' (Fig 2.2.19).

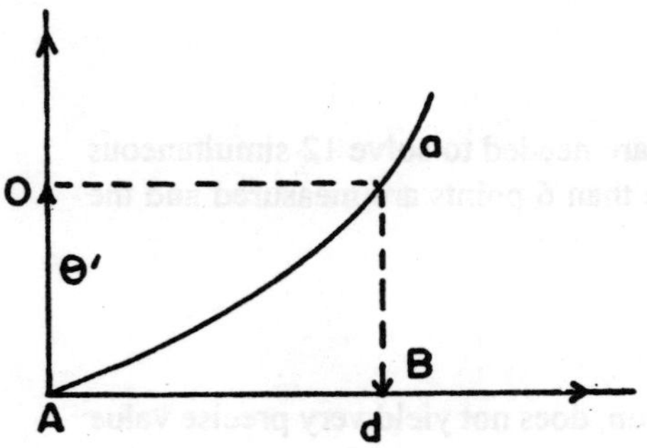

Fig. 2.2.19 : Distance Versus Angle Curve

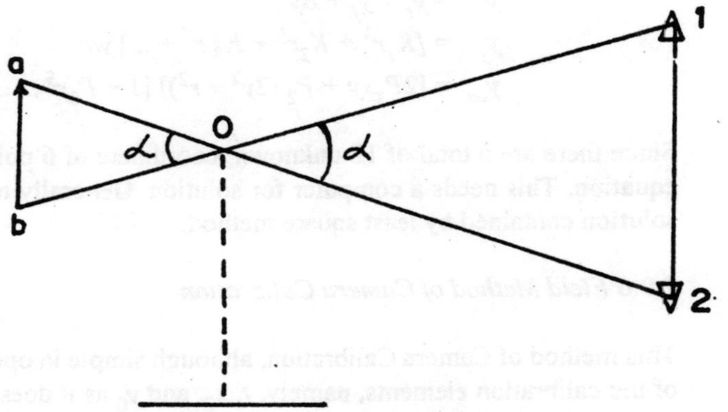

Fig. 2.2.20 : Field Calibration

2.9.5 *The Analytical Method*

As the name suggests the elements of camera calibration, namely, $C, x_0, y_0, k_1, k_2, k_3$, etc. are recovered through a set of calculations. It involves the basic projective equation between the plate co-ordinates, the ground co-ordinates, the camera orientation parameters and the exposure station co-ordinates. The equations are :

$$x - x_0 = C.\frac{a_{11}(X - X_0) + a_{12}(Y - Y_0) + a_{13}(Z - Z_0)}{a_{31}(X - X_0) + a_{32}(Y - Y_0) + a_{33}(Z - Z_0)}$$

$$Y - Y_0 = C.\frac{a_{21}(X - X_0) + a_{22}(Y - Y_0) + a_{23}(Z - Z_0)}{a_{31}(X - X_0) + a_{32}(Y - Y_0) + a_{33}(Z - Z_0)}$$

The observed photo co-ordinate x_r, y_r are corrected for refraction and lens radial distortion, namely

$$x = x_r + x_f + \Delta x$$
$$y = y_r + y_f + \Delta y$$

For atmospheric refraction, mathematical models are developed and hence Δx and Δy can be numerically computed. The lens distortion x_r consists of two parts, the radial (symmetric) and the decentred (asymmetric) part. The asymmetric part generally is much smaller than radial part and therefore can be neglected. However, for precise calibration, they are given by :

$$x_f = x_s + x_{as}$$
$$x_s = [K_1 r^3 + K_2 r^5 + K_3 r^7 + ...]\, x/r$$
$$x_{as} = [P_1 (r^2 + 2x^2) + 2P_2 xy ...]\, [1 + P_3 r^2 ...]$$

Similarly

$$y = y_r + y_f + \Delta y$$
$$y_f = [K_1 r^3 + K_2 r^5 + K_3 r^7 + ...]\, y/r$$
$$y_{as} = [2P_1 xy + P_2 (2y^2 + r^2)]\, [1 + P_3 r^5 ......]$$

Since there are a total of 12 unknown, coordinate of 6 points are needed to solve 12 simultaneous equation. This needs a computer for solution. Generally more than 6 points are measured and the solution contained by least square method.

2.9.6 *Field Method of Camera Calibration*

This method of Camera Calibration, although simple in operation, does not yield very precise value of the calibration elements, namely, f, x_0, and y_0 as it does not take into account the lens distortion parameters. As the name suggests, the camera is centered over a field station of known co-ordinates x_0, y_0, and z_0. Photograph is taken of 4 to 5 known well established ground points whose co-ordinates are also known in the same system as the camera station. The camera elements, namely, the focal length and the co-ordinates of the principle point are then computed through the image co-ordinates of the field points. Let $x_1, y_1, x_2 y_2, x_3 y_3$ be the image co-ordinates of the field station co-ordinates $X_1 Y_1 Z_1$, $X_2\ Y_2\ Z_2$ and $X_3\ Y_3 Z_3$ (Fig. 2.2.20). Let D_1 be the ground distance between stations 1and 2.

$$D_1 = \sqrt{(X_1 - X_2)^2 + (Y_1 - Y_2)^2 + (Z_1 - Z_2)^2}$$

Let 'd_1' be the photo distance given by:

$$d_1 = \sqrt{(x_1 - x_2)^2 + (y_2 - y_2)^2}$$

Let '0' be the camera station. Then the slant distance between 0 and station '1' is given (See Fig 2.2.20)

$$O1 = \sqrt{(x_0 - x_1)^2 + (Y_0 - Y_1)^2 + (Z_0 - Z_1)^2}$$

Similarly the corresponding photo slant distance is given by $\sqrt{(x_o - x_1)^2 + (y_0 - y_1)^2 + f^2}$

Similarly we get expression for distance O_2 and O_b. Then the angle 'α' subtended by the ground distance '*D*' is given by:

$$\cos\alpha = \frac{(O_1)^2 + (O_2)^2 - D_1^2}{2(O_1)(O_2)}$$

Assuming collinearity and no lens distortion we have also:

$$\cos\alpha = \frac{(O_a)^2 + (O_b)^2 - d_1^2}{2(O_a)(O_b)}$$

$$\text{Hence} \qquad \frac{(O_a)^2 + (O_b)^2 - d^2}{2(O_a)(O_b)} = \frac{(O_1)^2 + (O_2)^2 - D_1^2}{2(O_1)(O_2)}$$

This equation involves f, x_0, y_0 as the three unknown. Hence we need two more equations to solve the three unknown.

This is done by formulating two more equations by the ground stations 2 and 3 and their corresponding image points. The three simultaneous equation of the type given will enable the determination of f_1 x_0 and y_0. As will be seen above the equations are non-linear and therefore, we have to solve them by successive iteration starting with some approximate value of 'f' x_0 and y_0. The starting value of x_0 and y_0 can be taken as zero and the approximate value of 'f' as the distance between the camera len and the film.

2.9.7 *Dynamic Method of Calibration*

The calibration of Aerial Camera by field and laboratory methods using ground control points in flat plane (Horizontal or Vertical) has shown that there is a strong correlation between the calibration elements x_0, y_0, f. and the camera exposure station coordinates x_0, y_0, z_0. This results in inaccurate determination of the calibration parameter. It is, therefore, necessary to break this correlation. This has been shown that by using ground control in both flat and hilly terrain in a particular geometrical manner results in breaking the strong correlation between x_0, y_0, z_0 and X_0, Y_0, Z_0. This is known as the method of Mixed Ranges (MMR). This method is also known as Dynamic Method of Calibration as compared to laboratory calibration which is a 'Static' method. The Dynamic method has the additional advantage that the aerial camera is calibrated in actual field conditions of photography and not in ideal laboratory condition. While taking actual aerial photo, the atmospheric and other environmental conditions are very much different from the laboratory conditions. The atmospheric turbulence, uncertain refractions, different temperature, pressure and humidity condition at the time of exposure of aerial photography cause errors which are not there with fixed target method of laboratory or field calibration on the ground.

The Method of Mixed Ranges involves in selection of ground control points in such a way that the lines joining control point A, B, C, D, etc. on flat terrain pass through the ground control points E, F,G etc. on mountains meet at the exposure station '0' of the Camera Station. (see Fig 2.20.1)

This results in almost fixing the coordinates X_0, Y_0, Z_0 and hence breaks the correlation with x_0, y_0, f. The method model for the computation of x_0, y_0, f and K_1, K_2, K_3, etc is the same as that of the projective equations.

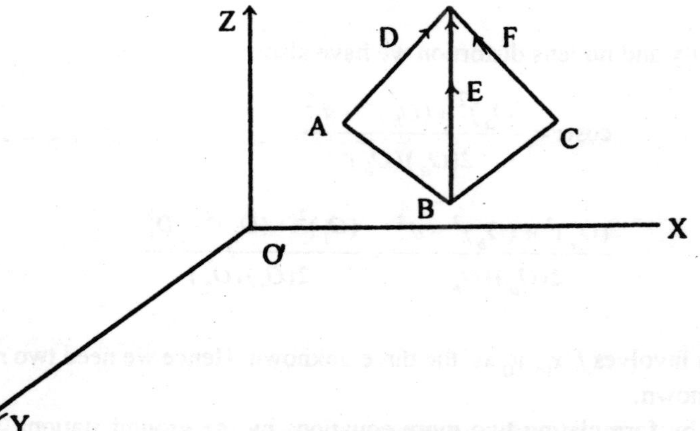

Fig. 2.20.1 : Dynamic Method of Calibration

The second method is known as the method of Vertical Wires. This, however, is not a dynamic method as the calibration is done inside a laboratory but it does break the correlation between x_0, y_0, f and X_0, Y_0, Z_0 because calibration done by ground control points in two dimensions, namely, vertical and horizontal. In this method vertical wire with weights are hung in different planes and photographs taken with markers on the wires. The co-ordinates of these markers are measured for the photographic image and then the projective equation solved for the unknowns which involve x_0, y_0, f, K_1, K_2, K_3, etc. A sufficient number of ground control points and their images are measured to get a least square solution.

3

STEREOSCOPY

3.1 Introduction

Practically the whole of air survey contouring and detail surveying is possible due to three-dimensional view available from two consecutive photographs when seen in a particular manner. The physiology of binocular or three-dimensional vision is difficult and quite complex and it is not fully understood as to how the mechanism in the human brain works to get space impression. It is not possible to explain 'why' but an attempt can be made to show how a three-dimensional view is obtained with the help of two eyes. Let us first consider the formation of an image at eye due to an object.

3.2 Mono-vision

The elements involved in a mono-vision and the image formation (Fig 3.1) are:

(1) Eye ball,
(2) Optic nerve,
(3) Visual centres of brain.

The eye ball with the lens rests and rotates in the socket of the eye and forms an image of external object at the retina. The stimulation from the retina in the form of electric pulses are carried by the optic nerves to the centres of the brain whereby the object image is sensed and viewed. The eye ball can contract or expand to adjust for its focal length (called accommodation) to form a sharp image at the retina. In front of the eye lens is the 'Iris' van automatic diaphragm which closes if the retina receives too much light. The diameter can vary from 3 to 8 mm. Near the optical axis on the retina is a "yellow spot" which is the most sensitive part of the retina.

The perception of relative distance of objects or three-dimensional view is limited to a few feet from the eye in a mono-vision.

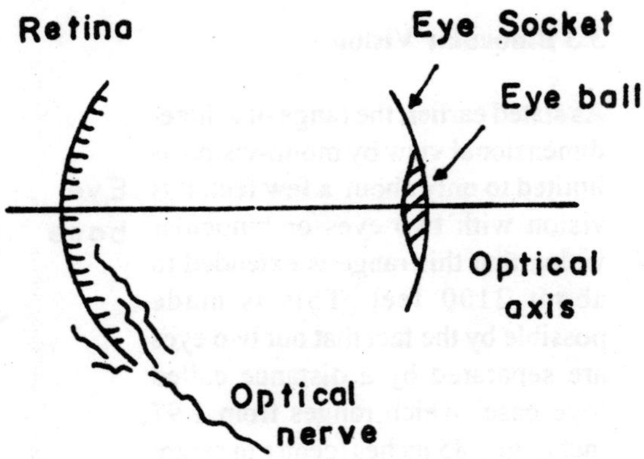

Fig. 3.1 : Construction of Human Eye

This is possible by various factors such as:

(i) Angle convergency: Near objects subtending larger angle at the eye than the objects at greater distance which subtend smaller angle. This changing angle is felt as an indication of the relative distance from the eye causing an impression of three-dimensional effect.

(ii) Degree of clarity of detail: The objects which are nearer appear very sharp and clear as compared to those which are further off. This sharpning of image or clarity of detail is also interpreted by the human brain as a measure of the relative distance and here the space concept.

(iii) By previous knowledge: A prior knowledge of the relative distances of the objects also creates and impression of space. The brain automatically stores this information with the image formation to judge which object is seen closer.

(iv) Accommodation: As started earlier, the capability of the eye lens to adjust its thickness and therefore the radius of curvature according to the distance of the object is termed as *accommodation*. The eye lens has to either contract becoming thicker, as seeing objects come closer and expand or become thin with a large radius of curvature to see objects at a greater distance. This contraction or expansion is also interpreted and correlated with distance judgement for three-dimensional space effect in a single eye. The best accommodation is obtained for objects at infinity when the eye is least strained, the near being at 150 mm and best possible at 250 mm which is called the distance of distinct vision (Fig. 3.2).

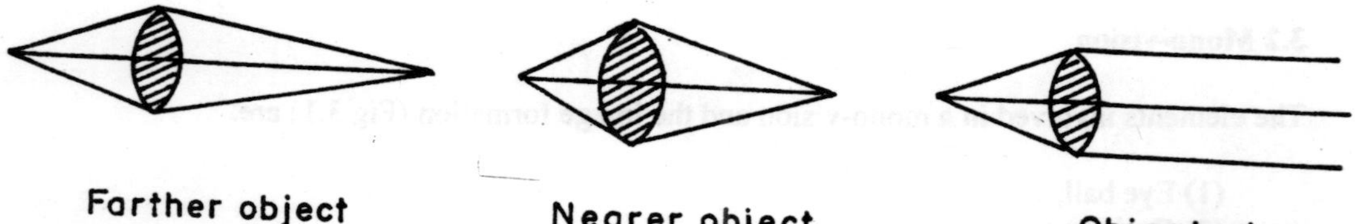

Fig. 3.2 : Eye Lens Optics

3.3 Binocular Vision

As stated earlier, the range of a three-dimensional view by mono-vision is limited to only about a few feet. It is vision with two eyes or binocular vision that this range is extended to about 2100 feet. This is made possible by the fact that our two eyes are separated by a distance called 'eye base' which ranges from 1.97 inches to 2.85 inches (centre to centre of eye balls). If there are two objects *A* and *B* subtending an angle θ_1 and θ_2 at the eye base, then it is $(\theta_2 - \theta_1)$ (see Fig 3.3) which determine the capacity of the eyes to distinguish these two objects as separate. It is now found that if $\theta_2 - \theta_1$ becomes less than 20 seconds of an arc the human eyes fail to resolve them as separate. Taking eye base (average) as 2.5 inches, the maximum distance up to which the relative distance can be appreciated is—

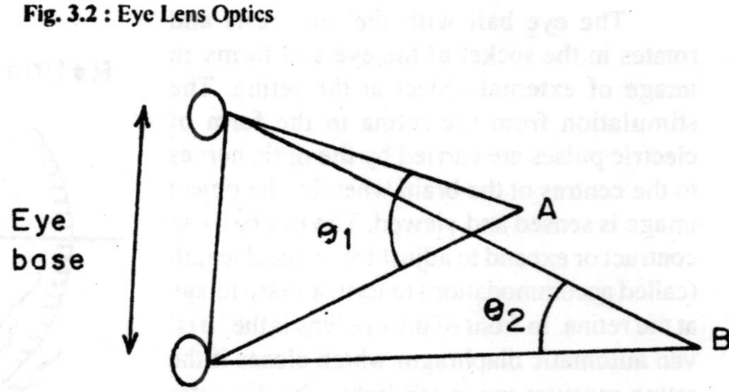

Fig 3.3 : Convergence of Eye Optical Axes

$$D = \frac{2.5}{20} \times 206265$$

$$= 2100 \text{ ft } (1 \text{ radian} = 206265'')$$

Other factors which help in enhancing the three-dimensional view in binocular vision are:

(a) Intensity of light (lighterd objects appear closer)
(b) Difference in colour (bluish objects appear further off)
(c) Size of object (bigger objects appear nearer)
(d) Mental illusions

The most important thing, however, in the formation of three dimensional effect is the slight different images as seen by the two separate eyes of the same objects. Referring to Fig. 3.3 we notice that the optical axis of each eye converges by different amounts with respect to the eye base which fixes the object *A* in space as if *A* is located in space by the intersection of the two optical axes of the two eyes. It is the two slightly differing views of the same object which is the essential requirement of three-dimensional image and realization. It is exactly this principle which is utilized in photogrammetry by taking two consecutive photographs of the same object from the different exposure stations that we see a three dimensional view under a stereoscope. This can be seen from the following set up also.

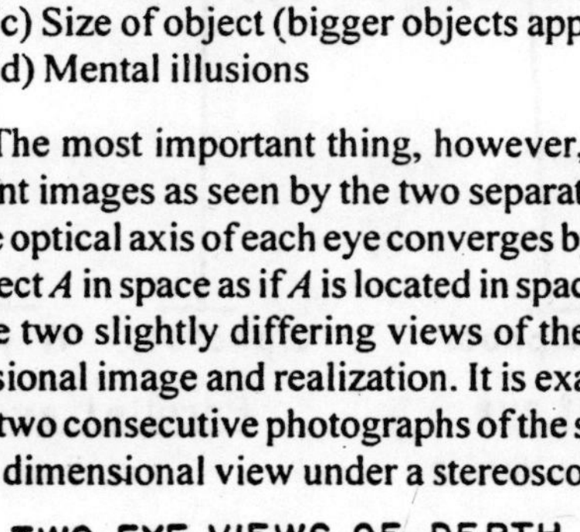

Fig. 3.4 : Image Formation by Two Eyes

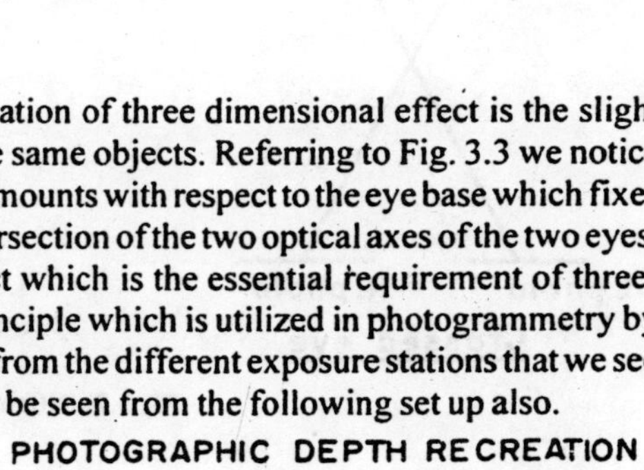

Fig. 3.5 : Image Formation by Equivalent Lens

Suppose we have a nail *AB* driven vertically into a wooden board. In the normal binocular vision an image *ab* is formed by the left eye *L* and another image *a'b'* by the right eye *R* as shown in Fig. 3.4. In Fig. 3.5 we have replaced the eyes by two identical lenses (1) and (2) and placed film to record the images *ab* and *a'b'*. Now in Fig. 3.6 we see these two images after developing the images by means of a cardboard placed between the two eyes *L*, *R* and the two photos so that the left image is seen only by the left eye and the right image by the right eye lens. By drawing the geometrical rays we notice that the three-dimensional image *AB* is reconstructed. This process is exactly reproduced while making maps from a pair of photos. The manner by which two images of the same object are merged into one to give three-dimensional effect is called "Stereoscopic Fusion". This is achieved by :

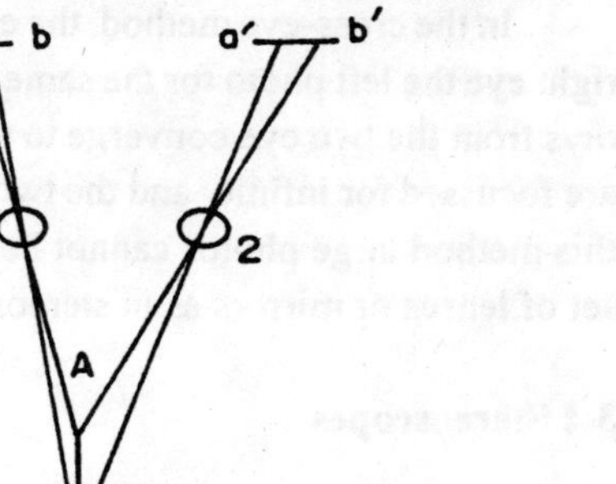

Fig. 3.6 : 3D Vision from a Pair of Photos

(a) Naked eye
(b) System of lenses and mirrors called stereoscopes.

We can get stereoscopic fusion by naked eye in three ways:
(i) Crossed eye (ii) Convergent eye and parallel eye as shown in Fig.3.7

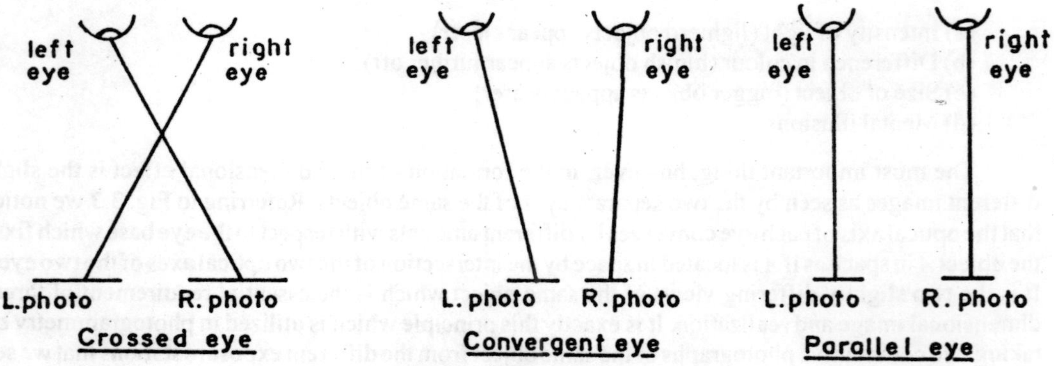

Fig 3.7: Different Types of Eye Viewing

In the cross-eye method, the eye balls are so moved that the left eye sees the right photo and the right eye the left photo for the same detail to form stereoscopic fusion. In the converging eye the two rays from the two eye converge to the same detail in the two photos whereas in parallel eye the eyes are focussed for infinity and the two photo images separated by a distance equal to the eyes base. By this method large photos cannot be handled. This is possible only where the effect is enlarged by a set of lenses or mirrors as in stereoscopes.

3.4 Stereoscopes

The separation of the images so that the left eye sees only the left image (photo) and the right eye sees the right image is achieved by means of mirrors and lenses in stereoscopes. The simplest type of a stereoscope is a mirror stereoscope shown in Fig 3.8 (a)

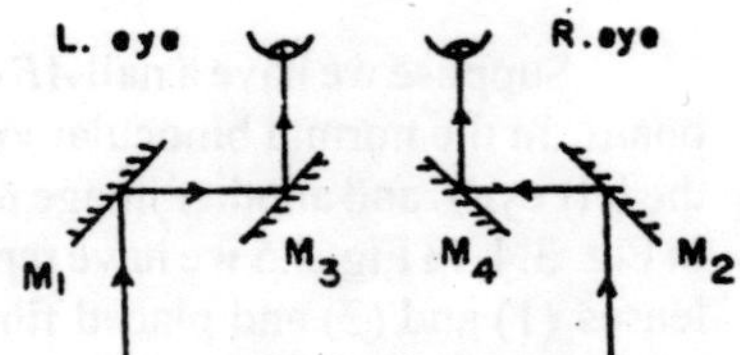

Fig. 3.8(a) : A Simple Mirror Stereoscope

The two mirrors $M_1 M_2$ reflect the photo images to the left and right eye respectively through two mirrors M_3 and M_4. The fusion of the images is obtained by moving the photos parallel to the eye base. Such a stereoscope has no magnification of the photo image. For the desired magnification up to a certain value, additional lenses with diagonal prisms can be used in place of the mirrors M_3 and M_4 of Fig 3.8 (b). The distance between the mirrors M_1 and M_2 is usually 240 mm (large enough for 9" × 9" photography). The use of lenses and diagonal prism increases this distance to 300 mm and gives about 0.8 magnification (which is rather, reduction). Additional telescopes placed between the eyes and the prisms give a magnification up to 8.

Lens or pocket stereoscope consists of two lenses separated by a distance equal to eye base (2.5" on the average). The photographs are placed (as shown in Fig 3.9) at a distance of *f*, the focal length of the lens *L*, with the result that the rays emerging after the lens *L* are parallel. These parallel bundles of rays are focussed at the retina by the eyes lens, viewing the objects at a distance of 250 mm for accommodation. The magnification of the image is therefore 250/*f*, with *f* = 100 mm we get a magnification of 2.5. This pocket stereoscope is cheap, portable and has a large field of view and a very clear and bright image. However' a pocket stereoscope has two big disadvantages: (i) *A limited magnification.* It is not possible to increase magnification with simple lens beyond 3 × and at the same time keep the lens aberrations low. Also the distance between the head and the photos becomes too small for adequate illumination without undue complication. (ii) The distance between corresponding points on the photos must be equal to or smaller than the eye base. With normal size photos this becomes difficult or impossible without bending or folding the photos.

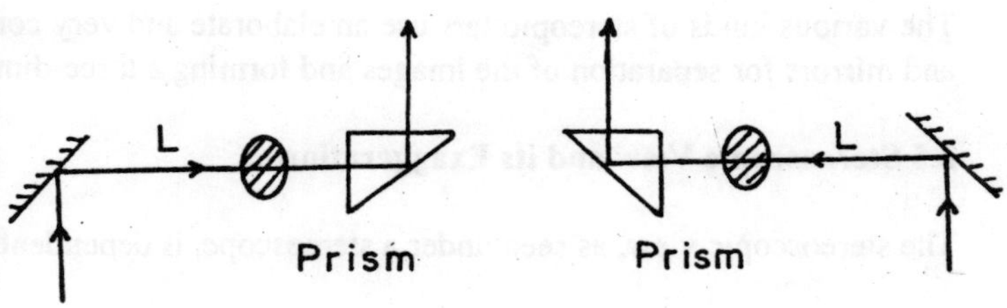

Fig. 3.8 (b) : Lens Stereoscope with Magnifier

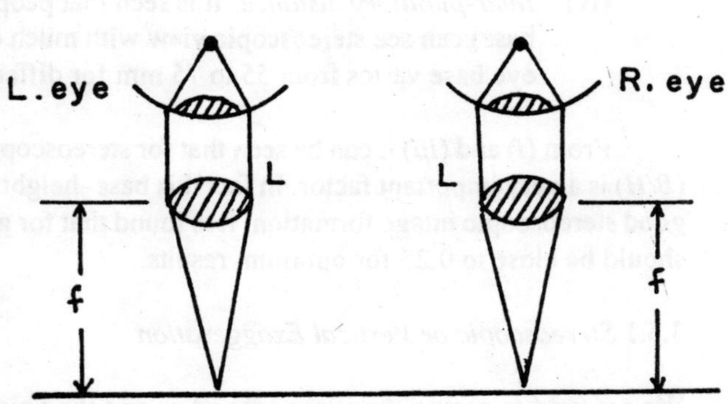

Fig. 3.9 : Lens Type Stereoscope (Pocket type)

3.4.1 *Anaglyphs*

Another method to separate the two photographic images is to have the two photos in two complementary colours, i.e. the left photo in red and right in blue green and then see them through a filter containing red and blue green lenses as spectacles.

Under stereoscopic fusion the three complementary colour (red, blue and green) fuse to give a white colour and three-dimensional view. This is done in the Kelsh Plotter. Sometimes the two images of red and blue-green can be printed on paper side by side and the view obtained by a red-blue spoctacle.

Vestograph is an arrangement in which the two images give out two types of polarised light, one polarised in the vertical plane and the other in the horizontal plane. Similar spectacles as for anaglyph can be used for viewing a three-dimensional effect whereby the left eye receives the vertically polarised light and right eye, the horizontally polarised light. Such a system while being used in stereoplotters give several difficulties such as additional polarisation due to the viewing surface with the result that this method has found no use except with the possibility of three-dimensional pictures seen in a movie hall.

3.4.2. *Stereoplotters*

The various kinds of stereoplotters use an elaborate and very complicated system of optical lenses and mirrors for separation of the images and forming a three-dimensional image.

3.5 Stereoscopic View and its Exaggeration

The stereoscopic view, as seen under a stereoscope, is dependent upon:

(i) *The air base:* Photos with greater air base produce better stereoscopic impression than those with a smaller base.
(ii) *Focal length of the stereoscope:* A stereoscope with smaller focal length produces greater magnification and hence a better three-dimensional appearance.
(iii) *Flying height:* Greater flying height gives smaller scale and hence little stereoscopic impression.
(iv) *Inter-pupillary distance:* It is seen that people with greater inter-pupillary distance (eye base) can see stereoscopic view with much ease than those with a smaller eye base. The eye base varies from 55 to 75 mm for different persons.

From (*i*) and (*iii*) it can be seen that for stereoscopic vision the ratio of air base to flying height (*B/H*) is a very important factor. In fact this base–height ratio *B/H* is always taken as an indication of good stereoscopic image formation. It is found that for good stereoscopic view this base-height ratio should be close to 0.25 for optimum results.

3.5.1 *Stereoscopic or Vertical Exaggeration*

We are used to seeing the space around us and the objects with our normal eye base of 2.5 inches. While seeing a three-dimensional view under a stereoscope the eye base is effectively increased by mirror or lens systems. As a result we see much sharper and steeper slopes under a stereoscope than they are actually on the ground. This enhanced three-dimensional view is called stereoscopic exaggeration or vertical exaggeration which causes exaggeration of vertical distances with respect to the horizontal distance and makes look objects taller than what they are. Vertical exaggeration increases with the base-height ratio *B/H*. Thus, greater the distance between the camera stations, the flying height remaining constant, greater is the vertical exaggeration. Several relations have been mathematically worked to get the vertical exaggeration factor *q*. Some of the relations are :

$$q = (B/Z)\left(\frac{250}{E}\right) \text{ (due to Jackson)}, \quad q = \left(\frac{B}{H}\right)\cdot\left(\frac{h}{E}\right)$$

$$q = \left(\frac{B}{Z}\right)\frac{D}{E} \text{ (due to Thurrel)}$$

$$q = \left(\frac{B}{Z}\right)\frac{250}{E} \; (D/C)$$

where

B = Air base, distance between camera stations in space
Z = Flying height over mean terrain level, also denoted by H
h = Distance at which we are conscious of stereoscopic three-dimensional view
D = Optical distance from eye to the photos in mm
C = principal distance (generally focal length) of camera
E = Inter-pupillary distance of the observer

Shadows also play a very important role in viewing a stereoscopic model. When the shadows fall toward the observer in a pair of photos seen under a stereoscope the objects appear in their proper relief. However, if we so align the pair of photos that the shadows fall away from the observer, the objects appear in inverse relief, i.e. valleys appear as ridges and ridges and mountains appear depressed as valleys and basins. This is called *pseudoscopic stereo vision.* The shadows also help in interpreting the nature and dimensions of the object. In order to get proper stereoscopic view the following requirements must be met :

(a) The y parallax should be very small. In other words, the camera axes at the moments of exposure should be approximately in one plane;
(b) The base-height ratio should be within limits;
(c) The scale of the two photographs should be approximately the same, although fusion may be possible with scale differences up to 15 per cent. For continuous observation and measurements differences greater than 5 per cent are found to be inconvenient and strenuous to eyes; and
(d) There should not be excessive x parallax and too much height difference as the human eye cannot fuse beyond a certain x separation of images. Also the two photos should have preferably the same colour contrast.

4

IMAGE INTERPRETATION

4.1 Introduction

4.1.1 *Principles of Image Interpretation*

Each image on a photo has its own characteristics and their merits differ from image to image and as such it is hard to lay down specific principles of image interpretation. Take for example a family portrait. Here every member of a family is recognized on the basis of tone, colour, shape and size of the image. In addition the interpreter has some pre knowledge of family members which may be called the 'Reference Level' of the interpreter. In the case of an aerial photo the characteristics of the image of earth's surface may again relate to tone, colour, shadow, texture, shape and size and other associations between features and their surroundings. In addition certain ground characterstics such as land form, vegetation, land use, drainage, erosion and lineaments help in interpreting the image.

4.2 Interpretation of Aerial Photo

It is easier to interpret an aerial photo if the interpreter is already familier with the area and he can easily correlate what he sees on the photo and what he knows is on the ground. This one to one correspondence is then stored in the mind of the person. The fundamental difference in capacity for interpretation for known and unknown areas stand in the mind of the interpreter can also be called the reference level and the successful interpretation of an aerial photo depends upon this reference level. This can be increased for each site. In addition a good sense of observation, imagination and patience do add to the qualities of the interpreter.

For any site investigation an interpreter should have a basic knowledge of geology, geomorphology and geotechnical engineering as the site investigation requires knowledge of physical and cultural features and their relationship to geology, geomorphology landuse etc. As each site is of different in nature, it is necessary to supplement the information content from his existing topographical, geological, soil and forest maps along with other reports of the site and last but not least the visit to the site for familiarization of the terrain.

4.3 General Procedure for Photo Interpretation

For aerial photo and remote sensed imagery interpretation the following procedure may be recommended:

(a) Preliminary examination
(b) Detailed examination
(c) Interpretation
(d) Compilation

In the preliminary stage it is necessary for the interpreter to become familiar with the site and its surrounding area. At this examination easily identifiable images are correlated with the ground features such as roads, rivers etc. The principle of working from 'whole to parts' is also followed here from the overall view of the terrain using aerial photos. This is achieved by making a photo mosaic of the aerial photos (by joining successive and overlapping photos and removing the common area). The next stage of detailed examination is to examine overlapping photos under a stereoscope to see the third dimension i.e. topography of the terrain and its variation. Overlays are then prepared by tracing from the photos on to tracing paper showing the features which have been identified.

Many times the stages of detailed examination and interpretation can be combined and can be carried out side by side.

Although the nature and amount of interpretation work will vary from project to project some of the common features to be noted from aerial photos which are common to any project work are:

(i) Topography such as hills, valleys, flood plain, lakes, steep and gentle slopes, depression, gullies quarries, embankments and coastal features etc.
(ii) General Geology such as different soil boundaries, soil types (whether alluvium, peat, clay, sandy or gravel etc.).
(iii) Structural Geology such as major joints, strikes, faults, dykes, rock types erosion, and bedded rocks etc.
(iv) Drainage and drainage patterns, springs, seepage, major rivers, streams and channels etc, marshy areas, ponds and lakes etc.
(v) Existing hazards such as abandoned mine sites, mining subsidence, trenches and burried foundation etc.
(vi) Site history such as earlier use of now abandoned buildings, wasteland and removal of vegetation etc.

The compilation stage consists of making a map from aerial photos and showing the features of significance as identified by interpretation. Since the scale of each photo differs, depending on the topography and tilt of aerial photos, any of the existing photogrammetric methods such as rectification may be employed to get a final map with symbols depicting the features of the terrain and other information about the terrain such as landuse etc.

4.4 Three Dimensional Image Interpretation (Qualitative) Method

The basic requirement here is a set of overlapping imagery and a stereoscope to obtain a three-dimensional view of the terrain. Information about the object is then collected based on the following interpretation keys and other converging evidence:

(*i*) *Tone :* Ground objects of different colour reflect the incident radiation differently depending upon the incident wave length, physical and chemical constituents of the objects. The imagery as recorded in remote sensing is in different shades or tones. For example ploughed and cultivated lands record differently from fallow fields. Tone is expressed qualitatively as light, medium and

dark. In SLAR imagery, for example the shadows cast by non-return of the microwaves appear darker than those parts where greater reflection takes place. These parts appear of lighter tone. Similarly in thermal imagery objects at higher temperature are recorded of lighter tone compared to objects at lower temperature which appear of medium to darker tone. Similarly top soil appears as of dark tone compared to soil containing quartz sand. The coniferous trees appear in lighter tone compared to broad leave tree clumps.

Tone, therefore, refers to the colour or reflective brightness. Tone along with texture and shadow (as described below) help in interpretation and hence is a very important key. Differences in moisture content of the soil or rock result in differences in tone. In a black and white photograph dark tone indicates dark bodies, namely, greater moisture centents and grey or white tone reflect the dry soil. The aerial photos with good contrast bring out tonal differences and hence help in better interpretation. Tonal contrast can be enhanced by use of high contrast film, high contrast paper or by specialized image processing techniques such as 'Dodging' or 'Digital Enhancement'. Some time Infra-red film can give better contrast but it can also reduce resolution and loss of detail in shadows.

Table 4.1 gives the tonal ranges for different terrain factors such as topography, geology, vegetation etc. for the reflectance characteristics and different tones as recorded in radar imagery.

(*ii*) *Texture :* Texture is an expression of roughness or smoothness as exhibited by the imagery. It is the rate of change of tonal values. Mathematically it is given as dD/dx where D is the Density and 'x' the distance measured from one arbitrary starting point, and can be measured numerically by the use of micro-densitometer. Changes of density 'D' in going from point 'A' of the imagery to point 'B' as measured by the micro-densitometer divided by the distance gives the texture values numerically. Texture

TABLE 4.1 Terrain Factors and Representative Tonal Ranges

Factor	Reflection Characteristics	Tonal Range
1. *Topographic*		
(a) Flat surface	Specular reflection if Surface is smooth: no return	Dark tone
(b) Sloping surface facing antenna/cemera	Relatively high return due to orientation effects	Medium to light tones
(c) Sloping surface facing away from antenna or camera	Relatively low return due to orientation effects	Medium to dark tones
(d) High relief	No return from shadow areas	Dark tones
2. *Geologic*		
(a) Rough surface	Diffused Reflection, medium to high return	Medium to light tones
(b) Smooth surface	Specular reflection if surface is flat: no return reflection influenced by topographic factors	Dark tone, lighter tones produced by orientation effects
(c) Natural corner reflectors produced by in bed rock by weathering	Maximum reflection, high return	Very light tones
3. *Vegetation*		
(a) Trees	Diffused reflection	Light tones
(b) Woods and Forests	High returns	Light tones

(c) Bush	Higher returns with increasing densing of occurrence	Light tones in number in sub humid areas medium to dark tone in arid area environments
(d) Natural grass	Diffuse reflections, medium to low returns, dry sparse vegetation produces less scatter than bush rich-vegetation	Medium tones in humid to subhumid areas. Dark tones in arid environment
(e) Broad leaf crops with high moisture content Small leaf crops	Diffuse reflection high returns Diffuse reflection medium return	Light tones Medium tones

is dependent upon (a) photographic tone (b) shape, (c) size, (d) pattern and scale of the imagery. Any slight variation of these can change the texture.

Texture can qualitatively be expressed as course, medium and fine .The texture is a combination of several image characteristics such as tone, shadow, size, shape and pattern etc. and is produced by a mixture of features too small to be seen individually because the texture by definition is the frequency of tonal changes. As an example, leaves of a tree are too small to be seen on an aerial photo collectively along with shadow they give what is called texture which in turn helps to differentiate between shrubs and trees, Texture sometimes can be very important factor in determining the slope stability. In the case of a humid ground, the blockage of water or bad drainage a characteristic texture results. Even spring and seepage of water from the base of clay give a kind of 'turbulant' texture. So is the case with mud flows. The term texture is also, sometimes, used to denote drainage density and the degree of dissection of land surface.

(*iii*) *Association* : The relation of a particular feature to its surroundings is an important key to interpretation. Sometimes a single feature by itself may not be distinctive enough to permit its identification. For example sink holes appears an dark spots on an imagery where the surface or immediate subsurface soil consists of lime stones,. Thus the appearance of sink holes is always associated with surface lime stone formation. An another example is that of kettle holes which appear as depressions on photos due to terminal moraine and glacial terrain. An another example is that of dark - toned arcuate features associated with a flood plain of a river which can be interpreted as in-filled oxbow lakes.

(*iv*) *Shape :* Some ground features have typical shapes due to the structure or topography. For example air fields and football stadium easily can be interpreted because of their finite ground shapes and geometry whereas volcanic covers, sand, river terraces, cliffs, gullies can be identified because of their characteristics shape controlled by geology and topography.

(*v*) *Size* : The size of an image also helps for its identification whether it is relative or absolute. Sometimes the measurements of height (as by using parallax bar) also gives clues to the nature of the object. For example measurement of height of different clumps of trees gives an idea of the different species, similarly the measurement of dip and strike of rock formation help in identifying sedimentary formation. Similarly the measurement of width of roads help in discriminating roads of different categories i.e. national, state, local etc. Size of course, is dependent upon the scale of imagery.

(*vi*) *Shadows* : Shadows cast by objects are sometimes important clues to their identification and interpretation. For example shadow of a suspension bridge can easily be discriminated from that of cantilever bridge. Similarly circular shadows are indicative of coniferrous trees. Tall buildings and chimmneys, and towers etc. can easily be identified for their characteristic shadows. Shadows on the other hand can sometimes render interpretation difficult i.e. dark slope shadows covering important detail.

(*vii*) *Site factor or Topographic Location :* Relative elevation or specific location of objects can be help to identify certain features. For example sudden appearance or disappearance of vegetation is a good clue to the underlying soil type or drainage conditions.

(*viii*) *Pattern* : Pattern is the orderly spatial arrangement of geological topographic or vegetation features. This spatial arrangement may be two-dimensional (plan view) or 3-dimensional (space).

Geological pattern may be linear or curved. Linear pattern are formed of a very large number of continuous or discontinuous short ticks which when viewed by eye appear to be continuous lines. Example of linear geological pattern are faults, fractures, joints, dykes, bedding planes, anticlines etc. (See Fig 5.5) Examples of curved features are plunging anticlines and folds. (see Fig 5.6)

Lineaments or lineations may be short, medium or long running for several hundred kilometers. These are very important expressions of the lithologic characters of the underlying rocks and the attitude of the rock bodies, spacing of planes of bedding and other structural weaknesses and the control extended by them over the surface features.

Vegetation pattern may be of the 'Block' type or 'Alignment' type.

The 'Alignment' type may be further subdivided into the Linear, Parallel and 'Curved' type.

Example of Block type are the timber trees in Montana, U.S.A. due to extensive outcrop of rocks of uniform character i.e. presence of unaltered quartz monozonite.

Alignments are due to narrow rockbands or faults. Since faults retain moisture, vegetation is aligned along the fault lines.

Example of topographic pattern are the typical drainage patterns (controlled and uncontrolled type). The uncontrolled type are those which are purely governed by topography, that is the slope whereas the controlled type are those which are governed by the underlying geological formations.

The well known drainage patterns are :

(i) Dendritic, (ii) Trellis, (iii) Annualar, (iv) Radial, (v) Rectangular, (vi) Parallel Type, (vii) Braided, (viii) Anastomotic, (ix) Asymmetrical, (x) Collinear.

Drainage patterns take an important place amongst the various interpretation elements, used as criteria for identification of geological and geomorphological phenomena. Factors to be considered are amongst other the density which is measured for the erodibility of the rocks; the amount of geological control on the drainage pattern and the integration and homogeneity of the pattern.

In alluvial terrains the anastomotic pattern (Fig 5.7) of meandering streams, cut off meanders, oxbow lakes and interlocking channels is the most common. The Yazoo pattern (Fig 5.7) occurs if the natural levees of the trunk river force the tributaries to flow parallel to the main stream before debouching. The dichotomic pattern (Fig 5.7) of radiating (centrifugal) drainage channels occurs in alluvial fans, Some channels may have a blind end because the water largely percolates into the coarse fan material. Other streams may then originate as springs in the lower part of the fan. Some deltas have a similar pattern. The braided pattern (Fig 5.7) develops where excessive sedimentation occurs e.g. due to a sudden decrease in gradient of the river which then is unable to carry on its load. The sediments then force the rivers emerge from the mountains and enter the alluvial plain. The rectangular pattern (Fig 5.7) is a system of interconnected stream channels formed in coastal lowlands when tidal currents occur. Special drainage type are amongst other the drainaged, phantom and internal lacunate patterns etc.

If in erosional terrain the influence of geological structure on drainage is negligible, the following main patterns are found. The dendritic (arborescent) pattern (Fig 5.7), resembling the stem and the branches of a tree, is the most common. The parallel pattern (Fig 5.7) composed of more or less parallel channels is developed if the influence of the general slope of the terrain is more pronounced. Sub-dendritic and Sub-parallel patterns (Fig 5.7) are transitional forms, where geological structure may have slightly influenced the trunk rivers. A radial pattern (Fig 5.7) also is not usually directly influenced by structure. It is either centrifugal (Volcanic cone: dome) or centripetal (depression).

The influence of structure begins when beds of different resistance are exposed by erosion. An annular pattern (Fig 5.7) then will result in case of a dome structure. It is composed of circular or ellipsoidal, subsequent drainage element located in the less resistant rocks, which debouch in the pre-existing and consequent, radial streams. The trellies pattern (Fig 5.7) is characterised by long, rather straight main rivers, many of which are parallel. The tributaries are short. This type originates if in sedimentaries straight strikeness and parallel main faults occur. The angulate and rectangular patterns (Fig 5.7) are characterized by many sharp angular bends of the streams which are due to faults or joints. Special types of patterns in erosional landscapes are pinnate, collinear, swallow hole, contorted, barbed patterns etc. Internal drainage patterns may occur in areas of important infiltration.

Other geomorphological indications are numerous. The watershed pattern e.g. a phenomenon to be considered in conjection with the drainage pattern, is especially useful in areas where little resistant beds of gentle to moderate dips occur. The dip slopes then are largely eroded, but the U or V shaped divides may still indicate the direction of dip and the general strike.

The dissection of the area (coarse-medium-fine) and the size, steepness and shape of a slope may also yield important information. The form and development of slopes depend as far as lithology is concerned on the resistance of the rocks against surfacial run off and against mechanical or chemical weathering. Factors influencing run-off effects are cohesion plasticity and permeability. The effect of mechanical weathering is governed by the massivity (fractures etc.) of the rocks, the grain size and the homogeneity of the grains (size, colour etc.). The rate of chemical weathering is influenced by the solubility of the rocks and minerals the susceptibility of these minerals to certain chemical processes etc. Resistant to superficial run off are e.g. most igneous rocks and sandstones. Non-resistant in this respect are clays, sands and shales (weak cohesion or great plasticity). Limestone is particularly influenced by chemical processes.

Another group of interpretation elements is in the cross-sections of valleys and other erosional features usually of small scale. The shape of gullies (See Fig. 5.8 a,b,c) is largely governed by the material in which they are formed. Their characteristics thus have some value for the determination of the kind of material occuring, provided that the other factors influencing their forms such as climate, vegetation and stage of development are comparable. The erodability of a soil is influenced by two factors viz. the mechanical friction between the grains and the physical/chemical cohesion. Medium to coarse sands and gravels have considerable resistance due to the high internal friction inherent to their grain size, whereas clays derive their strength from the cohesion. The material between 2 and 200micron (fine sands and silt), is according to LUEDER, easily erodable. The height of the slope is another important factor in this relation. If it is less than the critical height of the material occurring, a vertical slope will be maintained, whereas mass movements (sliding, slumping, etc.) will create a characteristic and more gentle slope profile as soon as the critical height is exceeded. The critical height ranges from 0 metres for dry sand and max. 1 metre for moist sand to max. 10 metre for material with a certain silt or clay content. Extremely high values are found in lees and volcanic tuffs (100 metres).

The following three characteristic types of cross-section exist. In non–cohesive porous material (sands, gravels) a V-shaped profile (See Fig 5.8b) with a low vertical cliff at the upper end of the slope is characteristic few branches occur. In cohesive, rather impervious material shales, clay the cross-section is charactrized by its width and its smooth forms. Many branches occur, cross-sections of gullies occurring in intermediate material (sandy shale etc.) have a moderate width and after smooth vertical sides (U-shaped), intricate patterns occur. The longitudinal profile of the gullies may also have some value for the estimation of the kinds of material occurring. Rather steep and short longitudinal profiles normally occur in non-cohesive prorous material, whereas long and gently sloping valleys, with almost unnoticeable valley-heads are characteristic for cohesive material of low porosity. The easily erodable material of intermediate grain size has normally a moderate gradient with abrupt and steep valley head. The characteristic longitudinal profiles and cross sections are indicated in figure 5.8c; Fig 5.9 shows a plot of Resistance to erosion versus the size of the eroded particles.

4.5 Grey Tone Criteria

The photographic grey tone is more limited an interpretation element than the above-mentioned group of landform (relief) elements. Definite conclusions usually are only arrived at in conjunction with other criteria. It should be borne in mind that only the tonal differences are important and not the absolute total values. The latter depend largely on the sensitivity range of the film emulsion used and upon the processing of the film. Tonal differences of geological origin are, of course, rather rare in areas covered by a uniform vegetation (tropical rain forest). The grey tone criterion is most valuable for geological purposes in non-vegetated areas. Part of the tonal variations then are due to the different rock or soil colour and another part is the result of differences are often particularly striking in semiarid countries. Capillarity largely influences the saturation and desication of the ground and thus is important in this field.

The *Patterns* of tonal fetures also may offer a clue, e.g. to reveal a creek system, joint pattern, etc. A comparison of densitometer measurements of the photographic image with reflectivity data of rocks or soils colected in the field, may be useful as an aid in improving the interpretability of an area.

Optimum use of the grey tone criterion requires sufficiently large tonal differences. It is not uncommon, however, that certain features having a low grey tone contrast are particularly important as interpretation criteria, whereas the high tonal contrasts are due to factors of non-geological interest (e.g. shadows). Electronic dodging by reducing those high contrasts, then may add considerably to the interpretability of the photos.

4.6 Associated Phenomena as Criteria

Vegetation and landuse features are the most important amongst the associated phenomena, which make up the third group of interpretaiton criteria, special tree/vegetation types may regionally be characteristic for a certain rock type or inversely, may not occur under certain lighological conditions. Zoning of the vegetation frequently indicates clearly the strike direction in areas of sedimentary or metamorphic rocks. Such vegetative indications in photogeology may either be due to the physical or the chemical characterisitcs of the soils or result from difference in soil humidity or permeability. Faults and fractures are often well visible from the air due to vegetation features and humidity conditions (see Fig 5.10)

Apart from specifie species, the vegetative cover, as a whole may offer a clue, by way of its characteristic density, height size and regularity.

An example of this phenomenon is. e.g. the much higher– though similar vegetation occurring in Suriname on Dolerite dykes than on the surrounding granites. Micro-vegetation sometimes is of special importance in arctic and semi-arid regions. Careful distinction should be made, however,between patterns of geological importance and others related to factors like human activity and topographic exposure to rain, wind or sun.

Vegetation on the other hand may also obscure a great amount of geological details, particularly if it forms a dense cover. A homogeneous cover is less disturbing than an irregular, dotten one and particularly less than the intricate pattern produced by intense landuse. It is for this reason that photogeology of intensily cultivated areas in N.W. Europe is sometimes more difficult than jungle covered areas, particularly those where sedimentary rocks occur. Many geological details can often be traced with remarkable details underneath a jungle of rather uniform height.

4.7 Evaluation of Various Criteria

The various interpretation criteria mentioned above, can be applied to the three types of geological/ geomorphological photo-interpretation : structural, lithological and dynamical interpretation.

Structural interpretation is particularly important where sedimentaries occur (oil-exploration). The understanding of the geological structure is usually arrived at during the process of delineation of boundaries and it thus precedes the lithological interpretation. Dip and strike observations are a main concern and are dealt with in more detail. Other indications for the structure are in the first place outcrop patterns., The actual outcrops of exposed rock only play a role of importance in non-vegetated countries, provided that the scale of photography is sufficiently large. Next in importance ranks the drainage pattern. Annular and trellis patterns frequently occur, with subsequent rivers located in the less resistant beds and particularly if the dips are moderate or steep. The length of tributaries sometimes is an indicaton for the dip direction as usually the longer ones are found on dip slopes, whereas the shorter ones occur on the face slope of the beds. Exceptions to this rule may, however, occur if the beds are steeply dipping. Dendritic patterns indicate the occurrence of horizontal beds or possibly very weak beds of any dip. Faults can often be detected from the air on the strength of horizontal displacement of the bedding, drag, scarps, drainage features, etc. Unconformities also can be pointed out when discendances of dip and strike, abrupt contact between different formations etc, occur. Care must be taken, however, not to be misled by cross bedding, or faulting.

Structural interpretation of metamorphic areas is much less revealing and usually confined to incomplete scattered features, the interconnection of which is difficult or not at all possible. Foliation and cleavage are common in these kinds of rocks. Contact zones, veins and plugs, are structural elements to be mapped in igneous areas. Cleavage can sometimes be observed. A particularly interesting aspect in igneous (and in some sedimentary) rocks is the mapping and interpretation of joint patterns. Two aspects can be considered viz. the frequency distrubution of joint directions (azimuth) or the regional distribution (delineation) of certain patterns of joint density characterisitcs.

The dynamic interpretation is quite a different aspect of photo-interpretation. The changes occurring in the landscape, due to various processes (river work, coastal processes, mass movements, etc.) then is stressed. This approach is particularly important for certain geomorphological studies and if rather rapid changes are concerned. It is advantageous to have two or more photo coverages from different years, or otherwise a reliable map and a set of photos from another period. Quantitative evaluation of the changes then will result from comparative studies. The dynamic approach is still possible, however, if only one photo- coverage exists. A number of subsequent positions of coastlines, natural levees of rivers etc. are often visible from the air and thus the trend of development can be studied.

Extrapolation of the observed changes, into the past or into the future is feasable. Extrapolation into the future is of particular interest for engineering purposes.

In practice the various aspects of interpretation are used in combination although the accent is not always on the same aspect. Direct evidence is sometimes obtained, but more important are usually

the conclusions drawn by deduction from indirect evidence. In mineral exploration e.g. can are deposits related to faults or veins and also goshen, often be easily detected from the air. Mineralization slumping is another direct indication. If ore deposite in the contact zone surrounding an intrusive body or hydrothermal deposits are concerned, direct indications are usually lacking and it will then only be possible to point out areas where the chances for mineral accumulation are best. Lateritic ores and placer diposits are detected mainly on the strength of their morphological appearance.

4.8 Resolution

The capacity to differentiate two very elosely situated objects is defined as resolution. Among other things the incident wavelength is one of the most important criteria for resolution. The shorter the wavelength the greater the resolution. High resolution gives better object discrimination and hence more information about the object. Thus an imagery with high resolution be of great use in identifying ground features of small extent such as small fractures, joint, buildings and nature of trees etc.

4.9 Spectral Response

The fact that imagery in different wave bands is available in remote sensing can considerably enhance the art of visual interpretation compared to black and white photography. The response of objects to different wavelengths being different, the examination of the different waveband imagery can help pick up the particular object. For exmple, if we were to differentiate between surface water bodies and vegetation a comparison of the four waveband imageries in band 4, 5, 6 and 7 will immediately show the presence of water bodies distinctly in band 7. This is because water has strong absorption for infrared waves, The band 7 imagery will clearly show water bodies distinct and promient than forest or vegetation areas (on the positive transparancies they will appear darker).

The nature of multispectral imagery help interpreting and collecting more information is respect of the following fields in the manner indicated below:

4.10 Application of Aerial Photo Interpretation

Aerial photos have been used for several applications. Using the principles of visual photo interpretation information about the earth's surface feature can be obtained. Some of the areas whereas aerial photos have been extensively used are in the areas of :

(a) Topographical mapping
(b) Geology,
(c) Soil mapping,
(d) Forestry,
(e) Terrain evaluation,
(f) Landuse/Land cover mapping,
(g) Agriculture,
(h) Water resources, and
(i) Environmental studies/flood damage studies.

(a) Topographical Mapping : The basis of topographical mapping using aerial photograph is the common overlap between two successive photos in the forward and lateral direction. The forward direction is the direction of the aircraft flight and the minimum forward overlap required is 60 per cent. The lateral overlap, at right angles to the forward direction can vary from 25 to 30 per cent.

The overlapping photos are placed in the socalled stereo projectors in such a manner that the model of the ground is recreated and the observer sees the three dimensional view of the ground. For this it is necessary to create geometrical conditions between the two photos in the stereo projector in such a way that the inclination between the two successive photo is exactly the same as at the time of taking pictures by the aerial camera. This is best illustrated by Fig 5.11. It is possible to draw not only the planimetry but also the contours at desired scale and interval by suitable selection of ground control points. These ground control points appear on the aerial photos. The biggest advantage of aerial mapping lies in cost and efficiency. Whereas a very large number of such control points are required for mapping by traditional ground survey methods, such as plane tabling, a much less density of control points is required by aerial methods. The time required by photo mapping is also much less compared to ground methods. At present, the accuracy achieved is so much that the aerial mapping has almost become a universal technique of mapping.

(b) Geology : The geological mapping involves both surface and subsurface mapping for mineral and other geophysical exploration. An aerial photo gives an excellent birds eye view, a so called 'synoptic' view of the terrain from a given height. Higher the elevation from where the photo has been taken greater is the synoptic view. In case of geological surface features it is some times very difficult to recognize it from the ground. For example a fault of width of a few metres may not be recognized while standing on the ground but if seen from a height the fault will appear very clearly on the photo. This is due to what is called the lineament effect. Human eye can some how recognize features if they extend over a long distance even though the width of the feature is beyond the resolution of the eye. Using the principles of photo interpretation and by the help of so called 'Key' it is possible to do geological work for the following:

(*i*) Structural mapping such as for Faults, Folds, Dykes, Joints, Dip and Strike: using the method of 'Parallax Bar' it is possible not only to determine the direction but also to calculate the slope and hence the dip and strike of formations. Similarly displacements due to big faults, folds, with anticline and synclines, fold axis etc. can be easily identified on the aerial photos. The classical joints and dykes, volcanic cones etc are also very easily recognized because of their characteristic shapes. Some of these are illustrated in Fig 5.12

(*ii*) *Rock Types :* The three major rock types, namely igneous, sedimentary and metamorphic rocks can be identified with the help of drainage pattern and other characteristric features like erosion pattern, Sand stone and limestone rocks show very poorly developed drainage pattern and typical karst phenomenon of sink holes (see Fig 5.13). These holes appear as dark round features on the aerial photos. Granite rocks appear as massive rounded domelke structures with typical drainage pattern and absence of vegetation or vegetation appearing in areas of joints. Volcanic rocks appear with radial drainage pattern and typical lava flow and volcanic vents. (See Fig 5.14 to 5.16). The metamorphic rocks have a banded structures which can sometimes be identified on the aerial photos. In general interpretation of metamorphic rocks is much more difficult compared to sedimentary (Fig 5.17) and igneous rocks.

(iii) Lithology : The types of information that an aerial photo provides for interpretation *lithological* purposes are :

(a) The photographic tone of the rock body to that of adjacent rocks,
(b) resistance to erosion,
(c) boundaries of rock types,
(d) topographic expression,
(e) boundaries of outcrops,
(f) the joints and their pattern,
(g) faults and their pattern,
(h) drainage pattern,
(i) the vegetation cover, and
(j) the lineament pattern.

(c) Soil Mapping : It is well known that soils are derived from rocks and that soils are in general . surface features and hence cannot be directly mapped the same way as in forestry, geology or topographic mappings. A photo will serve to prepare a Base Map on which ground information can be inserted and a correlation between the type of soil and corresponding tone and texture on the aerial photo be identified. Using this the experienced soil scientist can use aerial photos to his benefit. In addition viewing the photos under a stereoscope gives him additional 3 D view. Other factors which help in soil type mapping are the soil moisture content, soil texture, surface roughness, the presence of iron oxide and the organic matter content.

The unpredictibility and indirectness of relationship between individual landscape element and soils has led to an emphasis on the use of so called 'Physiographic Systems' in photo interpretation. Such a physiographic system is defined as specific set of physiographic conditions which can be inferred by the use of 'Converging evidence' produced by different individual landscape elements on the photos. These physiographic systems may be related more specifically to conditions created by stratigraphy, block faulting, ground water and surface water hydrology, geomorphology, erosion and weathering processes, wind action or sedimentology, but more generally they are related to combinations of these conditions and processes. An example of this is the physiographic system of Bhabar and Tarai below the foothills of the Himalayas, which is not only a hydrological system but has also aspects related to sedimentology and soils. An another well known example is the physiographic system produced by block faulting processes north of Dehradun which has both geological and sedimentological aspects, but which is also influenced by resulting erosion, weathering and seepage processes. The third example is the system produced by gently dipping Gondwana sandstones overlying Gondwana shales. In all these situations these physiographic systems are expressed on the aerial photos in not just one but in combinations of almost all the individual photointerpretation elements.

A model of the process and conditions governing certain physiographic system and their resulting soil patterns can generally be presented in the forms of a detailed cross–section. A model like this is established during detailed studies in sample areas. After it is fully understood, its influence on soil patterns studied and its different experssions on the photographs established, the model can be applied to the other parts of the survey area for which the sample is representative. The validity of this extrapolation of knowledge is then checked by some rapid traverses in the rest of the area. These traverses may take the form of a field check and a "predicted soil map" based on the physiographic model drawn up in the sample area. If the predicted soil patterns along these traverses prove to be correct we may conclude that the model is applicable. If not, either the model as a working hypothesis was not correct or the sample area was not truly representative. In the latter case we may have to select new sample areas and change our first interpretation.

(d) Forestry : The main application of photo interpretation to Forestry involves : (a) Preparation of a Base Map, (b) Identification of tree species, (c) Quantitative measurements about the density of trees in a given area, height of trees and crown shapes and volumes.

The principles of photo interpretation as explained earlier such as shape, size, pattern, shadow, tone and texture are applied for (a), (b) mentioned above.

Individual tree species have their characteristic shape and size. With some ground knowledge and experience it is possible to identify these on the air photos. Shadows of trees help to know their shape in profile. Changes of tone and texture also help in identification of species. Trees also give a peculiar pattern depending upon underground moisture condition. Trees along a straight line may be due to under - ground water channel. Trees also occur in clumps. Knowledge about tree height can easily be obtained using a simple parallax bar with viewing under stereoscope. Physiographic conditions also help in identification of tree types. For example, Sal trees generally grow on low hills upto 1000 metres and Pine trees upto 2000 metres or more of terrain heights above sea level.

(e) Terrain Evaluation : The study of terrain is essential and a prerequisite for proper planning and utilization of land resources. The purpose could be a short term military requirement for certain localized zones a long term peace time need like development and exploitation of mineral resources, availability of construction material, exploration for ground water etc. The aim of terrain study is to gather maximum and systematic information on various aspects of the ground so that proper evaluation of this information can be done to meet the requirements of different users. A system of classification of terrain is, therefore, necessary where a given area can be subdivided into basic units. The question becomes more important for an inaccessible area where the only available tool is the aerial photo and the concept of 'known to the unknown' will hold good. In fact the aerial photos, when seen under a stereoscope, bring the 'Ground' to the laboratory.

The two important units in terrain classification are Pattern and Facet. A Facet is the fundamental unit in the classification. It is desireable as a piece of ground possessing uniform physical properties for all practical purposes. It is classified on the basis of surface configurations, nature of surficial deposits, surface and subsurface water region, landuse and its associations with other terrain units. A landscape pattern is an area or areas of regularly occurring pattern of topography and surficial deposits including soils. The landscape pattern is recognized on the basis of geologic set up, climate and topography. The following information is recorded for each terrain unit :

Terrain Unit	:	Type of Information Card
Pattern	:	Pattern Card, Pattern Description, Climate
Facet	:	Facet Card, Ground Description, Surficial deposit and soils, Landuse, Vegetation, Soil Properties and Classification, Engineering Resources and Water Supply.

The detailed method of Terrain study is as follows :

Area of study

1. Library Work
   Collection of basic material and back ground information
2. Laboratory Excersise
   Scanning of airphotos, checking of quality, scale etc. study of maps and delineation of major units, preliminary list of landscape Patterns and Facets
3. Ground Reconnaissance
   Initial Field Traverses

4. Study of Aerial Photos
   delineation of facets and planning of field work
5. Detailed Field Work
   Checking of photo-characteristics, recording terrain data, collecting soils samples field tests for moisture content and soil strengths
   Final List of Pattern and Facets
6. Laboratory Tests
   Soil tests, rock identification etc.
7. Completion of Reports
   Confirmatory Recce, if required Finalization of report, Typing of Cards and preparation of maps
   Main Report, Appendices (pattern, Facets and information cards, Facet maps).

The process of photo-interpretation can be devided into steps like observation and measurements, logical reasoning and influence. The equipment required is simple and constitutes pocket stereoscope for quick scanning in the field mirror stereoscope for detailed work, parallax bar for height measurement and sketch master to transfer the interpreted data to the base map. In the case of terrain studies presenting in progress the details are directly transferred to existing toposheets.

The recognition elements used for photo interpretation aids to describe different terrain units are:

(a) Position in landscape and association with other terrain units.
(b) Morphology, surface configuration and micro relief.
(c) Drainage pattern, texture and density internal and external drainage.
(d) Erosional features and gully sections.
(e) Landuse and cultural features.
(f) Vegetation.
(g) Tonal variation and special photo textures and pattern if any.

(f) Landuse/Land Cover : The term landuse refers to the human activity associated with a specific piece of land whereas the term land cover related to the type of feature present on the surface of the earth. The United States Geological Survey has devised a classification scheme at different levels for Land use/Land Cover system for use with aerial photos. Examples of Level I and Level II are :

Level I	Level II
1. Urban or Built up Land	1.1. Residential
	1.2. Commercial and Services
	1.3. Industrial
	1.4. Transportation, Communication and Utilities
	1.5. Industrial and Commercial Complexes
	1.6. Mixed Urban
	1.7. Other Urban

Similarly under Urban or built up land levels I, II, III are :

Level I	Level II	Level III
Urban or Built up Land	1.1. Residential	1.1.1. Single Family
	1.2. Commercial	1.1.2. Multi Family
	1.3. Industrial	1.1.3. Group Quarters
	1.4. Lakes	1.1.4. Residential Hotels
	1.5. Parks	
	1.6. Orchards	
	1.7. Agricultural	

All these landuse/land cover types can easily be delineated on aerial photos seen under stereoscopic vision. The resolution or the smallest distance that can be identified depends upon the scale. The larger the scale of photos greater is the clarity and resolution. In fact for land use/land cover work photos on large scale such as 1: 10,000 to 1: 5000 are recommended. Colour photos enhance the features much more and hence give much more information. Shadows play an important role in identifying multistoried houses and tall structures. Ground verification follows the photo interpretation map.

(g) Agriculture : The three major areas in which photo interpretation can help in the discipline of agriculture are :

(i) Crop condition assessment, (ii) Crop type classification, (iii) Crop yield estimation. Crop type is characterised by characteristic pattern and texture on an aerial photo whereas crop condition i.e. healthy or diseased are identified by virtue of tonal and grey level changes. The crop can be damaged due to several causes such as insects, moisture excesses, iron deficiency, nitrogen deficiency, soil salinity and air pollution. The crop yield can easily be determined by determining the area under cultivation for a particular variety.

The photo interpretation steps involved in agricultural studies relate to determination of drainage pattern and analysis, erosion pattern and analysis, photo tones, textures and vegetative feature and their pattern.

(h) Water Resources : The application of photo interpretation techniques to water resources involve two types (a) mapping surface water bodies, (ii) subsurface or ground water potential. The first part is simple as surface water bodies like streams, rivers, lakes etc. can be easily identified on the aerial photos. Water bodies appear darker in tone compared to rest of the features because of the simple fact that most of the sunlight that enters a clear water body is absorbed within about two metres of the surface. The degree of absorption depends upon the incident wave length. This infrared light in the region of 1 to 2 micrometer wave lengths is absorbed within a length of a metre for the surface.

The ground water location on the other hand is not so simple as this is a sub-surface feature. The indicators of ground water are the topography and vegetations namely presence of springs and wells and other seepages. Present photo interpretation techniques can not be applied for estimation or determination of ground water depth., The other features of the interpretation techniques are the delineation of watershed and its assessment for reservior selection and snow cover mapping which help in determination water available from snow melt. The underground or burried stream can also be mapped for vegetation patterns on the surface along their streams and which also help in locating possible ground water zones.

(i) Environmental Studies : Under the heading the areas of study are (i) Water pollution, (ii) Deforestation and denudation, (iii) Industrial pollution. Water pollution is caused by organic waste from domestic sewage and industrial wastes, production of excessive algae and water weeds and sediments brought down by rivers etc. Some times pollution can often be seen on aerial photos and delineated due to different tones and textures. The pure water appears with light grey and polluted

water with darker tone. Deposits of oil on water also show darker tone. Use of aerial photos for flood damage can also be done by taking aerial photos before and after floods. Areas prone to successive flooding can be marked and preventive measures can be adopted.

(j) Land Resources Assessment using Aerial Photos : Aerial photographs have extensively been used for the assessment of Land Resources. The technique basically involves interpretation of air photos, the analysis of land form, vegetation pattern and land use pattern. This is supported in the final analysis by field investigation, available literature and statistical testing. Aerial photos are used to establish "Land Systems" A Land system is a uniform area through out which there is a recurring pattern of homogenity of given features such as topography, soil and vegetation. A change in the pattern determines, the boundary of a Land system. The Land system boundary depends to a great extent on the boundary of different land forms which can be detected from aerial photos.

The Land form boundaries usually coincide with the breaks in ground slope.These changes, or break in slope can easily be seen on a stereoscopic pair of photos. The other keys which determine the Land form are the topography such as high lands, low lands, hilly areas, major drainage patterns, changes of slope, linear features, flood plains, wetlands, gullies, joints, strikes, faults and rock exposure etc. Table 4.1 gives the symbols used in preparing a Land form map.

The information as obtained during Terrain Land from analysis is plotted in black on transparent overlays and printed with the negative of the mosaic of aerial photos, generally on the scale of 1: 25,000. The pattern of land form units on the mosaic are then grouped into provisional land systems which are subsequently studied in the field. The boundaries are finally compiled on 1:50,000 scale maps.

Normally the vegetation pattern is in equlibrium with the environment of the area concerned. A change in environmental conditions results the change in vegetation pattern. A change in soil type or climate both can bring changes in vegetation pattern. The vegetation maps will therefore, show where there are similar areas of same vegetation.

The first step of a vegetation survey, the object of which is to map the distribution of the vegetation, is to establish the relationship between different vegetation species. This can be done on the ground and from aerial photos for the various boundaries between species.

The technique of identifying land form and vegetation patterns, as described above enable us the area to be divided environmentally. The next is to determine the manner in which the land is being used. This information about land use is very helpful in planning for development. In preparing such land use maps we have to demarcate the boundaries of different land uses, such as cultivated, uncultivated and uncultivable lands, industrial and urban areas etc. There could be further subdivison, such as in cultivated land there could be area of dry land cultivation, seasonally flooded grasslands, alluvial land or estates of plantation. Similarly uncultivated sub–division could be recent fallow, fallow land, swamp grassland, seasonally flooded grassland, long term fallow land, or uncultivated land of low fertility. The uncultivated land could be steep and rugged country, lakes, ponds, rivers and streams, very much eroded land and wasteland with boulders etc.

The depiction of various landuse categories could be done by 'Dot' distribution method. The Land Resoruces Division of the Directorate of Overseas Survey U.K. uses the following formula to calculate the number of dots for a natural area to be determined within selected error limits as :

$$D = \frac{N}{AP}$$

Where $$N = \frac{(100 - P) \times 38400}{P_x E^2}$$

D = No. of dots per photo

AP = the number of air photos

P = the percentage of the total area within a natural area or category occupied by the most critical land use category.

E = the percentage area within which results can be expected to fall in 95 per cent of cases.

The number 38400 is a constant or student's Distribution statistics taken at 95 per cent level of probability. The computation and plotting can then be done with electronic computer and plotter. The plotter will plot each land use category within each natural area. The sample dots for the Land use category being analysed in relation to the co-ordinates of the principal point of the air photo can also be done. The result is a dot distribution map for the land use category.

A combination of Land form, Land use and vegetation analysis gives a good idea of the land resources of the area under consideration. The accuracy of the method, however, depends upon the accuracy of the fundamental air photo interpretation (Table 4.2).

4.11 Interpretation of Satellite Imagery

Since the satellite imagery is available both in graphic forms (on contact prints or film negatives and positives) and in Digital form (on CCT's) there are two possibilities for interpretation. For the graphical form the same technique is used as for aerial photographs. However, due to very small scale of imagery (1:1 million or so) special emphasis has to be laid on additional help for the imagery on different bands or channals. For example, water features appear quite dark on Band 7 imagery compared to other bands. Use should also be made of additional imagery obtained at diffferent dates. This helps in forestry and vegetation studies as the colour and leaves of trees change with time. These also are helpful in other areas such as natural hazards, flooding , landslide, earthquakes and other feature which change with time. The satellite imagery of the same area available every 18 days for landsat and for similar time for other satellite. The repetitive imagery and imagery in different spectral bands are two main advantages of satellite imagery photo interpretation. The main drawback is the small scale of imagery which render identification of small features impossible. For example an image of a 1 mm in size of the satellite imagery of 1:1 m scale is of 1 km size of the object. Thus individual building or feature of 80 m in dimensions are extremely difficult to identify. But there is one advantage in this case. It is that of linear image. A road of 30 or 10 m in width is too narrow to be seen as such but the fact that it appears as a linear feature can help in its identification. In fact mapping of lineaments using the satellite imagery has greatly improved the geological interpretation because the satellite imagery, because of the large area it covers, gives a good synoptic view of the terrain, so necessary for geological mapping.

The Digital method, using statistical clarifier and computer aided mapping, is possible due to availability of digital data on CCT's which is not the case in aerial photography. This Digital technique is capable of providing thematic map with various classes associated with the terrain such as water, vegetation, soils, built up area. Although the resolution is limited to fixed size the fact that the computer can recognize 256 levels of brightness compared to 8 or 10 by human eye makes digital clarification a very powerful tool in interpretation of satellite imagery.

TABLE 4.2 : Land Form Analysis Legend

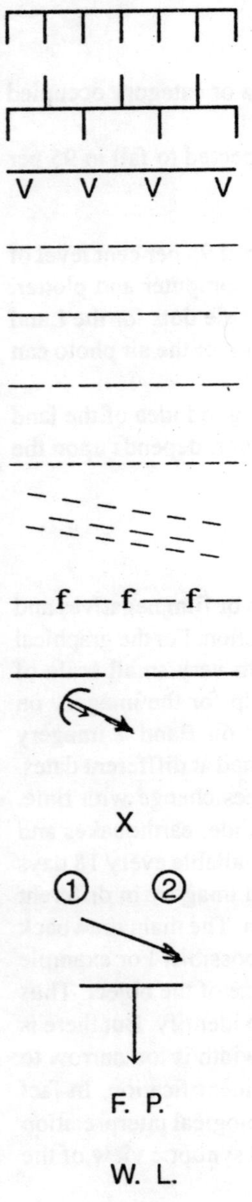

- Convex break slope-(steeper side ticked)
- Ridge
- Cliff
- Concave break of slope
- Transitional boundary between contrasting terrain
- Linear feature of probable geological origin
- Geological boundary
- Strike trend
- Fault
- Major joint direction
- Direction of dip or slope of land surface
- Rock exposure
- Successive flats, numbered from the lowest
- Eroded gully, arrow to gully head
- Waterfall, arrow downstream
- Flood Plain
- Wet Land

4.12 Quantitative Interpretation

So far we have discussed mostly quantitative aspects of photo interpretation. Quantitative interpretation involves laws of geomorphology. Some aspects of these laws, which are applicable to drainage basins are given below. These help to arrive at in interpretation of various types of basins marked on the air photo. A low ruggedness number expresses rather ill developed drainage and less mountaineous terrain. Similarly a highly complex terrain with large drainage will speak of high ruggedness number. Method of obtaining some of the numerical parameter are given as follows:

By use of aerial photos it is possible to demarcate basins or drainage divide by observing a pair of overlapping aerial photos. Under stereoscopic fusion it is also possible to delineate the streams and channals of various basin. Having done it is then possible to carry out numerical analysis of the basin. Some of the important features from the point of view of photo interpretation are (i) the basin area, (ii) the basin shape, (iii) the drainage density and the (iv) ruggedness number.

(i) Basin Area : This can be easily determined by use of a planimeter and the tracing of the basin boundary. The size of the area determines the stream flow and sediment yield. There is a relationship between the drainage area and the length of this main steam. This relation measures from the start of the main stream, in the direction of the flow is given by:

$L = KA\mu$ where L is the length of the main stream, K and μ are constants and 'A' the area of the basin. The value of the constant can be obtained by least square. The investgations made in U.S.A. gave the values as :

$$L=1.66A\ 0.6$$

(ii) The shape of the basin area is described in many ways:

(a) Length to Width ratio is L/W where L is the length of the main stream and W the maximum width of the basin.

(b) *Circulity Ratio* : A/A_L where A is the basin area and A_L is the surface area of a circle possessing the same perimeter of the basin.

(c) *Elongation Ratio* : $R_c = D_a/L$ where D_a is the diameter of a circle having the same area of the basin and L the maximum length of the same.

(iii) *Drainage Density* : This is defined as $D_c = EL/A$ where EL is the total length a summation of all channels of the basin and A the area of the basin.

(iv) *Ruggedness Number* : This is the product of local relief and drainage density. The local relief is generally measured as diffrence between the maximum and minimum elevation of this basin. The number suggests steepness of slope and the ruggedness number becomes large for larger drainage density and relief and is a measure of heavily dissected terrain unsuitable for roads or railway lines.

5

KEYS AND EXAMPLES

5.1 Introduction

The accuracy of interpretation to a large extent depends upon the experience of the interpreter. This, in turn, depends upon the ability to associate and correlate the photo image and the ground object. Most of us (in the Northern Hemisphere) are used to seeing objects with shadows falling towards the north. Therefore to obtain the best results in interpreting the aerial photos, they should be oriented such that the shadows fall towards the observer, as if the light source is at the upper left. In that case objects having shadows on the near side will be seen elevated and those having shadows on the far side will be seen depressed. If this is not done objects will be seen in reverse slopes and with a stereoscope this is called Pseudoscopy.

5.2 Keys for Ground Object Such as River and Stream

By keys is meant the factor which will help in quick interpretation and recognition of the ground objects from their corresponding photo images. They have been developed based on the *characteristic* images of certain objects which are indicative of the object already having been seen by the interpreter. For example an orchard will have trees planted in rows with fence boundaries. Similarly the cultivated field will have clear markings and lines that appear in lighter tone compared to uncultivated and barren areas. Also ground with moisture will appear in darker tone compared to dry areas.

The following type of objects will have features which are described below:

5.2.1 *Rivers and Streams*

These have uniform water (black tone) will show meanders (in plain areas). Other associated features are the presence of sand bars, falls, rapids, bridges, dams and docks, oxbow lakes. (See Plate No. 5, Plate No 6 and Plate No. 12)

5.2.2 *Canal*

These are easily identifiable by their characteristic straight courses, dark tones, small bridges, roads by the side of bank (sometimes) and trees lined along the canal. The gradient will be generally low and smooth and the width being fairly even and uniform. There may be side constructions, locks and wells. (See Plate No. 9)

5.2.3 *Water Reservoirs, Lakes, Ponds and Water Ditches*

These are characterized by dark tone of uniform nature except where there is sun reflection. Near the ditches there may be natural vegetation.

5.2.4 *Marshes and Swamps*

These are typical in having growth of long grass with photographic tone as very dark. There may be small stream or drains emptying their water content into marshy areas. The marshes and swamps will have lowest level with depression when seen against the adjoining slope of the terrain. (See Plate No. 11)

5:2.5 *Snow and Ice*

They give characteristic strong sunlight reflection and hence appear very bright and white on the black and white aerial photos. They can be distinguished from white clouds by cloud shadow. (See Plate No. 10 and Plate No. 13)

5.2.6 *Beach Areas*

These are characterized by the sharp dividing line between sea water and the land. The sandy portion appears with very light tone whereas the sea water with characteristic waves and slightly darker tones.

5.2.7 *Railway Lines*

They appear as thin lines, straight in alignment. Wherever there is a change in direction it is marked by gradual change in direction with smooth easy curves of very low curvature. In undulating country the railways are marked by shadows of cut and fill. They are further identified by railway bridge, railway station on the sides, on large scale photography, number of track, side tracks, switches, cross over and sidings can be identified. (See Plate No. 9)

5.2.8 *Highways, Roads etc.*

These appear with characteristic straight lines of darker tone. They can be differentiated from railway line by having larger curvature at the turning and with deeper slopes compared to railway tracks. Road bridges will be conspicuous with absence of large garder which are easily identifiable from railway bridges. They are also differentiated by their characteristic right angle or other narrow crossings and intersections. Large scale photography can enable the observer to see the nature of the road surfacing and its type and width for classification. (See Plate No. 9)

5.2.9 *Transmission Lines*

Power and other transmission lines are identifiable by the presence of tower and clearance made, specially in wooded areas. The change of direction is sharp and not by curves as in railways and roads. With stereoscope and parallax bars it is possible to determine the height of tower using a pair of adjoining photos. (See Plate No. 14)

5.2.10 *Airports*

The photo image clearly shows the wide and straight runways with a right angle or oblique intersection of other runway and hangers, airport tower and other buildings. The clear surroundings and fences also help in recognition. The runway appear in light tone and the surrounding clear terrain in slightly darker tone. (See Plate No. 16)

5.2.11 *Towers and High Buildings*

These are easily identified by their shadows. The nature of towers and buildings can be recognized by their characteristic shadows and their heights can be determined by the parallax method. The shadow will also reveal the sharp corner of the buildings indicating the geometry like being rectangular, square, round etc. The structures on the roof like chimney, porches etc. can also be seen.

Houses in rural areas are identified by their proximity to roads and most often surrounded by trees. They appear generally in darker tone than the surroundings hutments and other clay structures are also identifiable from the tone and geometry of structure. (See Plate No. 17)

5.2.12 *Ruins and Archeological Sites*

These can be identified by their linear markings open (without roof) structures and tonal value which on the ground are hard to recognize sometimes. Old forts and its surroundings have very clear images on the photo.

5.2.13 *Industrial Sites*

They are marked by big structure, chimneys and smoke plumes. The discharge from these buildings and chemical plants can be seen emanating from the buildings which may be properly drained or may be cleared of by zig zag open drainage.

5.2.14 *Rural and Urban Areas*

These are marked by density of structure buildings and the extent on the ground. Rural and small villages can be easily identified with smaller size of buildings with less density whereas urban areas will be marked by mixed nature of buildings but characterized by heavy density interspersed and criss-crossed by roads and lanes.

5.2.15 *Urban Area Analysis*

The characteristic Landuse pattern such as high density populated areas, orchards, roads, rivers, low density populated areas, industrial sites, cultivated and non-cultivated areas, residential and non–residential boundaries can help in carrying out the urban area analysis.

5.2.16 *Faults*

Although difficult, sometimes, to recognize and identify on the grounds, faults can be easily located on aerial photos by their lineations which are reflections of rectilinear depressions. They are sometimes seen as sudden changes of drainage or vegetation pattern. They appear with darker tone and show displacement of one sort or the other. These displacements can be rock types or soil types too. (See Plate No. 3)

5.2.17 *Fractures*

Shear zones marked by fractures express themselves on the aerial photography by small breaks in linear or non-linear forms. Persistent and short linears, probably representing the surface traces of various fractures arranged in various superimposed or intersecting systems can be easily identified on the aerial photo. (See Plate No. 8)

5.2.18 *Lineaments/Linears*

A lineament is any line on an aerial photograph that is structurally controlled. This includes, for photogeological purposes, streams, beds, trees or bushes etc. The lineament may be due to beds, mineral banding, veins, faults, joints, unconformities and different rock boundaries. The lineaments should not be confused with non geological features such as rails, roads, canals, animal tracks, field boundaries and paths which will also appear in linear features. The short ticks arranged in continuous or with breaks and appear with lighter tones. The intersections of these linears indicate the presence of shear and faulted zones. The area around the intersection have been found to be mineralized. The analysis of these lineaments, their strike direction and density have helped in detection of oil bearing zones. The lineaments may be of three classes i.e. Mega, long and short. Mega lineaments may run for hundreds of kilometer and their presence indicates large shear zones which also indicate presence of underground oil. Long lineaments run upto few kilometres and are indicative of geological stressed area. Their intersections have indicated presence of hot springs and minerals. There is a distinct difference between 'Linears' and 'Lineation'. Lineation refers to the geological features which are just true lines in space such as elongation of pebbles, the trace of beddings on clearage surfaces or axially oriented crystals. Bed rock linear on the other hand represent the surface of traces of geological planer features as faults contacts, joints and bedding planes.

5.2.19 *Strike*

It is the line of intersection between the geological feature and the horizontal. It is the compass bearing measured from north. On an aerial photo it can be measured by orienting the photo with respect to north. For dipping planes the strike may be measured by joining any two points on the same plane at the same elevation. (See Plate No. 4)

5.2.20 *Dip*

Dip is the slope (tangent of the vertical angle) that a bedding plane makes with the horizontal. The dip direction is always perpendicular to the strike direction. The dip angle can be measured from a pair of adjoining photographs (with 60% forward overlap) by observing the 'X' parallax difference using a parallax bar and then computing the height difference between two points of a dipping bedding plane. The horizontal or sloping distance between these two points can be determined from the scale of the photos. The tangent of the dip angle is the ratio of height difference by the horizental distance. (See Plate No. 4)

5.2.21 *Joints*

A joint is a type of fracture along which there has been little or no movement. The distinction on an aerial photo between joint and fracture is that the fracture is a stronger and longer linear whereas the joint is a short one and mostly the joints are seen as criss–crossing linears. (See Plate No. 4)

5.2.22 *Bedding Planes*

These may be flat or tilting. The flat planes follow contours whereas the tilting areas appear as prominent ridges and bands of different tones and colours. The linear, as seen, consists of bedding joints and showing difference between adjacent strata.

5.2.23 *Synclines, Anticlines*

They can be identified from the directions of dip of the bedding planes. The nature of the drainage following the dipping planes also helps in recognition.

5.2.24 *Folds*

These are easily recognized when a fold occurs in a single photo in its entirely or when the erosion of rock of the structure takes place. Also the nature of drainage helps in identifying the fold. Another helpful feature is the curving around of streams around the nose of the fold with the convex side indicative of the direction of the plunge of anticlinal fold.

5.2.25 *Sedimentary Rocks*

These are mapped from their characteristic bedding nature as seen on the aerial photos. Because of differential erosion the image gives an impression of bands. As a result of weathering more resistant rocks appear higher in relief and less resistant type are seen as lowered. Tone also plays an important role in differentiation when the topography is not very expressive. Shales and fine grained rocks appear with dark tone whereas coarse grained rocks appear with lighter tone. Drainage also helps in identification. Most sedimentary rocks have dendritic pattern of drainage. The vegetation pattern do sometimes help in differentiation. For example, different vegetation species grow on limestone and quartzite formation. The consolidated and unconsolidated types of rocks are identified by the type of landforms such as sand dunes, eskers, alluvial fans, river terraces etc.

5.2.26 *Igneous : Extrusive Type*

The identifying features are the characteristic landforms besides drainage texture and massiveness of rocks. The basaltic flow may show darker tones.

5.2.27 *Igneous Intrusive*

Here dykes reveal themselves as straight or curved ridges and show as elevated feature because of stronger resistance to erosion. Dykes can also follow fractures in igneous rocks and may have distinctive vegetation pattern.

5.2.28 *Volcanic Cones*

They show very clearly on aerial photos by their conic structure with radial drainage pattern flowing outward from the top of the cone.

5.2.29 *Granite*

At low altitudes it expresses itself as hummocky with rounded topography with uniform vegetation and dendritic drainge pattern. (See Plate No. 13, Fig. 5.14, and Fig. 5.15)

5.2.30 *Metamorphic Rocks*

These are sometimes very difficult to identify on aerial photos because of lack of any particular key for identification. When these rocks are derived from sedimentary formation, bedding may be the only clue. Sometimes occurrence of widely spaced lineations at right angles to the regional trend may be an indicator.

5.2.31 *Gneisses*

They give a banded appearance and drainage pattern in angularly dendritic due to fractures foliation or due to glaciation. These may show up with highly dissected hills with parallel ridges with steep slopes.

5.2.32 *Schist*

They show up with structurally controlled rectangular drainage pattern with parallel gullies on highly eroded soils. Quartzite forms very steep sided, knife edged ridges which are generally the highest in the area.

5.2.33 *Terraces*

These are seen elevated level land deposited by streams fed by melting glacier. In the case of fluvial terraces, which are the old emanants of flood plains, the typical appearance is flat topped and scarped terrace land form.

5.2.34 *Moraines*

These are seen as boulders of varying height and of material such as sand, clay or gravel which have been plowed up and pushed ahead by glacial action.

5.2.35 *Kames*

These are glacier feature with steep sided mounds and dumped through holes.

5.2.36 *Esker*

It is a snake like ridge of varying height from 6 to 30 metres of gravel and sand deposited by streams which had run on through or under a glacier. It is easily identified on the aerial photos as it can cross hills and depressions. It has a uniform light tone with no erosion or drainage development but has its own internal drainage. Because of steep slopes there is no cultivation seen on an esker.

5.2.37 *Till Plain*

It is a smooth to gently undulating area of material as found on a moraine. It shows a plastic effect due to glacial action and appears on a photo with a smooth texture and tone. As comparison to glacial till the tone appear mottled one, which is characteristic of glacier features.

5.2.38 *Glaciers*

These are rivers of ice but with no apparent movement of ice. They are characterized by medium uniformly gray tones and show no sign of drainage, erosion, vegetation or land use. The topography consists of a series of lobate shaped rolling ridges and look like extremely ropy viscous fluid very slowly oozing down a valley. (See Plate No. 10)

5.2.39 *Gullies*

These are characterized by their typical shape of cross section. The V-shaped gullies develope in sand and gravel, U-shaped in silty soils and long gullies with rounded cross sections develope in silty and clay soils. Gullies, sometimes, are hard to recognize and the experience of photo-interpreter may be the only clue. Some of the other helpful clues, besides the shape of the cross section are the length, depth, width, plan view and profile.

5.2.40 *Sink Holes*

These are characterized by their shape, density and tone. They appear as circular or elliptical in shape with light gray to dark tone and of sufficient density to be noticed by the photo interpreter. They indicate lack of any drainage because of the soluble limestone formation where they occur. The drainage is internal with highly alkaline ground water, vegetation and land use are not very helpful keys. Sometimes short streams may lead into sink holes and drainage may occasionally occur along valley walls. (See Fig. 5.4)

5.2.41 *Flood Plains*

These can be seen with an overall level relief with a gentle downward gradient. They are characterized by great variation in soils and are subject to flooding at periodic intervals. Since the flood plains are formed by the normal process of meander development of stream and rivers and by over the bank flooding, the aerial photo will show such features.

5.2.42 *Forest Cover Types*

The identification and interpretation of forest cover type and plant species depends on the quality, scale, the season of photography and the type of film used for aerial photography. The shape, texture and tone of (See Plate No. 16) forest cover, as seen on photo, may be influenced by the topographic site. Also the time of day, the haze of the atmosphere, sun angle and cloudy weather effect the image quality. The important keys that help the photo interpreter are the texture (smoothness or coarseness of the image), the contrast, colour, the relative size of the around canopy at the scale of photography and the location of the area under study.

5.2.43 *Forest Species*

The identification of forest individual type depends to a great extent on the familiarity of the photo interpreter with crown size, the characteristic shadows which the trees show on the images. The knowledge of the cross sectional view of the trees as seen on the ground and their characteristic shadow as seen on the photo images can help a lot to the interpreter. Various forest agencies have developed keys with the help of typical silhouttes and the sketches of the overhead view for the tree species.

5.2.44 *Forest Tree Volume Estimates*

The forest tree volume can be estimated by knowing the exact scale of photography.

5.2.45 *Plant Stress*

By plant vigor and plant stress is meant the degree of health of plant. It depends upon the moisture content, soil salinity, soil fertility and the plant disease caused by insects. Infrared and false colour photography have been found to be more useful in this connection. Because of loss of water or other reasons an unhealthy tree will be at a higher temperature compared to healthy vegetation. It will emit radiation of longer wavé length i.e. in the infrared region. In black and white photography the unhealthy vegetation will appear generally of lighter tone compared to healthy vegetation which would be of darker tone.

5.2.46 *Sand Dunes*

These are wind deposit material and found in desert and shore lines. There are three types:

(a) Barchan, (b) Longitudinal, (c) Transverse (See Plate No. 7)

(a) Barchan
These are identified on the aerial photo by their characteristic crescent shape and are found in areas of strong wind and less of sand. The horn points downward.

(b) Longitudinal
These are ridges which extend downward from an obstruction. Their length is in line with the direction of the prevailing wind.

(c) Transverse

These are formed by gentle wind blowing over areas of abundant sand. They show up as scalloped ridges perpendicular to the direction of wind and tend to move forward. The photographic tone of all dunes are light except where covered by vegetation.

5.2.47 *Loess*

It is a wind blown deposit of silt found on the leeward side of the desert. These may also be found on highly dissected topography with streams. They provide good soil for agriculture. These are identified on the aerial photos as U shaped steep gullies. If there is a drainage it is mostly dendritic.

5.2.48 *Polluted Streams*

Streams carrying pollution start from man made sources such as factories or sewage outfalls and are easily identified on aerial photos as sharp contrasted tonal changes between the concentrated effluents and the receiving water.

5.2.49 *Wet Soils*

These appear with dark tone and if cultivated show smooth texture.

5.2.50 *Dry Soils*

They appear with light tone and barren uncultivated land may have a rough texture.

5.2.51 *Intrusive Rocks*

Acid, Basic and Dykes : Acid intrusive rocks are relatively light toned and have a rectangular joint pattern. At some places they are resistant to erosion than the country rocks. On aerial photographs the appearance of such large scale rectangular jointing is commonly associated with acid rather than basic intrusives.

Since dykes are rock bodies which have been intruded along fractures or planes of weakness in the earth's crust, many of them have some of the characteristics associated with joints or faults. Any dissimilarity between the dyke rock and the country rock may be indicated by a variation in tone, vegetation or relief.

5.2.52 *Stratigraphic Thickness Determination*

Where sufficiant exposure of rock bedding is seen, it is possible to determine the stratigraphic thickness using a parallax bar by measuring the parallax difference between the top and bottom of a strata. Where beds are dipping, the stratigraphic thickness can be determined by first computing the dip of each bed and then determining the parallax difference between some two points, one at the top and the other at the base of the beds and finally calculating the thickness according to the Figure 5.35 . It can be easily computed that the stratigraphic thickness 't' is given by :

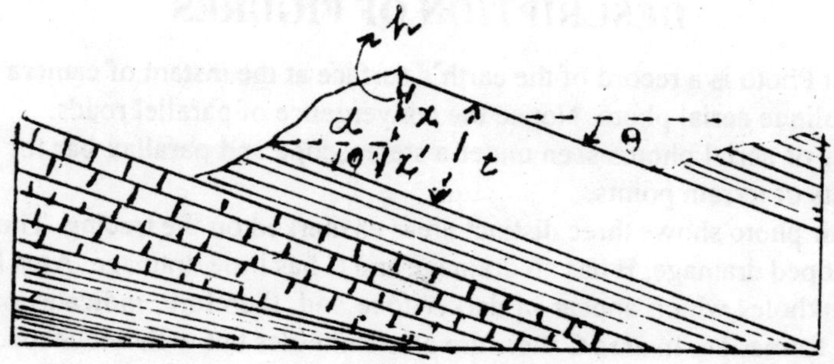

Fig. 5.35 : Stratigraphic Thickness Determination

$t = x + x' = h \cos \theta + d \sin \theta$

Here h = the difference in elevation between a point on the lower contact of bed and a point in the dip direction at the upper contact of the bed and θ is the dip angle.

5.3 Examples

The examples that are given herewith are to illustrate the principles discussed above. Some of the examples have overlays or tracings. These tracings should be placed over the corresponding photos by proper alignment. References have been provided in the description to locate the area of reference. Plates also illustrate some of features for interpretation of aerial photos.

DESCRIPTION OF FIGURES

Fig. 5.1. Aerial Photo is a record of the earth's surface at the instant of camera exposure.

Fig. 5.2. An oblique aerial photo. Notice the convergence of parallel roads.

Fig. 5.3. A pair of aerial photos seen under a stereoscope and parallax bar for measurement of heights of terrain points.

Fig. 5.4 The air photo shows three distinct areas as marked on the tracing. The area A has well developed drainage, B has no drainage and C has little drainage. Area B is well marked by sinkholes which appear in darker tone and, therefore, indicates presence of limestone formation. In area C there are also sinkholes but with wider space. The direction of the main stream is effected by the presence of fractures, indicating a change in composition of the limestone. Area A has dendritic drainage pattern with beddings dipping to south and south west. There is absence of vegetation except along valleys where it shows dark tone. The photo shows the area in the state of Texas, USA of scale nearly one inch to a mile taken with a camera of focal length 5.2 inches. The field data has confirmed the presence of limestone alongwith sandstone and more alterations overlain by limestones (overlay).

Fig. 5.5. Example of a linear fault traversing the whole and central part of the photo. As a result of faulting the left part is at a higher level.

Fig. 5.6. Photo Scale 1 : 23,600
Area : Wyoming, U.S.A.
Feature Illustrated : A small area of Jurassic rocks is exposed in the centre of this elongated dome that is largely outward dipping Cretaceous beds composed of shale and some sandstone. The beds are tightly folded along the southeast plunging anticline axis. The lowlands around the dome are underlain by Cody shale that is largely concealed by alluvium and terrace deposits.

Fig. 5.7. Main drainage patterns — lowland, structually controlled and freely developed.

Fig. 5.8. (a) A characteristic erosional patterns.
(b) Cross-sectional view of erosional pattern.
(c) Profile of erosion.

Fig. 5.9. A plot of Resistance to erosion versus size of the eroded particle.

Fig. 5.10. Vegetation pattern. The vegetation occurs chiefly along streams or low lying areas indicative of moisture holding soil and characteristic rock type.

Fig. 5.11. Creation of a three dimensional model in a stereo projector by a pair of overlapping aerial photos.

Fig. 5.12. Gently Dipping Sedimentary Rocks Offset by near vertical Fault (Utah), Scale 1 : 20,000. Line separating areas of contrasting photographic tone is trace of fault. The straightness of the fault trace indicates that the fault has approximately a vertical dip. Note vertical offset of dark toned shale bed A and difference in erosional character of topography on off sides of fault at B. Faint trace of fault in alluvium at C is locally marked by differences in drainage on opposite sides of the fault. Light toned sandstone interbeds, D, cap local areas and exhibit senated margins as a result of closely spaced joints. Fine textured drainage is typical of the poorly resistant shale and thin sandstone interbeds. (Overlay)

Fig. 5.13. The slightly dissected eastern edge of the Southern High Plains U.S.A. is dotted with shallow Sink holes (Karst Phenomenon) which appear as dark circular holes on the upper part of the aerial photo. The underlying indurated bed rock is limestone and sandstone. These rocks are largely concealed.

Fig. 5.14. Sakura—Jino Volcano Japan. The photo shows a wealth of interesting detail and should be studied carefully The main valcano is a triple cone with two, probably younger, craters of almost equal size and a smaller (probably older) one wedged in between them. The larger ones, with creaters, may have developed from adventive craters. On photo 980 – a longer lava flow has built up a peninsula by invading the sea. Cultivated land and settlements were probably destroyed here. The wrinkled surface of the flow suggest ropy lava of a viscous type. Higher up the slope a collapsed lave tube is seen, surrounded by a cracked-up area strikingly resembling the creracing of a cascading glacier and being due to the slow downward movement during refrigeration. Domes, plugs and spatter cones are seen and a blow hole, probably a gas vent surrounded by mineral deposits (light tone). Older lavas are partly covered by vegetation.

Upper part of the Volcano is covered with fresh ash (light tone). On 979-80 an adventure cone is breached by a lava flow, on to which an another, somewhat younger flow has spilled over in a cascade branching off the main flow. This flow has a slightly darker tone than the older one. Several small vents are seen (not cone forming). Surface of flows again strongly resembles that of glaciers. The difference is only in tone (and substance). The small stream along the edge of the flow has been faced to alter its coarse as the old valley was invaded and now forms a young incision. Note the strange wall like rim of the flow. The flow has built up a peninsula in the shape of a birds foot delta. The older flow levels abruptly in a steep escarpment. The phenomena described point to the presence of viscous lava. Note pattern of cultivation (innumerable small plots) which is explained by the extreme density of settlements along the Coast and the presence of fertile volcanic soils.

Fig. 5.15. Excellent volcanic crater and cone containing Deriba Lake (Africa). Extensive Erosion by streams.

Fig. 5.16. Active Lava Slopes (Japan).

Fig. 5.17. Shale in Semiarid Climate Area (Utah)

Scale : 1 : 20,000

Fine-textured drainage is typical of shale and other fine-grained clastic rock types. Relief is commonly subdued and divide areas gently rounded. Note that rounding of some divide areas may not be conspicuous because of vertical exaggeration of the stereoscopic model. For example, the relief at B is only 70 ft. The fine textured drainage and erosional topography suggest plastic soils. The numerous angular crenellations in minor tributaries probably reflect closely spaced joints. Their light-toned bands A are expressions of bedding.

Fig. 5.18. The stereogram (pair of overlapping photos) shows clearly the loop (meandering) of the River Colorado in Utah State USA. The dipping bedding planes are clearly seen along with the banks of the river. A normal fault cutting the smaller loop can also be seen. Curved joints can also be seen inside the bigger loop.

Fig. 5.19. Subsurface Structure Reflected in Surface Drainage Characteristics (Texas)

Approx. Scale 1 : 65,000

Subsurface structures at A and B are suggested by drainage characteristics of the area. Streams flanking the structures at A curve around the structures in their headwater portions. Tributary streams drain radially off the structures. In addition the crudely circular pattern of more highly dissected ground and the pattern of dark photographic tone C which results from a concentration of vegetation suggest subsurface structure.

Compressed meandors are present over subsurface structure at B. Also note stream deflection down stream from D which is a further suggestion of subsurface structure in area B.

Fig.5.20. Area of Sparse Outcrops underlain Largely by Gently Folded Sandstone, Conglomnate, and Shale (North Alaska)

Approx. scale 1:20,000

Dip slopes as marked by B are characterized by few streams in contrast to back slopes on which a system of numerous sub-parallel streams has developed. Drainge as marked in C in the dip slope direction is generally course textured except for profuse channels developed at heads of tributaries. Drainage on the back slope is fine textured. The textural difference or drainage density difference, rather than any specific drainage pattern, stands out the back slope with its fine texture drainage is predominantly a shale section in contrast to the sandstone and conglomerate of the dip slope. Note horizontal offset of light toned sandstone beds by near vertical faults illustrated at A, transverse to the strike. In the lower portion of the photo sandstone formations are marked by D&E.

Fig.5.21. Mt. Fujiyama–Japan II-28

Note flat bottom of deep, extinct crator and the relatively smooth outer slopes with no strong dissection. There are several bridle paths with rest houses at interval and temples on rim of creator.

Fig.5.22. Pakistan (West) 1/21

Scale :1:40,000

Alternation of predominantly argillaceous zones with occasional sandstone beds and well stratified, more competent, ridge forming beds: Strong incision due to lack of vegetation. In central part beds are roughly horizontal, but assume a moderately high dip very rapidly on either side. Note drainage pattern in large alluvial fan and dunes near lower edge.

Fig.5.23. India 3" to 1M 1/20

Topographic expression of shale and argillaceous sandstone under tropical conditions in an area of very heavy precipitation. Strong incision despite dense cover of vegetation, resulting in a number of small captures. The area was formerly covered with tropical rain forest and the numerous clearings are artificial. In centre of image, the similar incisions on either side of the straight ridge and the trend of the ridge proper suggest a high angle of dip, which is steep though not vertical, since the face slopes are shorter than the dip-slopes. This formation is overlapped in the east by a younger group (probably quarternary) with a very different drainage pattern. In the west a sandstone ridge swings around as part of the closure of an anticlinal fold.

Fig.5.24. Drainge characteristics in surfacial materials

State Wyoming Date 31.10.1944 C = 6"

Approximate Scale 1:28,000

Strong contrast in drainage densities of areas A,B and C. Area B has dense fine texture drainage, typical for fine grained deposits. The tone is medium grey, with small dark spots due to vegetation.

Field Evidence: The area consists of a clayey soil underlain by shale. The many drainage channels flowing across area B disappear in area C where only the main drainage channels persist. This drainage is typical for granular material of high permeability. The tone is medium grey with occasional lighter patches. Dark spots due to vegetation can be observed.

Field Evidence of Area C: This area consists of sand dunes partly covered by vegetation and stabilized. The dunes show combinations of longitudinal and barchan forms. Capping the fine grained deposit of Area B are those of area where the coarse drainage pattern indicates a layer of granular permeable material. The tone is medium grey with darker patches due to vegetation. Surface drainage is not completely absent probably becasue the thinness of this deposit.

In area D the sand cover becomes thinner and light grey toned material can be seen to pierce through the thining sand.

Fig.5.25. State Utah Stereogram No.173

F = 6"

H = 15,750

RF = 1:42,500 b = 0.215 ft

Map Ref: U.S.G.S. Tidwell NW 7.5' Quadrangle

Black Dragon Canyon was cut by the San Rafael River through cliffs of Jurassic sandstone composing the eastern flank of the San Rafael Swell. Strata dip east to South east (toward top and upper right of the stereogram) and the angle of the dip is much steeper to the right than to the left. Exposed strata range from the Traiassic Moencopi formation (bottom) to the upper Jurassic Morrision formation (top). Spectacular flatirous are formed by the late Triassic Navajo sandstone. The Moencopi is a light coloured unit immediately overlain by dark coloured Chinle sedbeds. Near the base of the flatirous, medium grey Jurassic Carmel limestone directly overlies light coloured Navajo sandstone. The river valley just below Black Dragon Canyon is in the Summer rille formation.

Flatirous, higher and larger to the left where the dip is lower, show fracture due to three directions of jointing one parallel to the strike and two oblique with the strike. These joints result in a series of sharp V's pointed in an up-dip direction. Several small water gaps notch the flatirous of Navajo sandstone. Incised meanders are well developed in Black Dragon Canyon.

Fig. 5.26. Dt. of photo: 30.8.1940

State Utah Stereogram 148

F = 6"

H = 18,100ft RF = 1:36,200 b = 0.200ft

Map Ref: U.S.G.S. Garlisle SE 7.5' Quadrangle

The conspicous pattern of intersecting joints developed in the Permian Cedar Mesa sandstone divides the outcrop into a series of knife-edge blocks. As many as three intersecting systems of joints are visible. One system of joints is curved, although the cause of the curvature is not known. In this region laccolithic intrusions, such as the Abajo Mountains, are known and jointing might be the result of an unexposed dome of salt igneous rocks.

Note: This explanation for the curvature of the jointing does not apply in stereogram (104) of the *Loop*, and also in view of the gently and uniform dip its validity seems doubtful.

Fig. 5.27 SINK Stereogram No. 133

State Kentucky F = 6" H = 10,200

RF 1:20,400 b = 0.244ft

Map Ref: U.S.G.S. Horse Cave 7.5' Quadrangle and Mammoth Cave 7.5' Quadrangle.

The dripping Springs escarpment crosses part of western Kentucky a short distance east of Mammoth Cave National Park and forms the southern border of the Eastern Interior Coal Basin. Here, late Mississipian sandstones of the lower Chester formation overlie thick series of Meramec limestone of middle Mississipian age. Mammoth Cave and other caves in the area are excavated in the Meramec formation. Normal stream valleys developed on the capping sandstone, but later development of sinkholes and caves in the limestones provided underground drainge for these valleys. A pair of dry solution valleys can be seen stereoscopically in the upper center of the stereogram and some sinkholes can be seen in the lower part of stereogram. Sinkholes of unusual depth some as deep as 180 ft, characterize the upland behind the Dripping Springs escarpment.

Fig. 5.28. State Puerto-Rico Stereogram No. 170

F = 6" H = 12,650ft Rf = 1:25,360 b = 0.291 ft.

Map Ref: A.M.S. Rio Camuy Quadrangle 1:30,000

Excessive solution of thick Tertiary limestones in the warm climate of the West Indies has resulted in an intricate pattern of *Karst* topography. Between the sinks, limestone remnants rise as sharp hay stacklike peaks. This process had rendered a substantial area of Puerto Rico unsuitable and, indeed, nearly inaccessible. Stereoscopic observation is of great assistance in visulizing this intricate surface. A narrow strip parallel to the line of flight and including the principal points of both photographs appears blurred. This is probably due to a defective vacuum system in the camera magazine, or to a tiny stream of warm air from the aircraft engine exhaust.

Note: Karstification in the northern part seems much stronger than in the south. In the south bedding can be clearly seen due to alternation of light and medium toned layer.

In this part there is also some surface drainage. It seems probable that the limestone is less pure here or interbedded with marly layers. In the northern part numerous lineaments can be seen, these might be caused by more resistant reins.

Fig. 5.29 Tanganyika II-1

F = 6" H = 19000'

Very complex arrangement of an inactive (or extinct) volcanic group. There are no recent flows and vegetation has been encroaching upon all the old flows. The relatively most recent ones are in the east and in the west, while the oldest ones are seen in the upper centre of photo 5272, where there is a cluster of craters, plugs and cones. These flows have already been attached by erosion and have shallow incised drainage channels (radial arrangement). Younger ones have still retained, to some extent, their fluivial texture (flow lines), but are also covered by vegetation. Many old breached crater rims are seen. The highest cone with its crater breached by a flow has built up in an old Caldera of which only a small part of the rim is preserved. There is some other interesting erosional detail such as the many nick points at the end of deeply incised gorges and marshy watershed with uncertain direction of run off, indicating different stages of erosional cycles.

Fig 5.30 State South Dekota Stereogram !74

F = 6"

H = 10,300ft

RF = 1:31,000 b = 0.187ft

Map Ref: U.S.G.S. Sheep Mountain Table 7.5' quadrangle.

This stereogram shows a good illustration of the stream erosion cycle. Hart Table (right) is a remnant of a late Tertiary or early Pleistocence, erosion plain now several hundered feet above the major valleys. This youthful surface is being destroyed by active dissection in small gullies. Hart mountain is a narrow, detached remnant of this table land on a drainage divide. Complete destruction of the table land plain produces regional, early maturity, well displayed in the badlands above Hart Mountain. Small gullies dissecting the slopes join to form larger valleys and meandering channels and narrow flood plains are evident less than a mile from their heads. A dark area (top centre) along a larger peak had been reduced to low relief or late maturity. A new grass covered plain several hundred feet below Hart Mountain might be called either an old age area or a pediment. Slight dissection of this low plain is shown in the lower centre, where climatic change, or slight uplift, has caused rejuvenation of the drainge. Strata present are terrestrial clays and sands of the White River Oligocene. The slopes of Hart Mountain and adjacent badlands are concave upward and belong to the Bruler formation, while lower hills in the uppper centre are convex upward and belong to the lower Oligocene Chadron formation.

Fig. 5.31 Zion Canyon USA Stereogram No.147

F = 6" H = 15,000 ft. RF = 1:45,000 b= 0.301ft (right)
= 0.305 ft (left)

Map Ref: Zion National Park 1:31,680, USA

Zion Canyon is excavated in the Jurrasic Navajo Sandstone, which is nearly 2000 ft thick at this location. Underlying this are red beds of Triassic age which crop out in the lower walls of the Canyon. The sandstone is cut by a spectacular series of north-south (top to bottom in the stereogram) joints along which deep and very narrow Canyon have been excavated. The great White Throne (centre), a monolith of sandstone over 2000 ft high, is bounded by narrow canyons on two north-south joints (Zion Canyon and another narrow Canyon) in a joint system trending N60° E.

Fig. 5.32 Sediments & Quarts diorite

State : California

f = 6" Approximate scale 1:20, 000

Three units have been indicated A, B,C

Massive and poorly bedded unit 'A' had a coarsed textured, dendritic drainage and a dark to medium grey photo-tone. Scarce vegetation occurs only along the main drainage lines. Wedging out, light toned interbeddings help to determine the dip, which is to the NW.

Field Evidence: Beds A consist of conglomerate. From the photo-characteristics they appear to become less resistant and probably finer grained to the top.

Unit B shows no strafication; the photo tone varies from medium to dark grey, with occasional irregular lighter toned lenzes. The finely textured dendritic drainage seems to show preferred directives, probably indicating wide spaced jointing with NW-SE and NE-SW strikes.

Field Evidence : Unit B consist of quartzdiorite.

An important fault offsetting both rock units runs along the main valley.

Unit C consist of terrace remnants and mantle cover, its photo-tone is medium to light grey; there is no vegetation, except along the larger valleys.

Fig. 5.32a *Playa odd drainage*. The most striking feature is the centripetal, radial drainage pattern around the many shallow depressions showing a lighter tone than the surrounding country, they may be saltmarshes.

Fig. 5.33 *Crystalline Rocks*

State : Wyoming C = 6" Approximate scale 1 : 60,000

A single rock unit is exposed within the area. It has a medium to light gray photo-tone, vegetation is scarce and the topography irregular.

There are numerous joints and fractures in various different directions, which stongly control the drainage. The larger fractures show by stream alignments, rectilinear depressions and vegetational alignments. Older fault zone A has been offset by younger fault B.

Field Evidence : The area consists of crystalline, locally gneissic rocks.

No signs of gneissic banding can be detected on the photographs.

Fig. 5.34 Overlays

Fig. 5.35 Stratigraphic Thickness Determination.

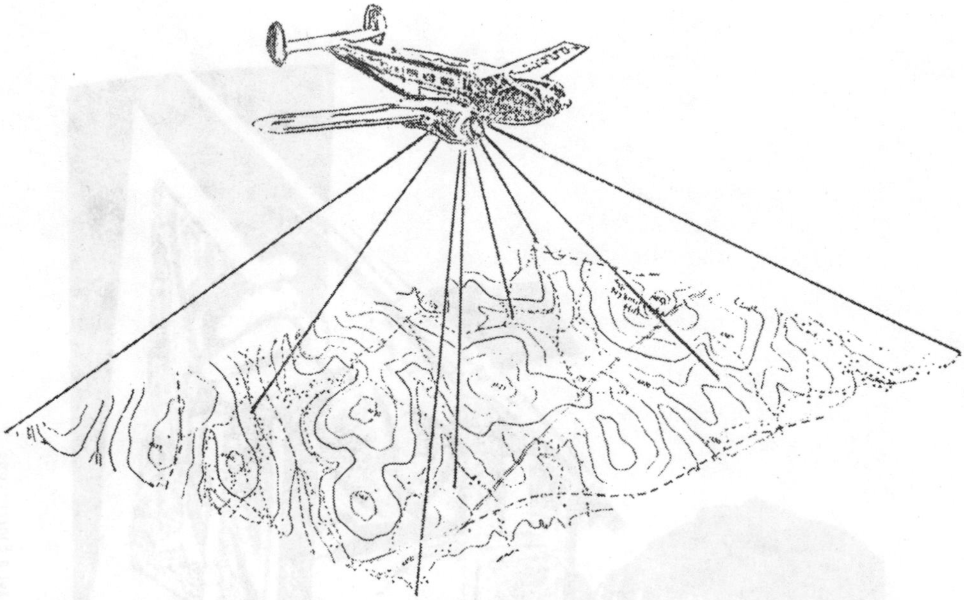

Fig. 5.1: Aerial Photo is a Record of the Earth's Surface

Fig. 5.2: An Oblique Aerial Photo

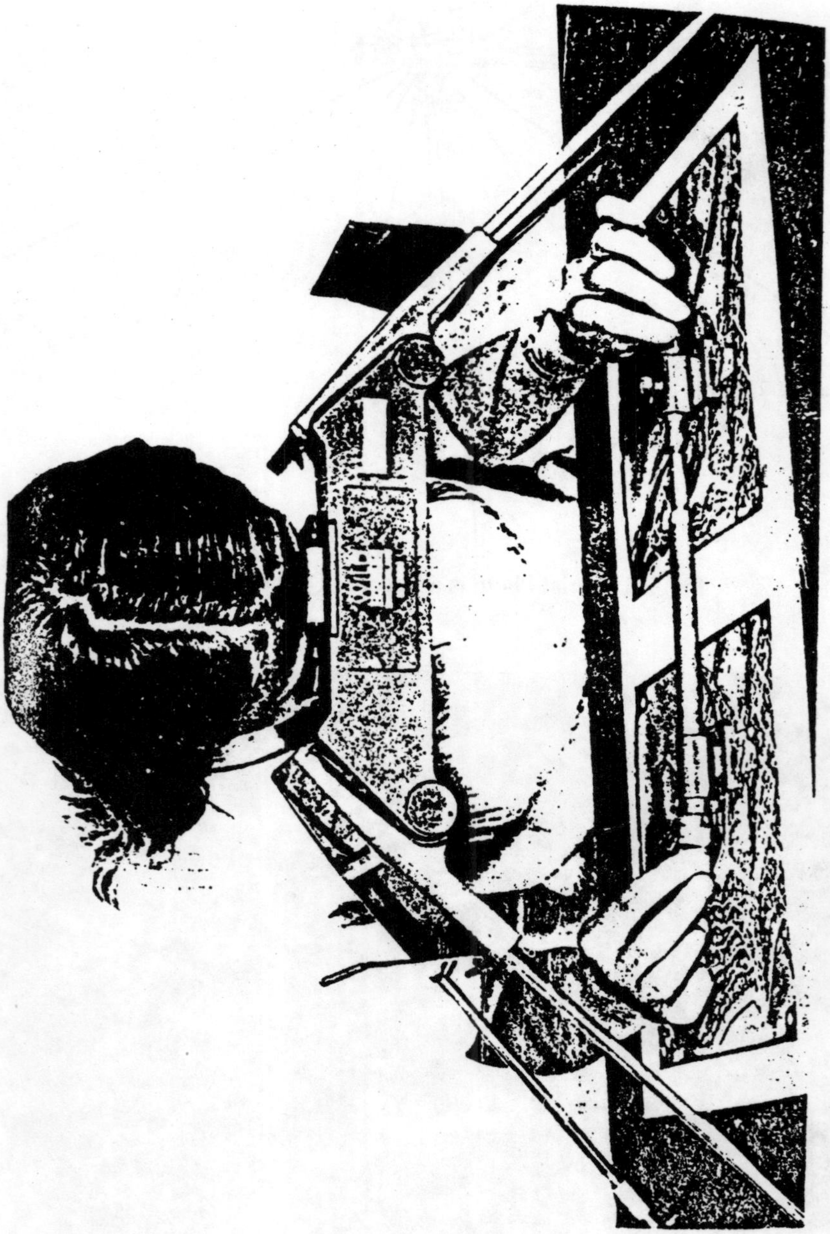

Fig. 5.3 : A Pair of Aerial Photos Seen under a Stereoscope

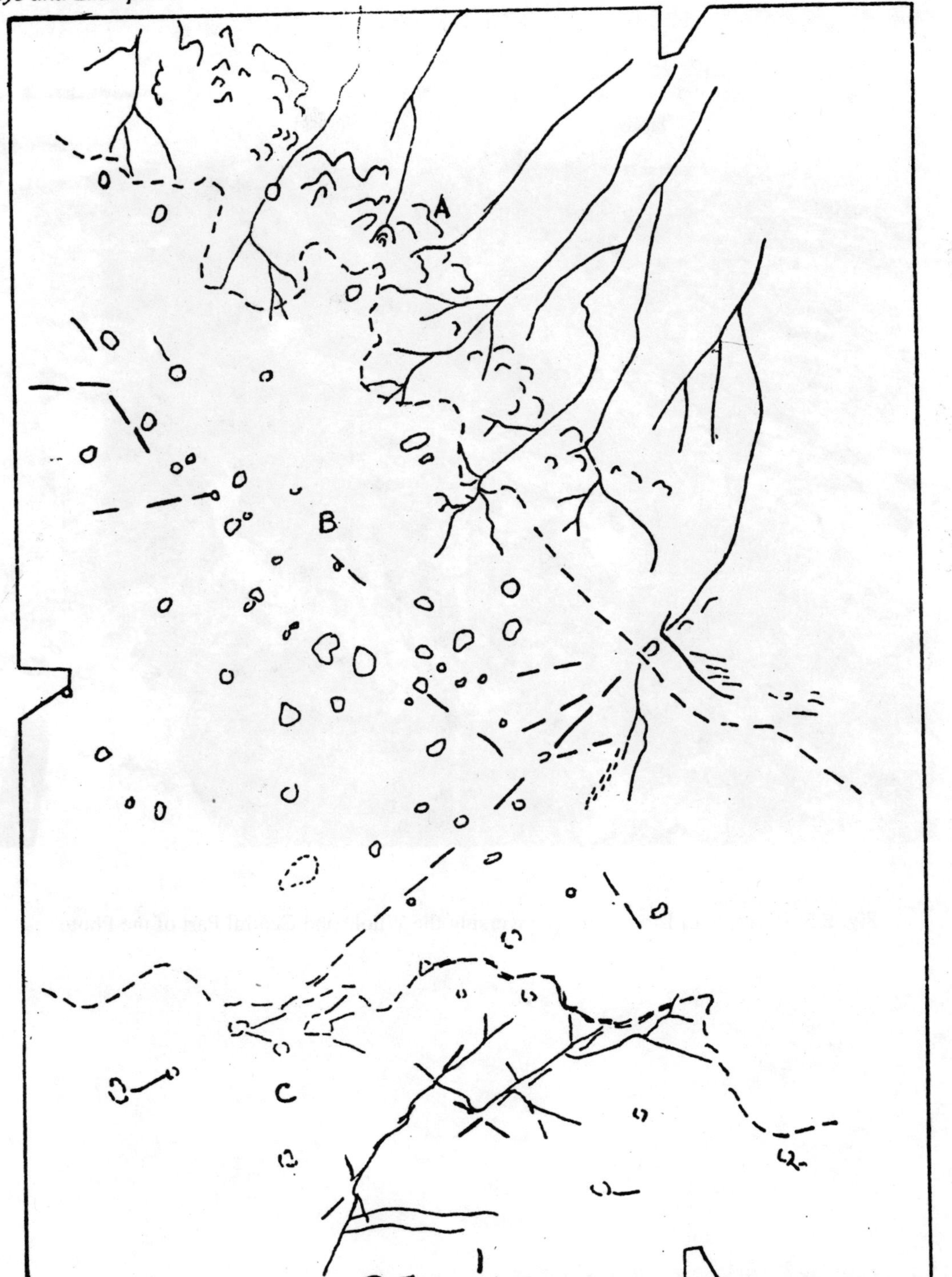

Fig. 5.4 : An Air Photo Showes Three Distinct Areas (Overlay)

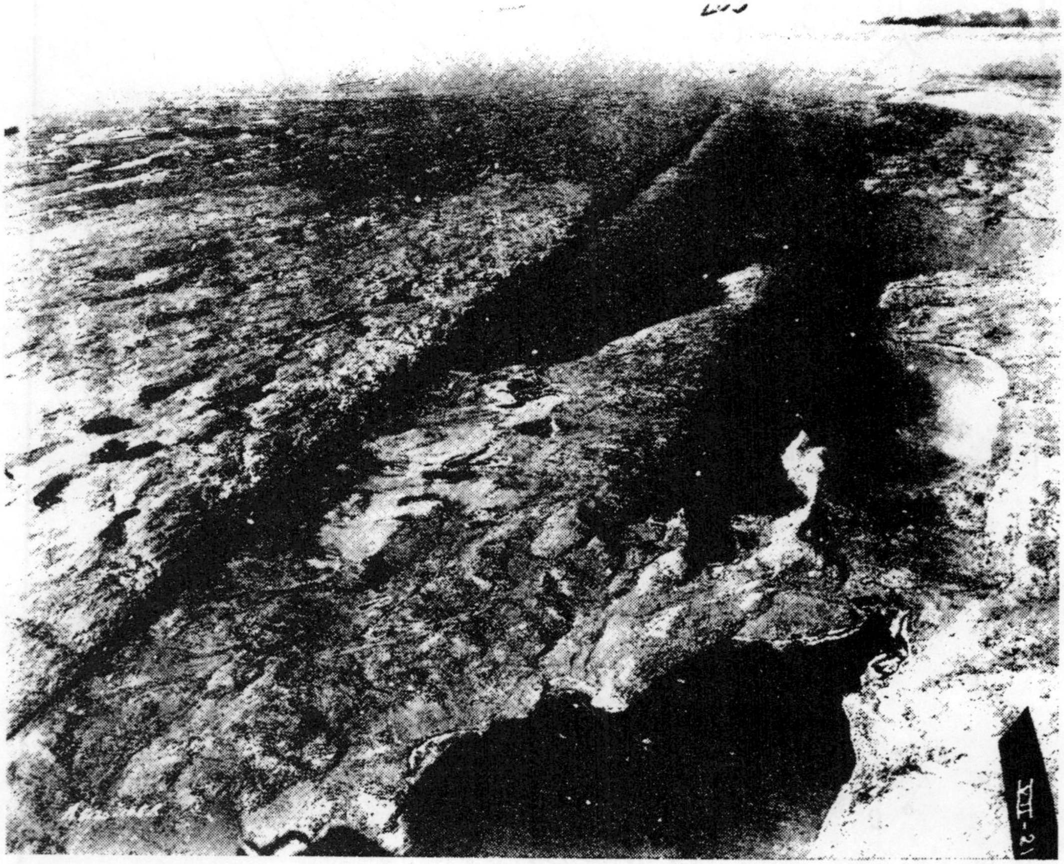

Fig. 5.5: Example of Linear Fault Traversing the Whole and Central Part of the Photo

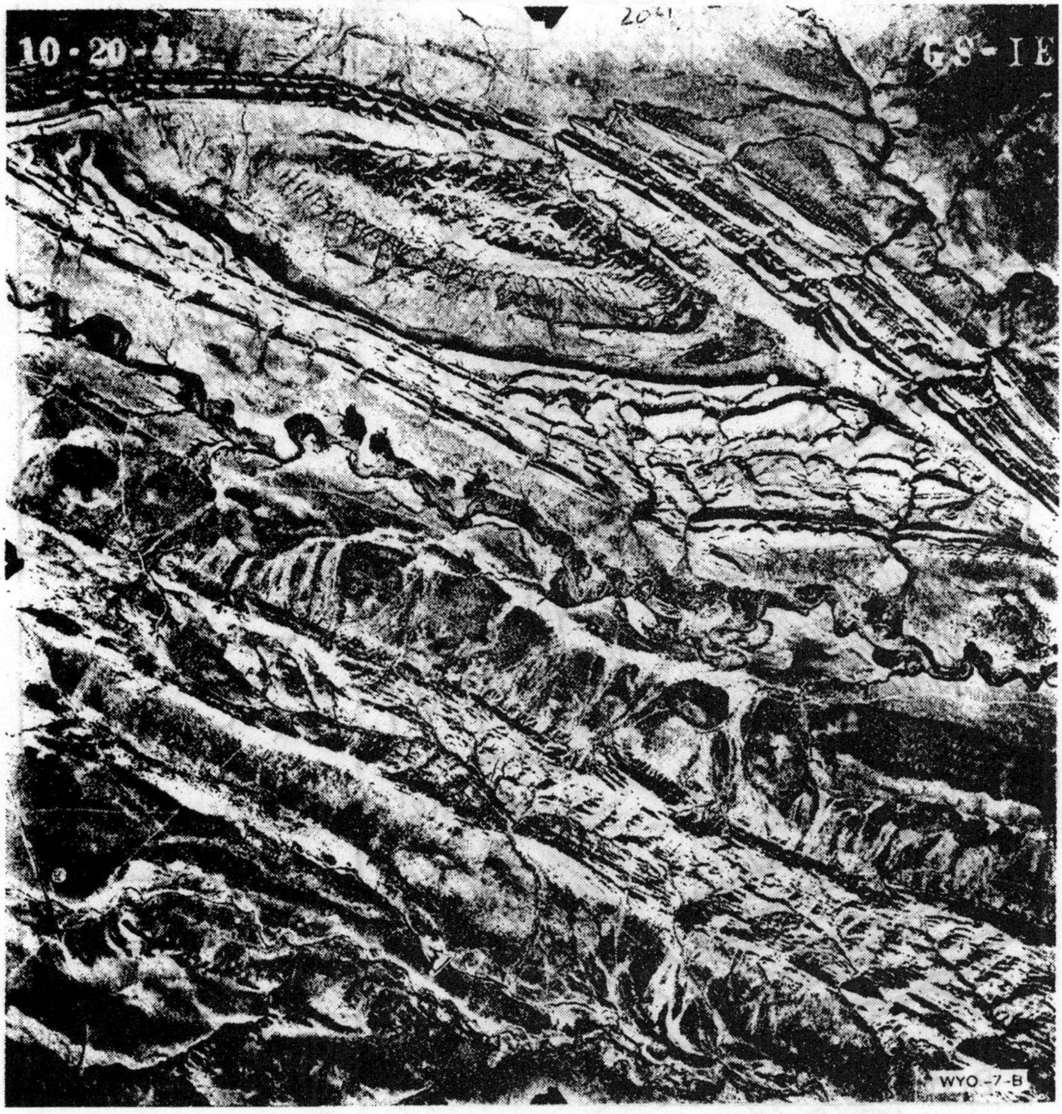

Fig. 5.6: Feature Illustrated

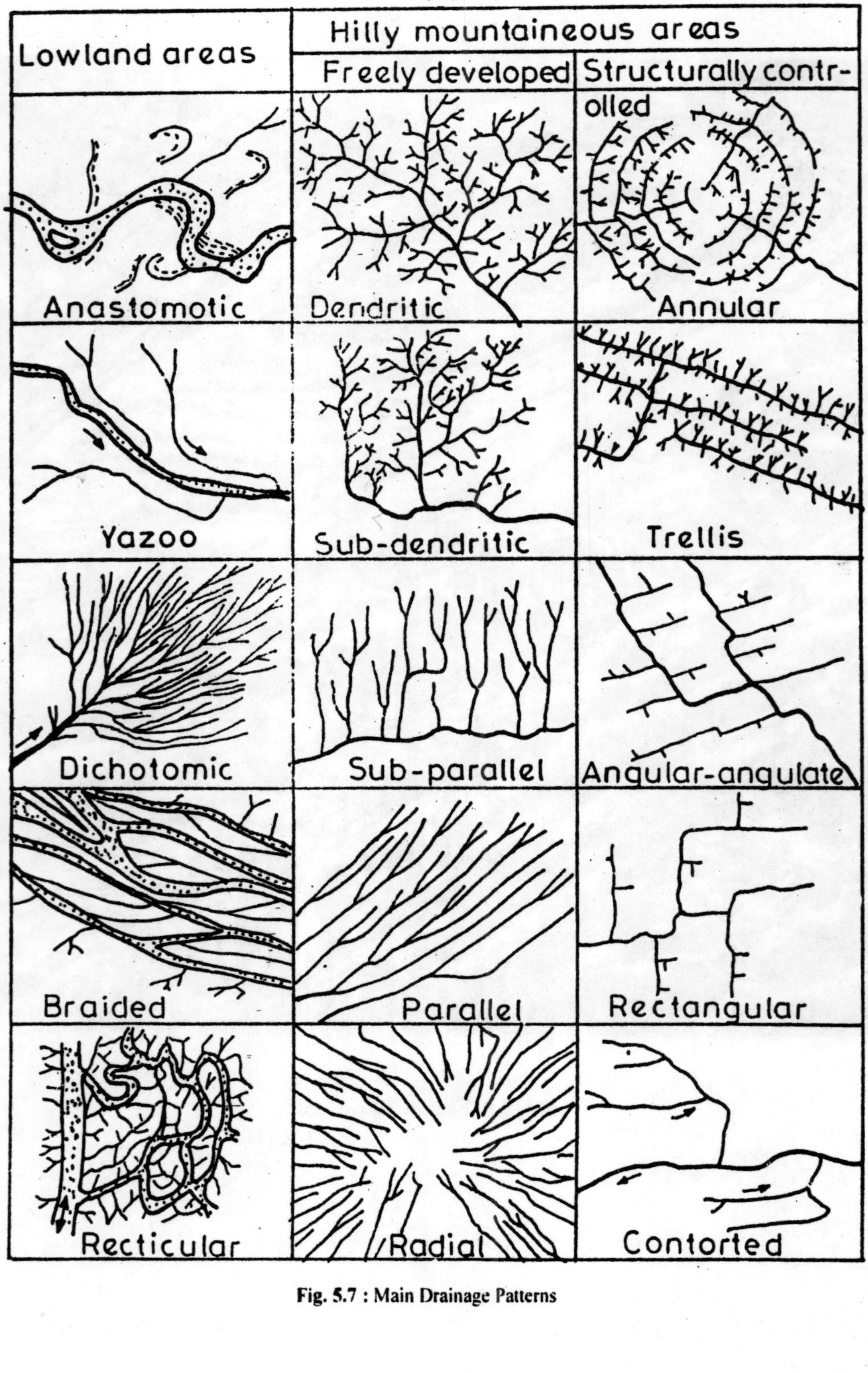

Fig. 5.7 : Main Drainage Patterns

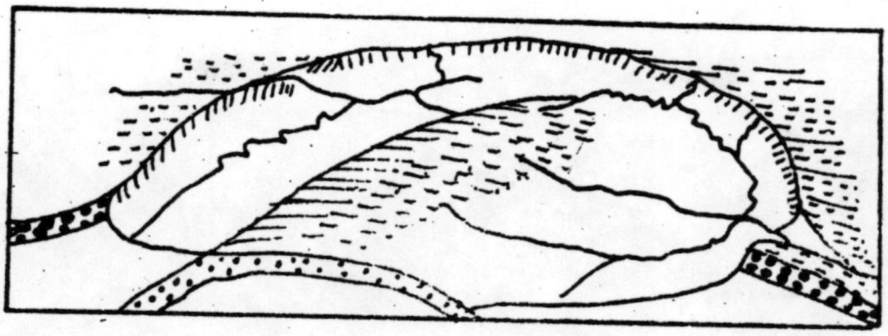

(a)

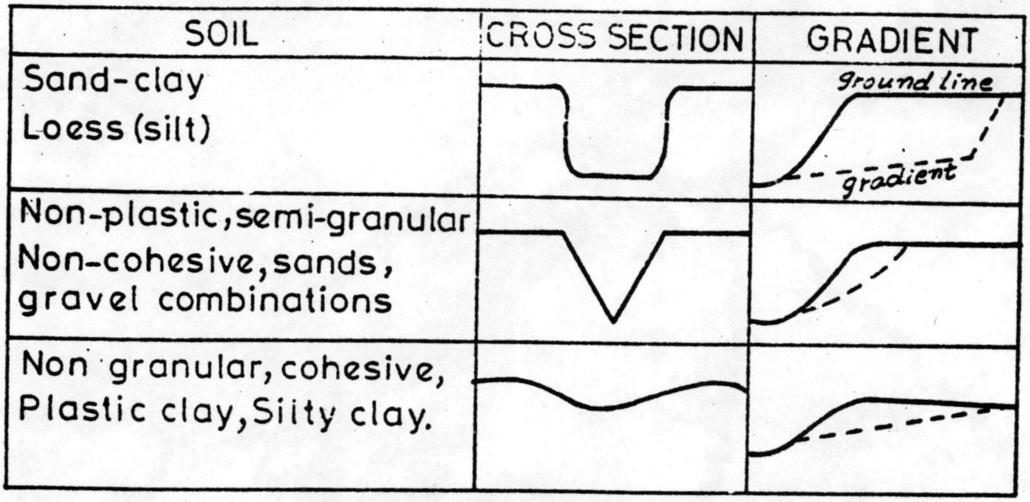

Fig. 5.8 : A Characteristic Erosional Pattern

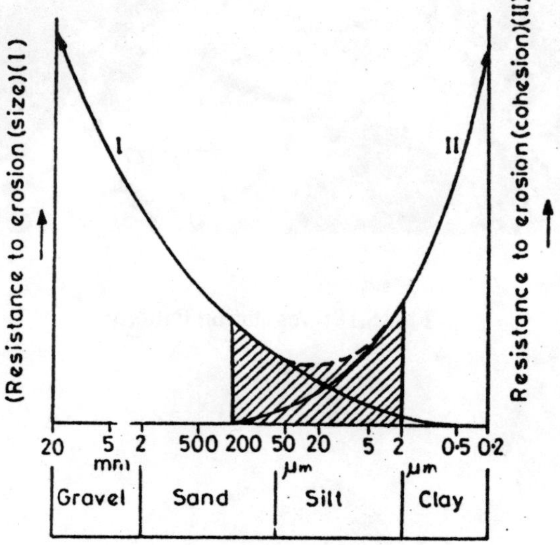

Fig. 5.9 : A plot of Resistance

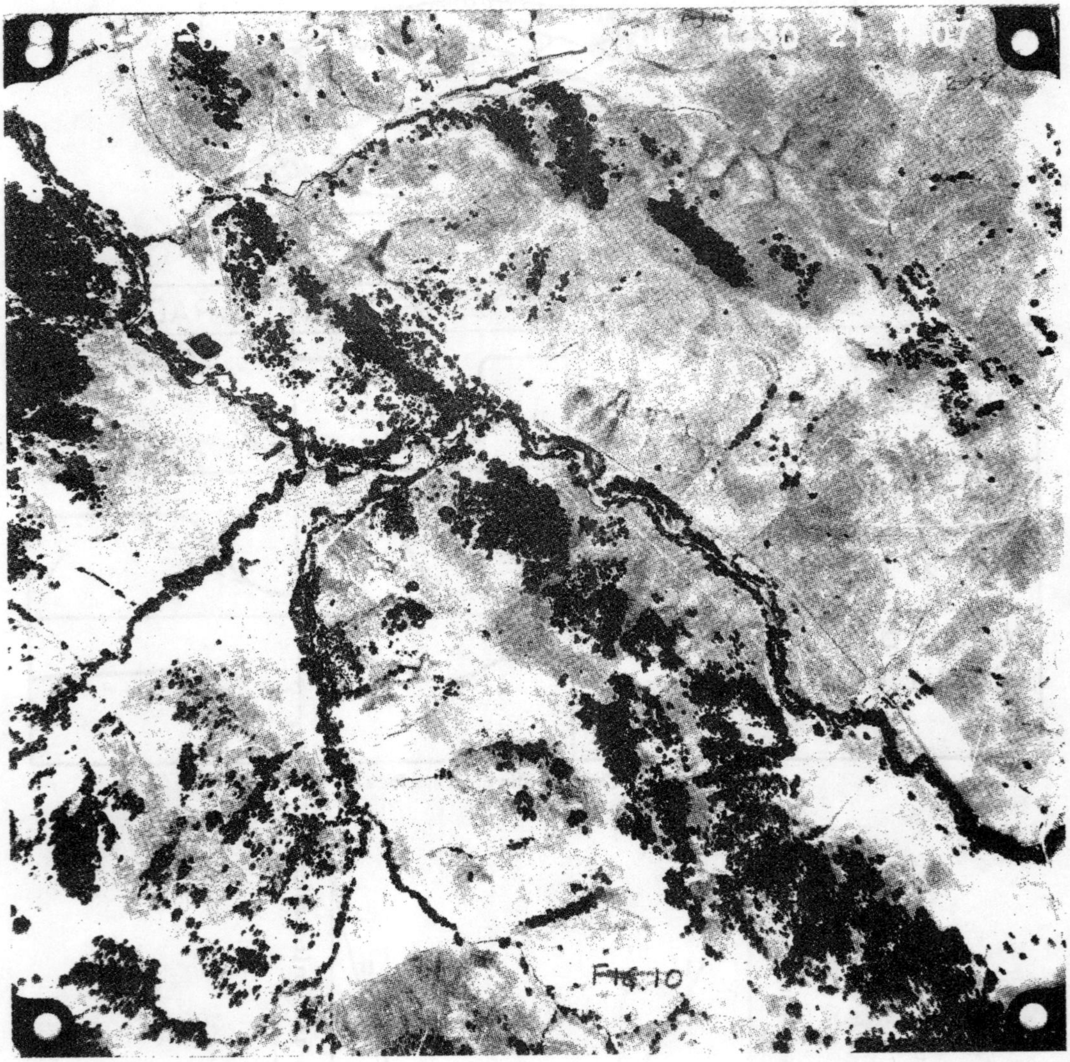

Fig. 5.10: Vegetation Pattern

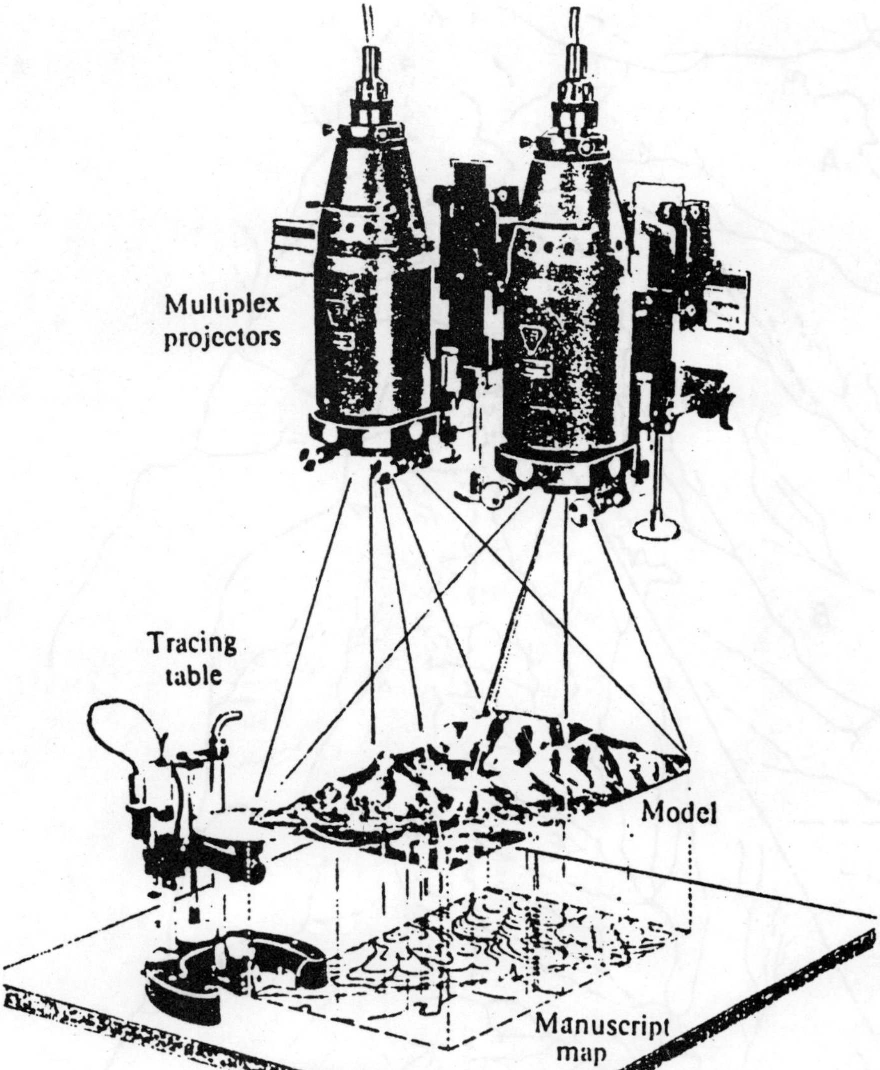

Fig. 5.11 : Stereoscopic Plotting Instrument (*Courtesy* of U.S. Geological Survey)

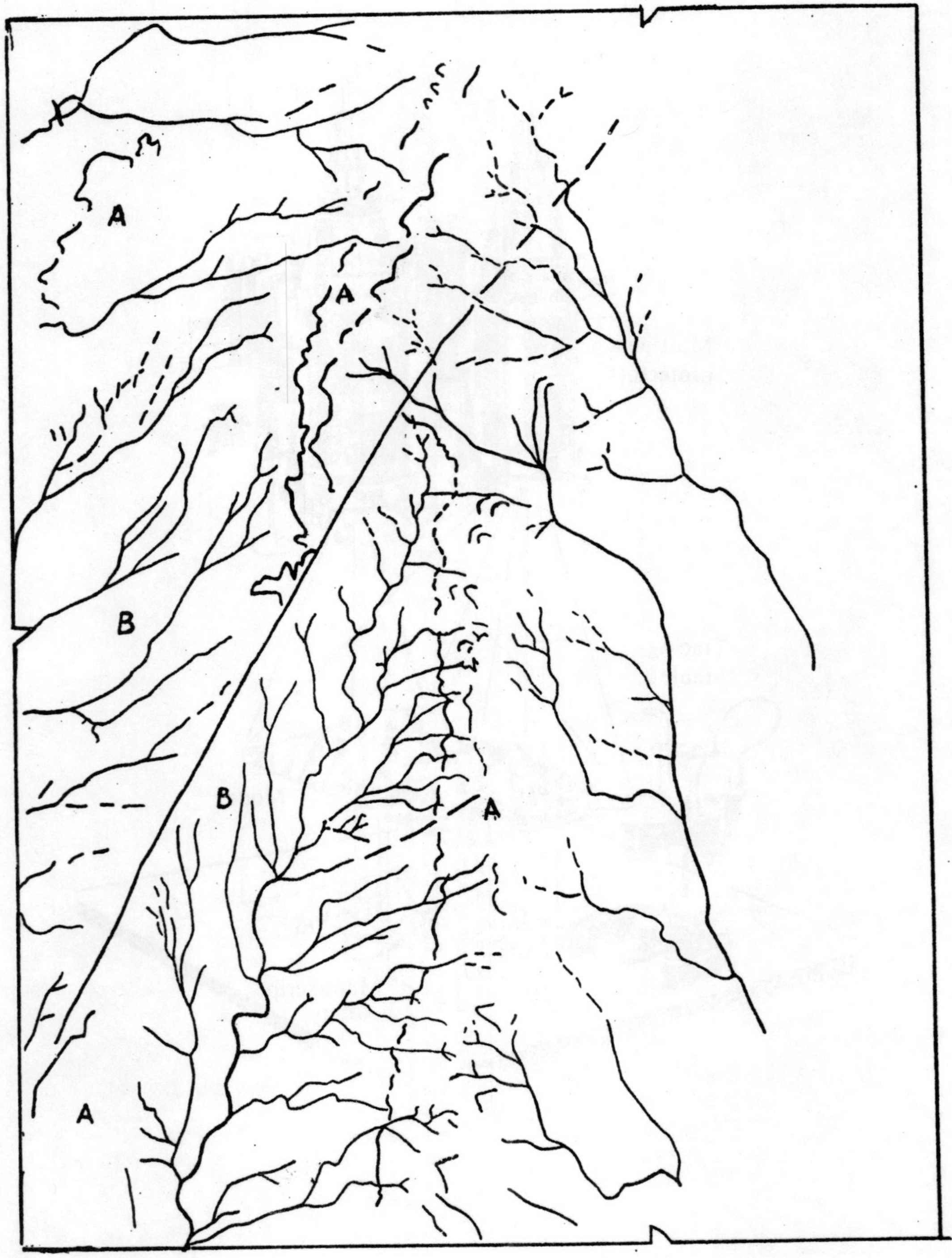

Fig. 5.12 : Gently Dipping Sedimentary (Overlay)

Fig. 5.13: The Slightly Dissected Eastern Edge of the Southern High Plains (U.S.A.)

Fig. 5.14: Volcano Sakura-Jino (Japan)

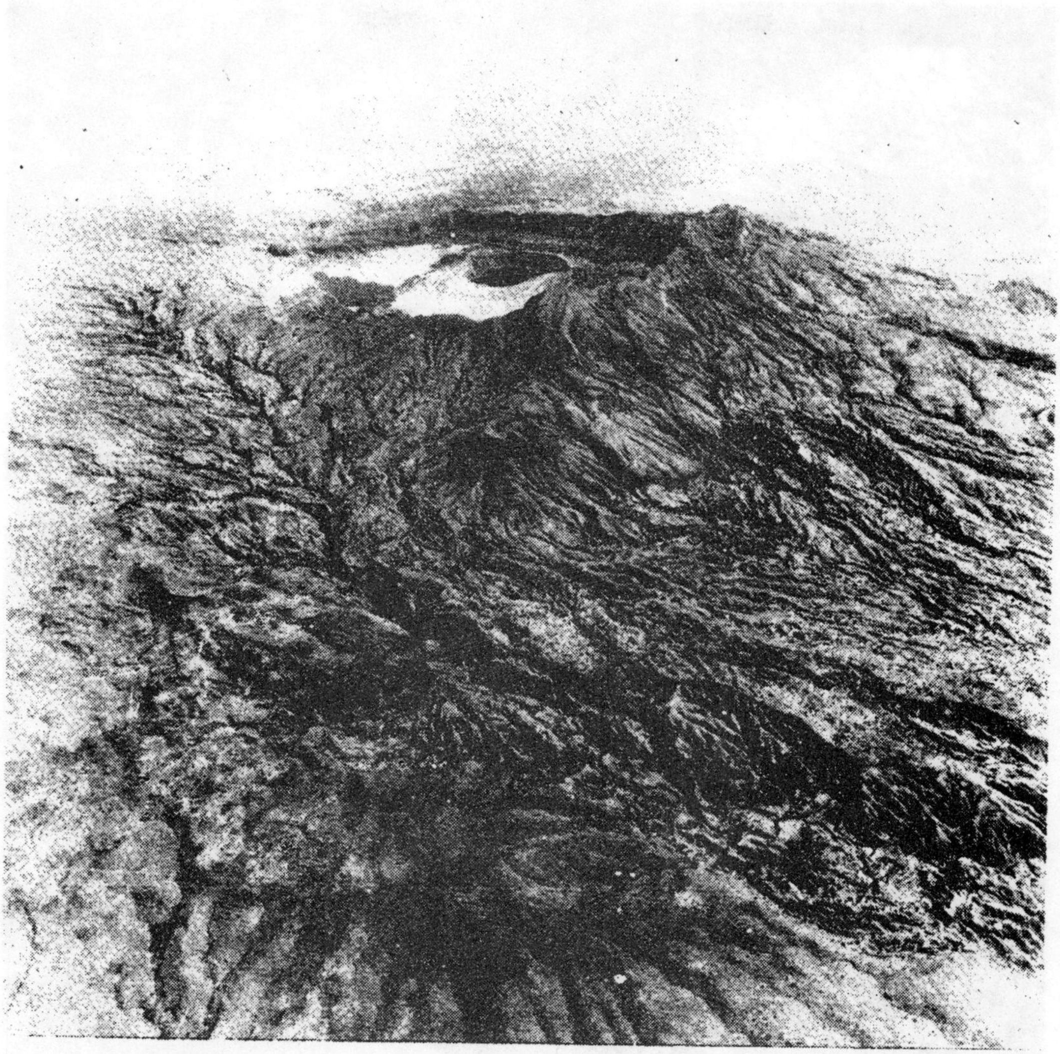

Fig. 5.15: Excellent Volcanic Crater and Cone Containing Deriba Lake-Externsive Erosion by Streams (Africa)

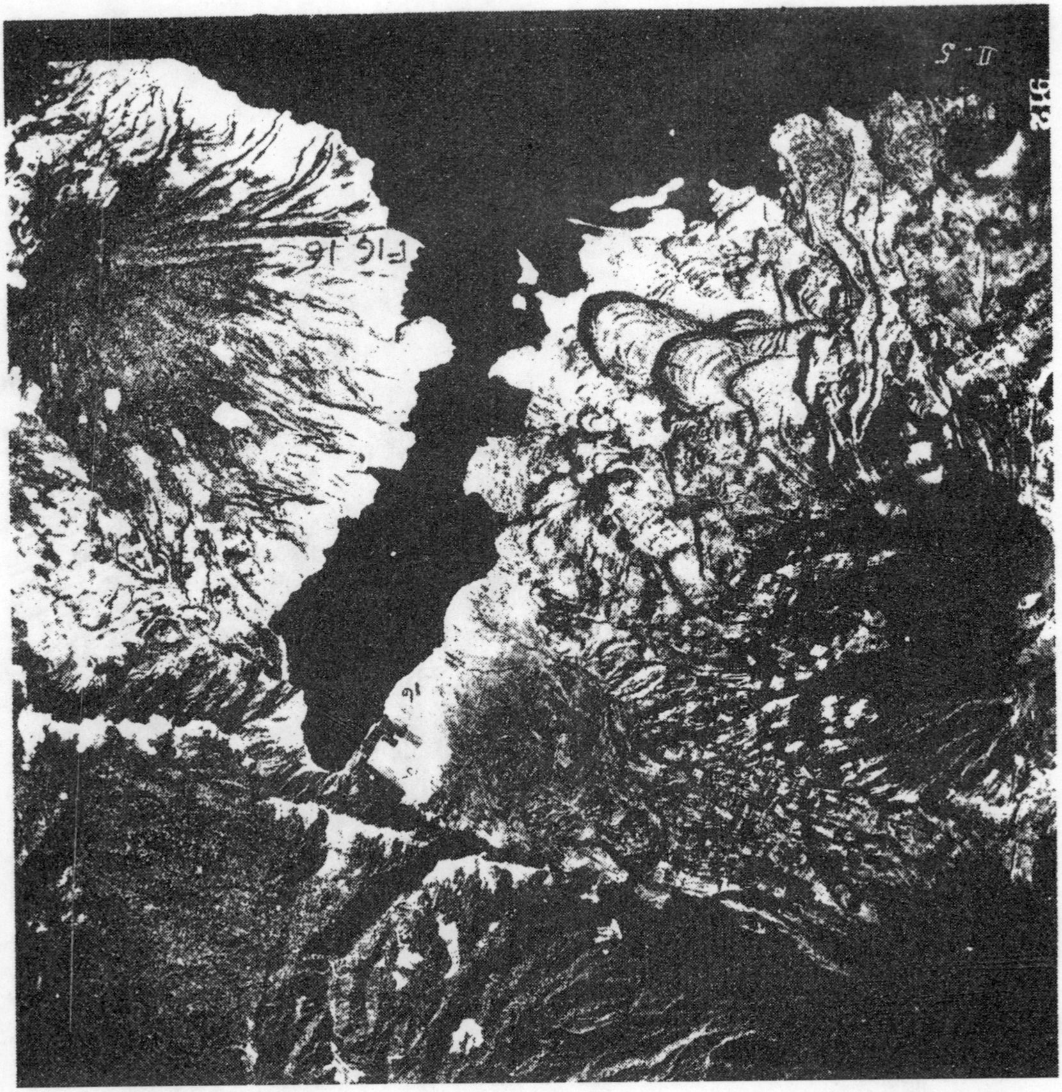

Fig. 5.16: Active Lova Slopes (Japan)

Fig. 5.17: Shale in Semiarid Climate Area (Utah)

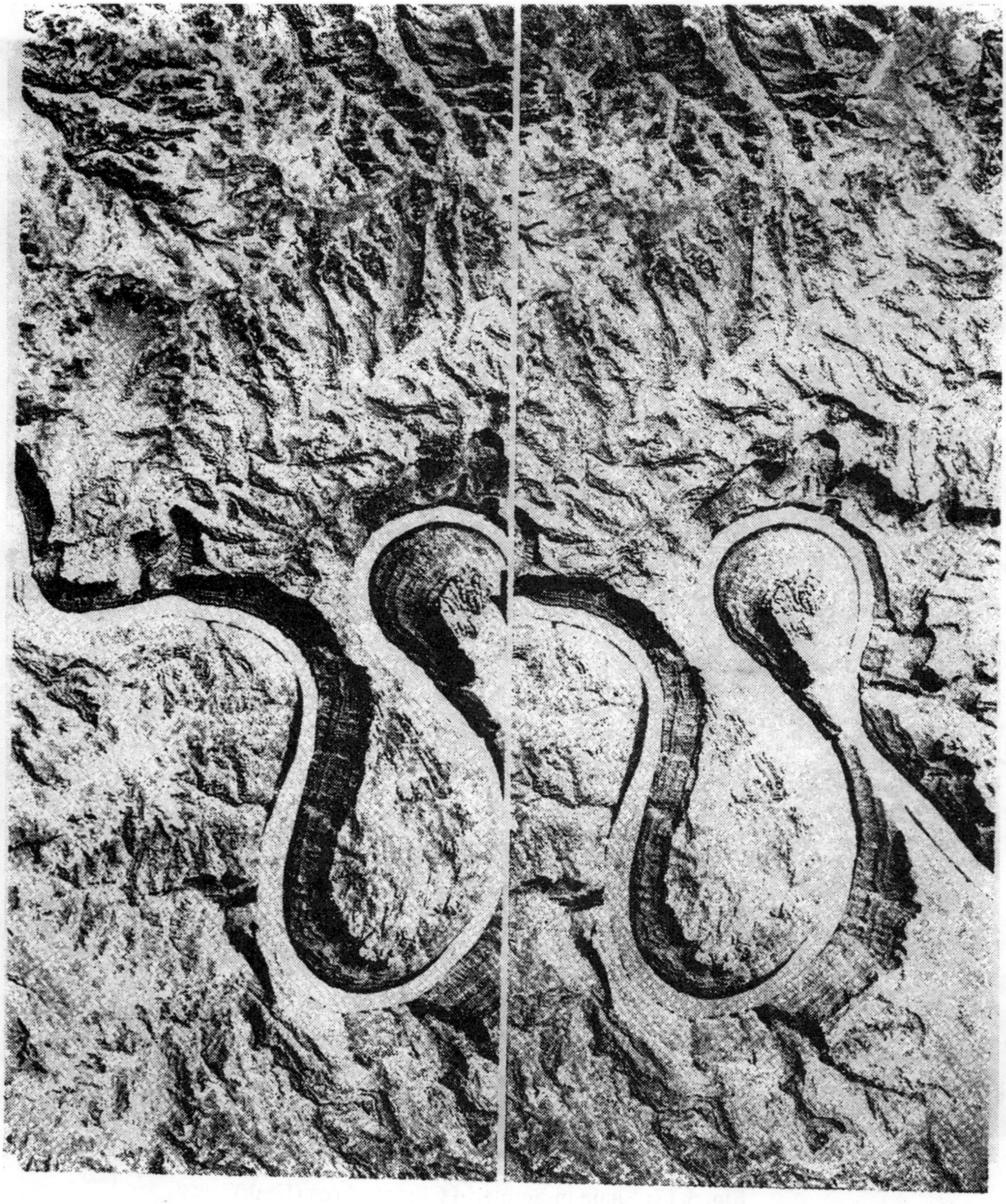

The Loop
San Juan County, Utah, U.S.A.

August 30, 1940
RF = 1: 41, 900 H (=) 20, 900 feet

Stereogram No. 104
Prepared from USDA-SCS aerial photography by the University of Illiois Committee on Aerial Photography.

Fig. 5.18: The Stereogram (Pair of Overlapping Photos)

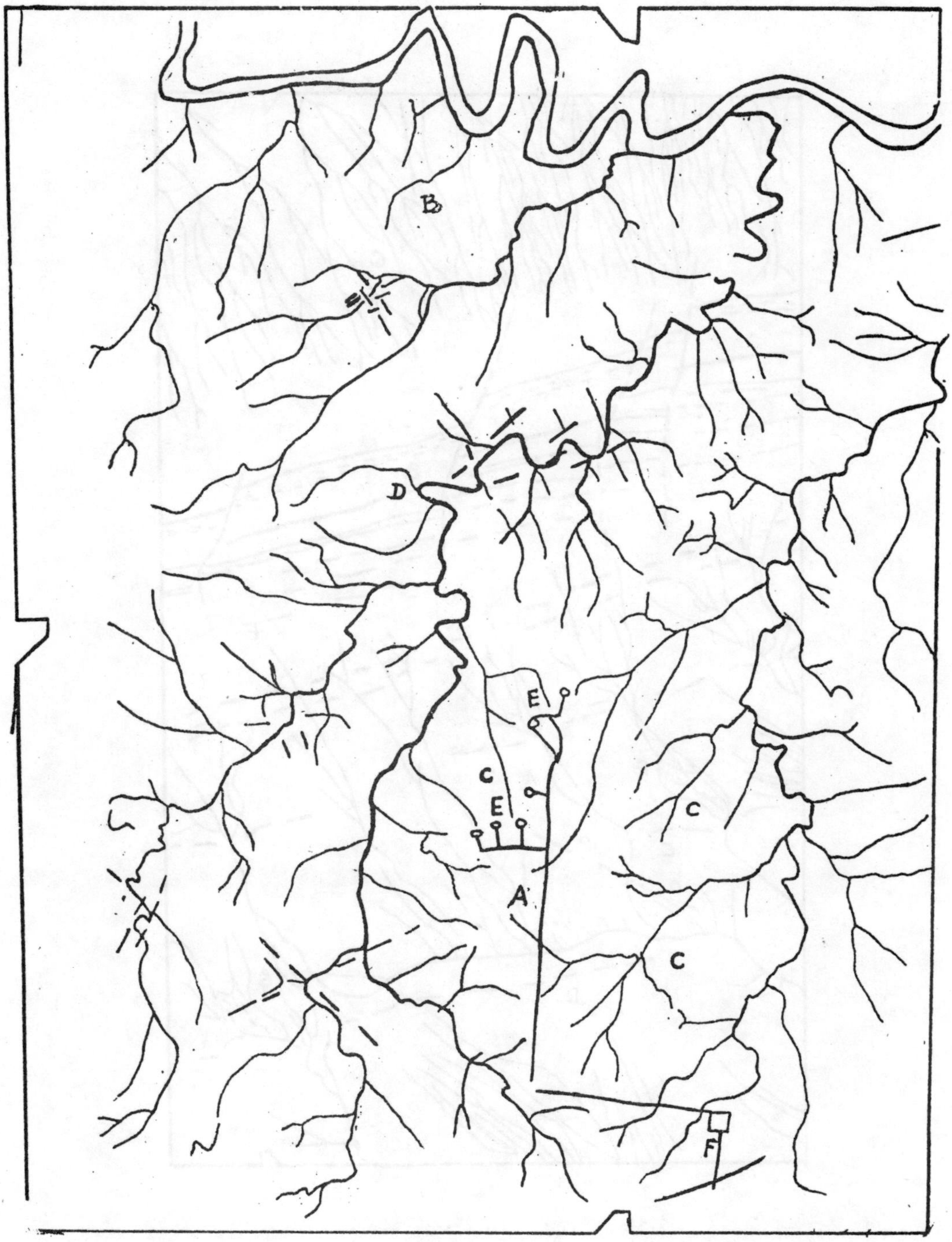

Fig. 5.19 : Subsurface Structure (Overlay)

Fig. 5.20 : Area of Sparse Outcrops (Overlay)

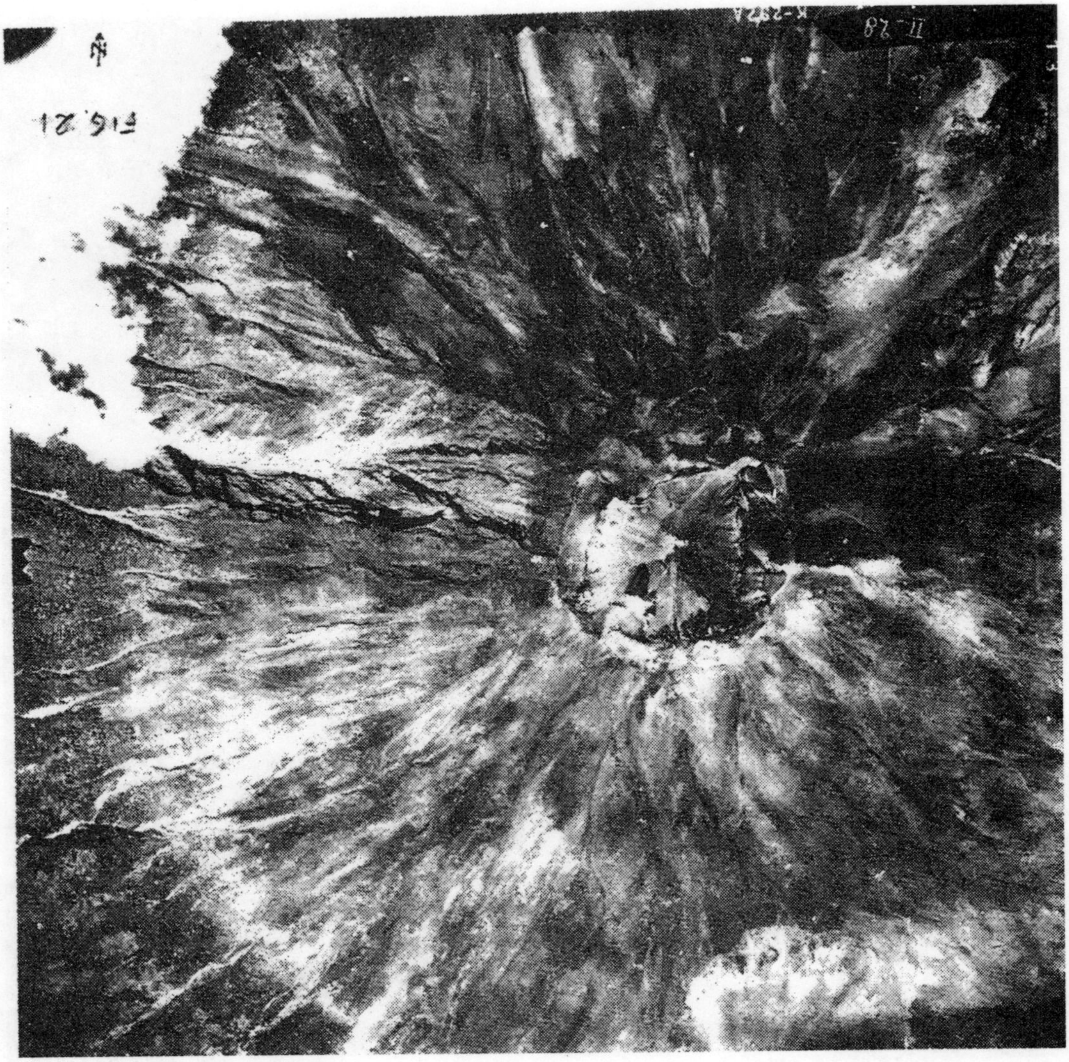

Fig. 5.21: Mt. Fujiyama (Japan)

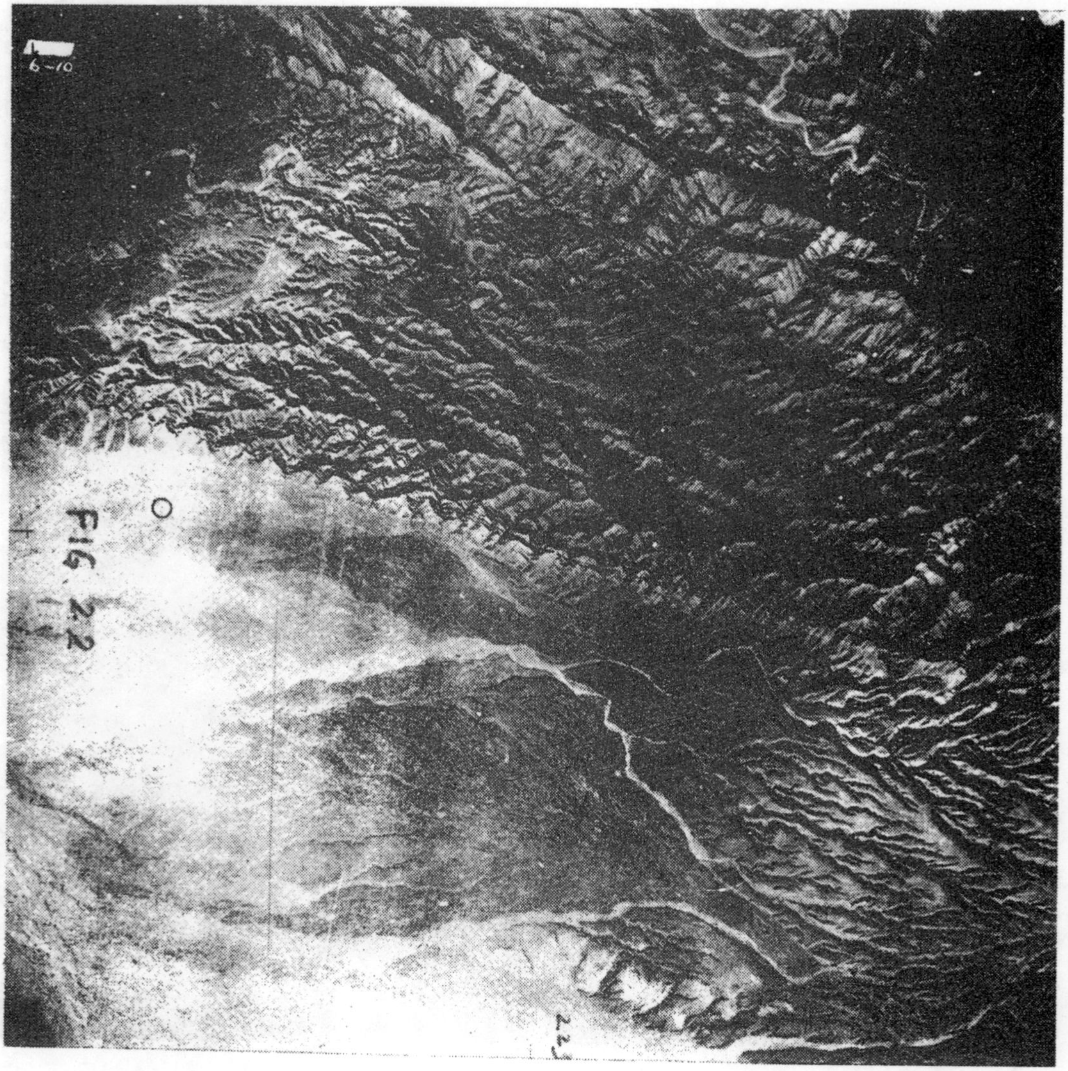

Fig. 5.22: Alternation of Predominantly Argillaceous Zones

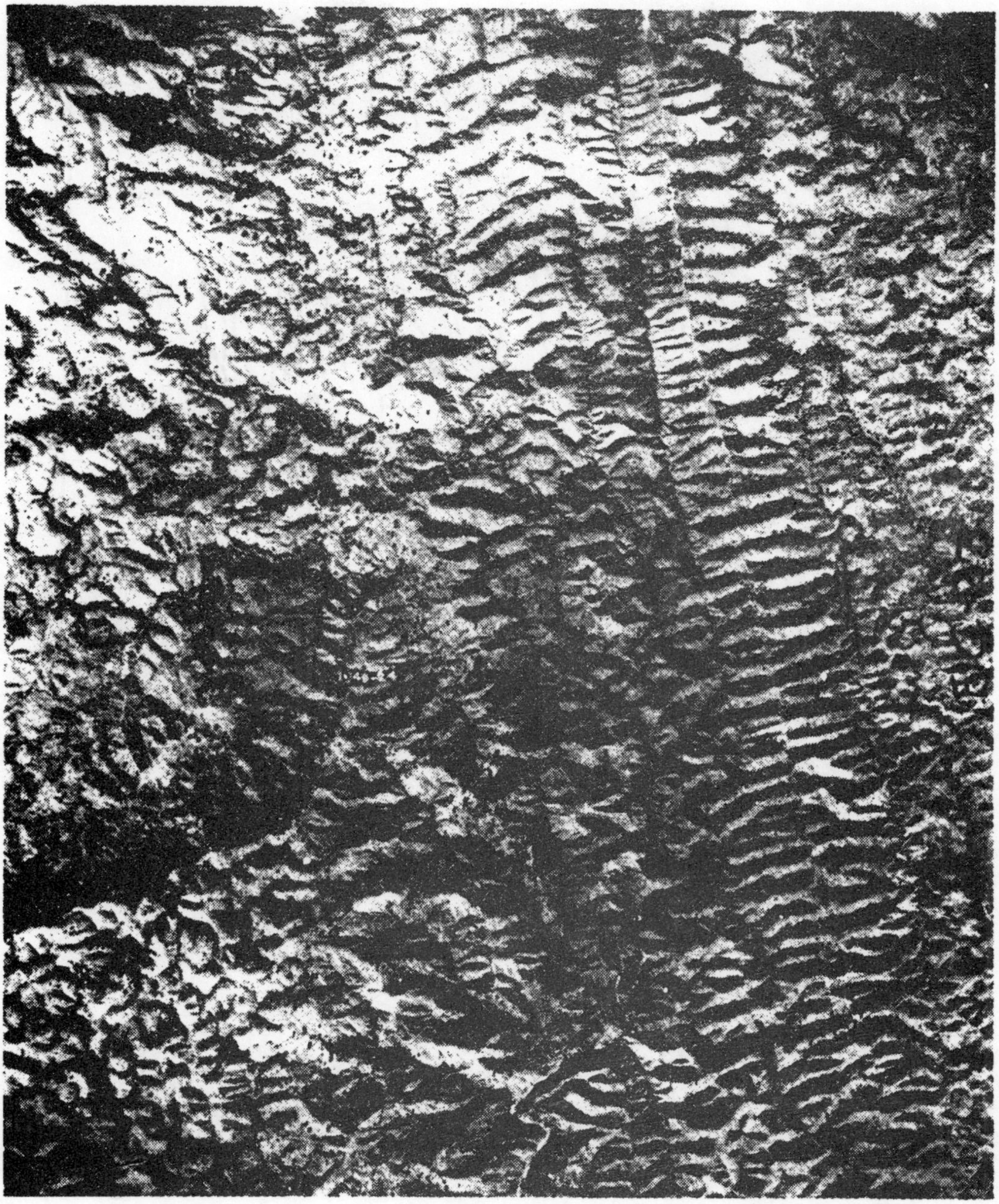

Fig. 5.23: Topographic Expression

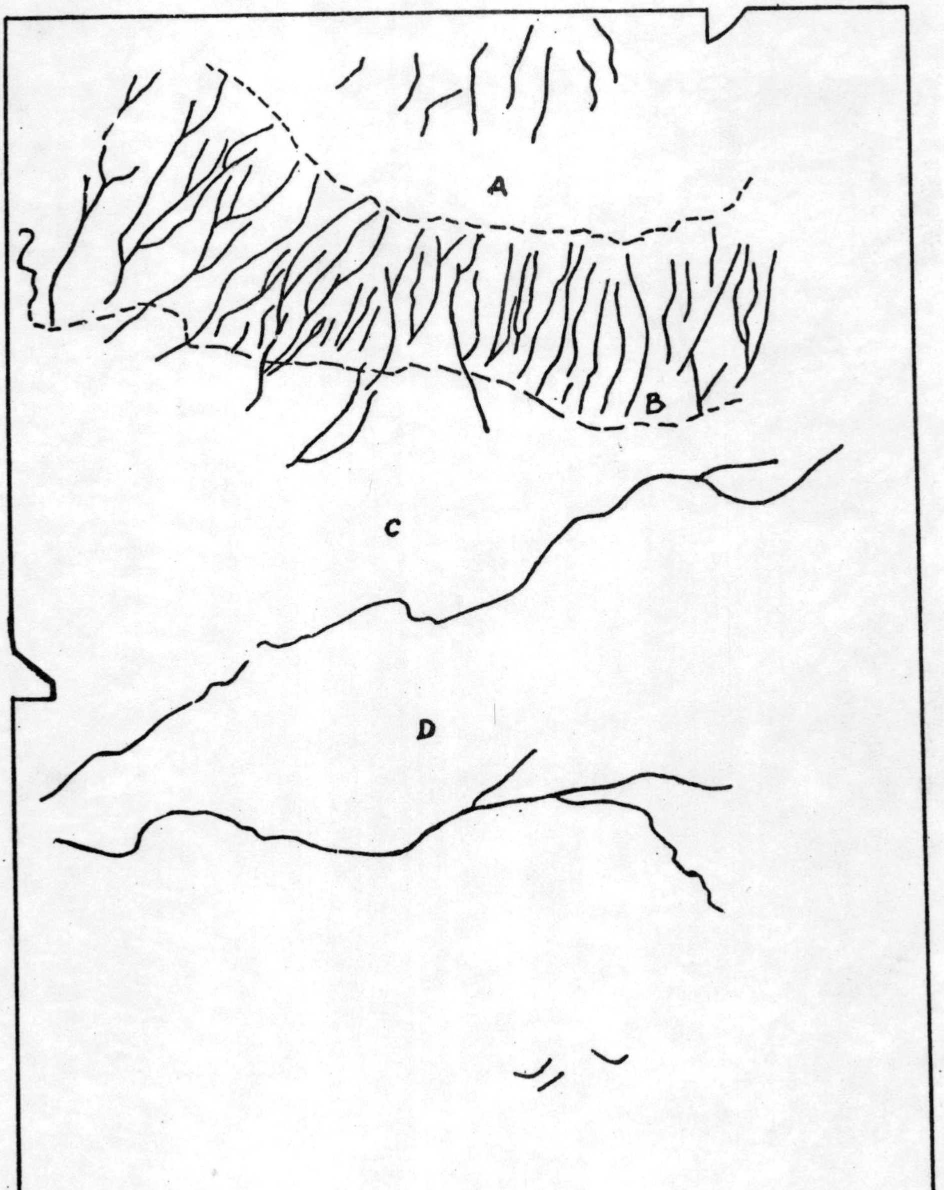

Fig. 5.24 : Drainage Characteristics in Surfacial Material (Overlay)

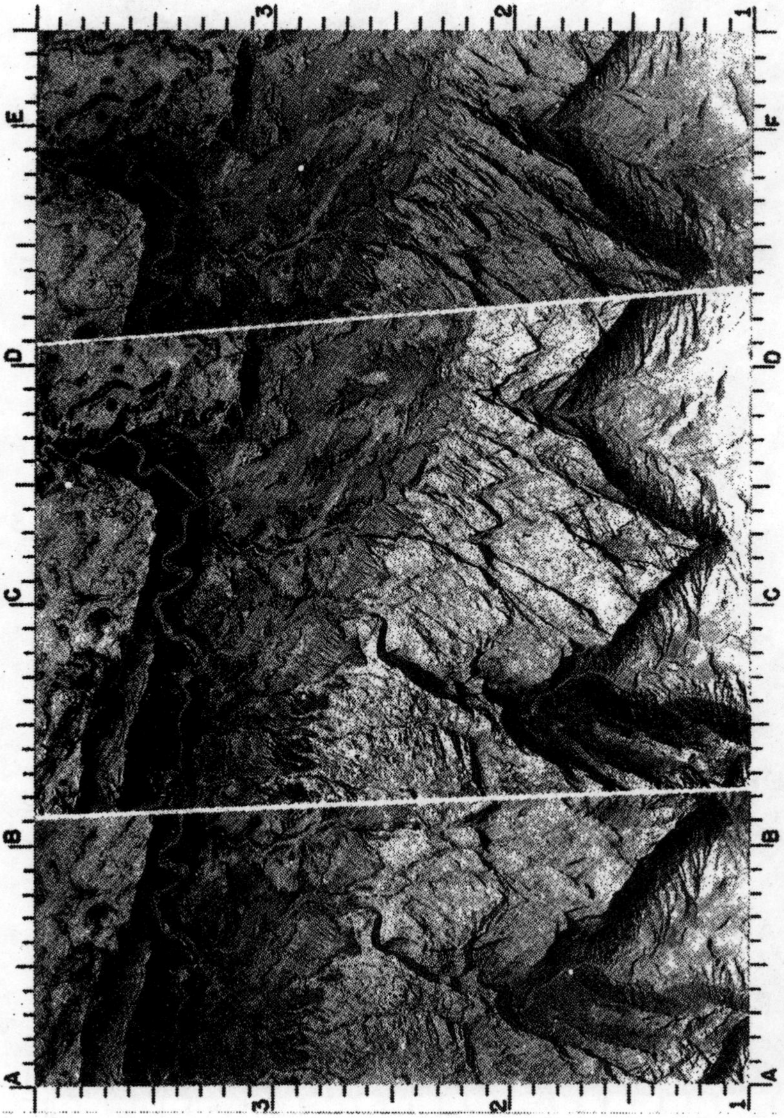

Black Dragon Canyon
Emery County, Utah, USA
July 6, 1938
RF = 1:42, 500 11 = 16, 300 feet

Stereogram No. 173
Prepared from USDA-SCS
photography by the University
of Illiois Committee
on Aerial Photography.

Fig. 5.25: Black Drayon Canyon, Emery County, Utah, U.S.A.

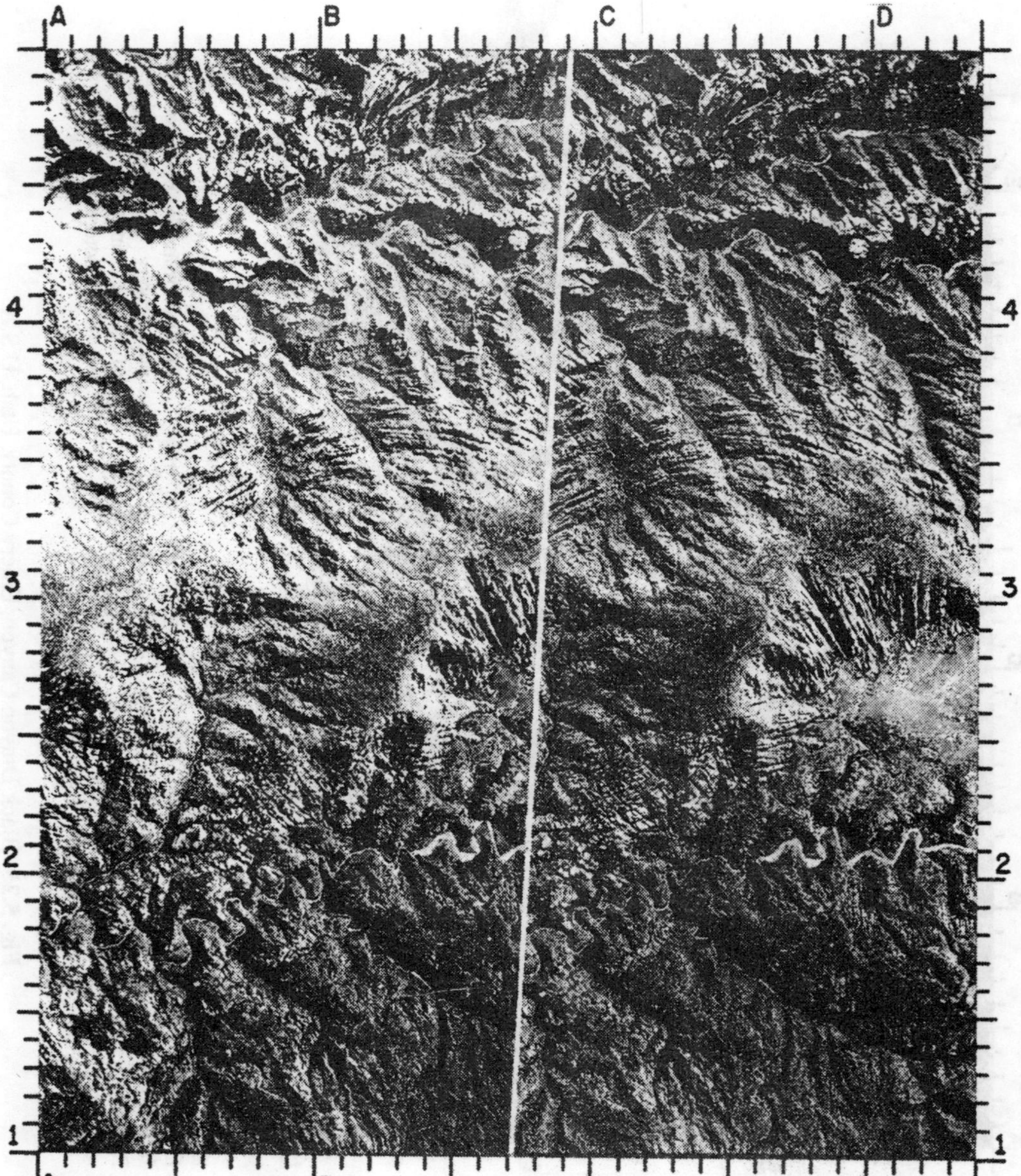

Salt Creek Canyon
San Juan County, Utah, USA
August 30, 1940
RF = 1: 36,000 H (=) 18, 900 feet

Stereogram No. 148
Prepared from USDA-SCS
photography by the University
of Illiois Committee
on Aerial Photography.

Fig. 5.26: Salt Creck Canyon, San Juan County Utah, U.S.A.

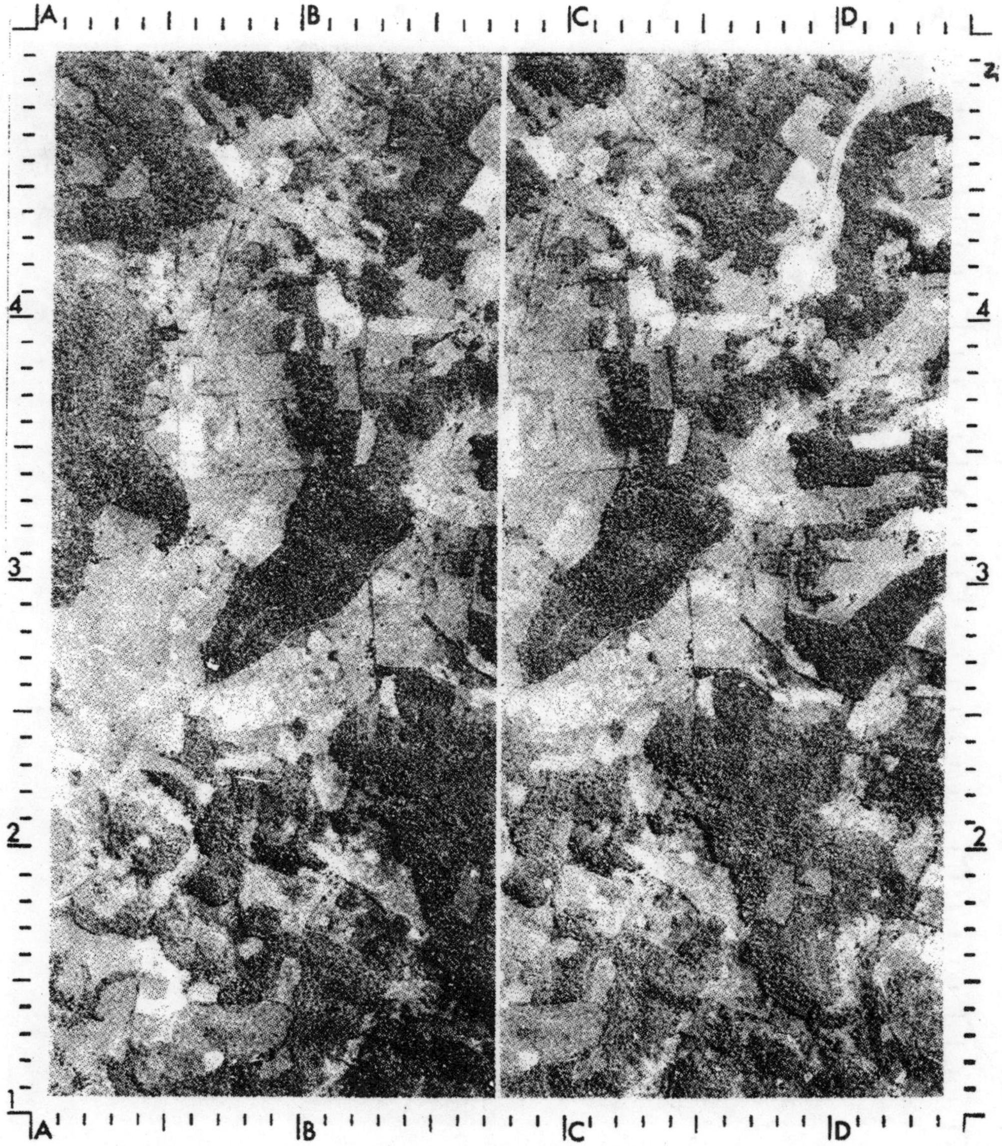

Sink
Hart County, Kentucky
October 17, 1938
RF = 1: 20, 400 H = 14,000 feet

Stereogram No. 133
Prepared from USDA-AAA
photography by the University
of Illiois Committee
on Aerial Photography.

Fig. 5.27: Sink-Hart County, Kentucky

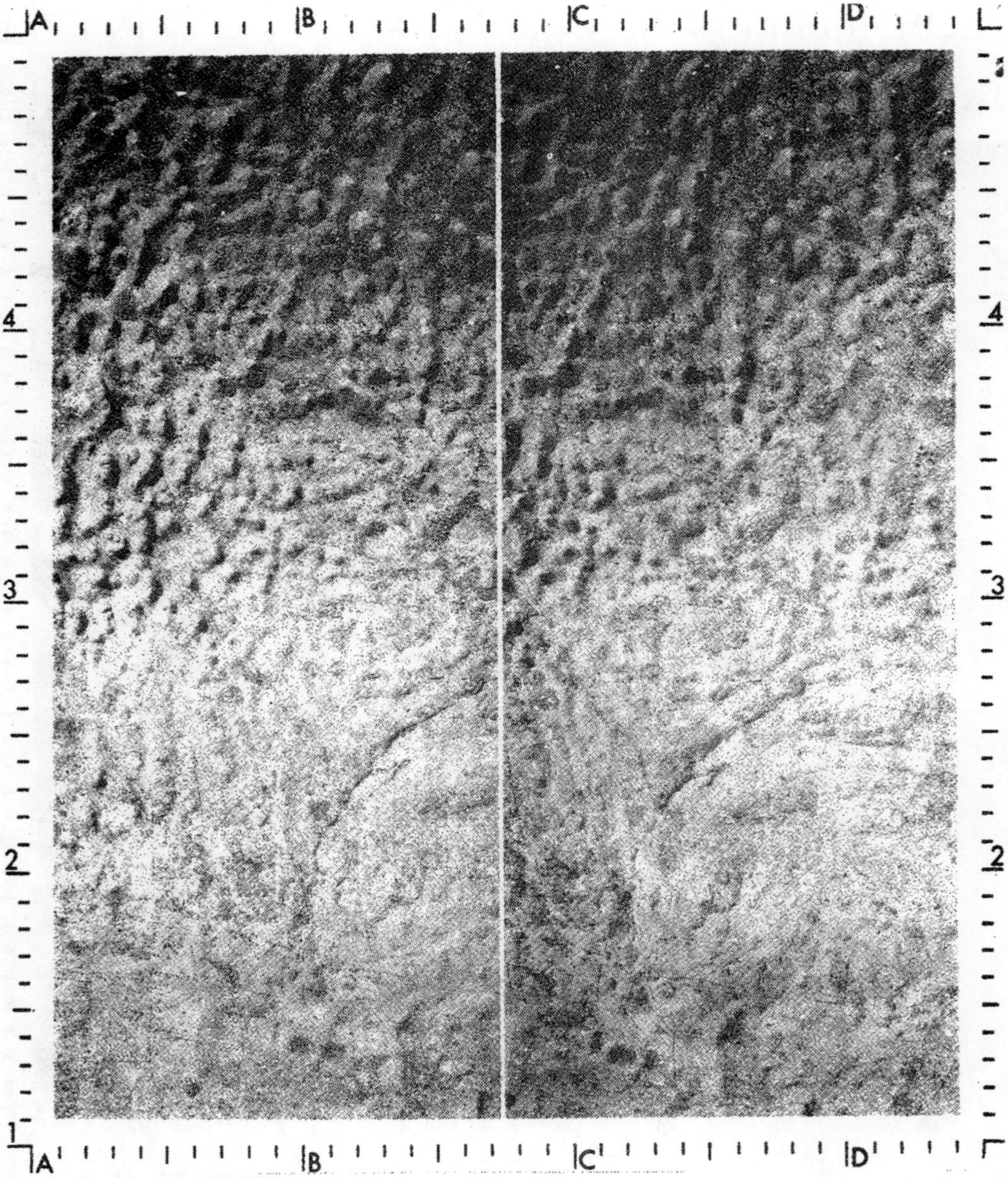

Haystack
Puerto Rico
Date : 1941
RF = 1: 25, 300 H = 10,900 feet

Stereogram No. 170
Prepared from Puerto Rican
photography by the University
of Illiois Committee
on Aerial Photography.

Fig. 5.28: Haystack, Puerto Rico

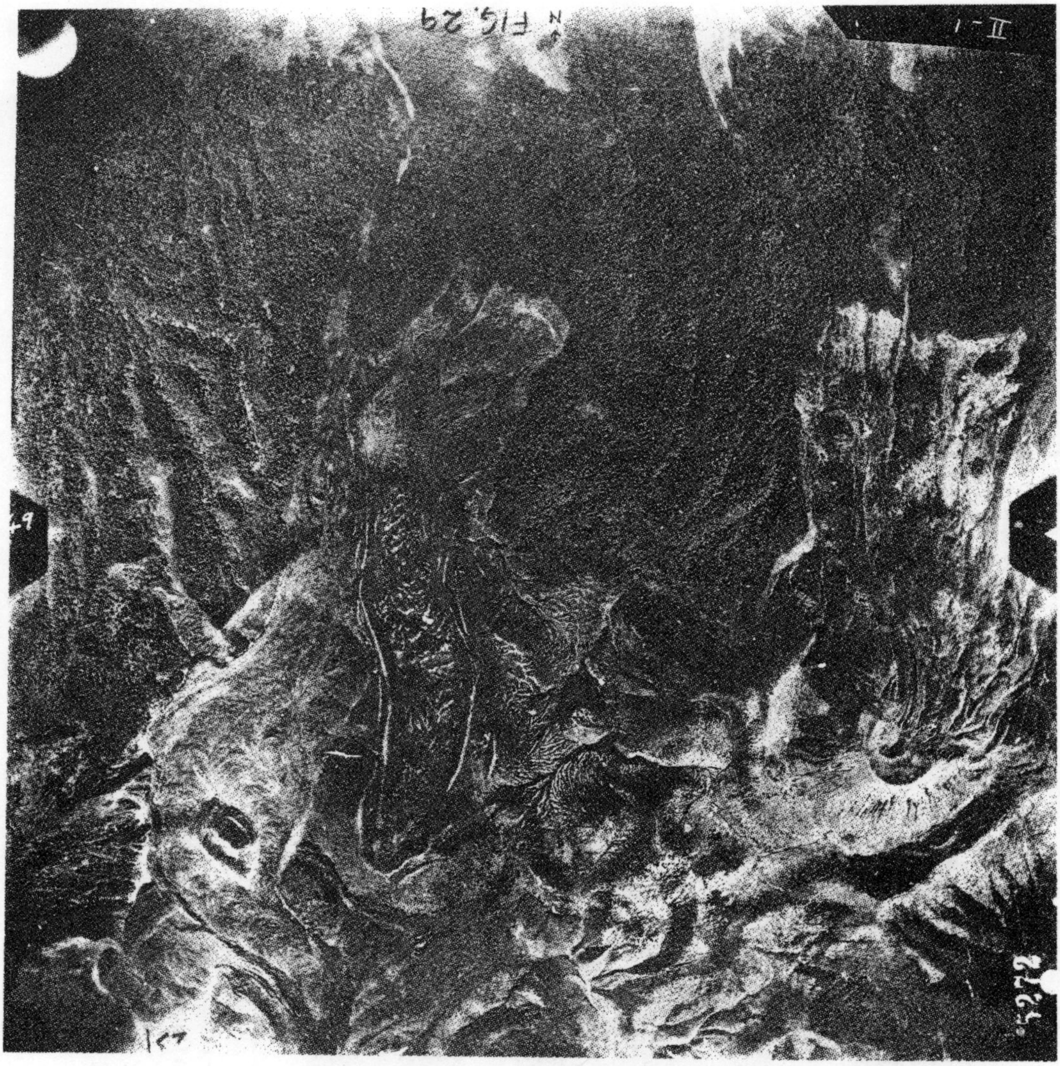

Fig. 5.29: Tanganyika

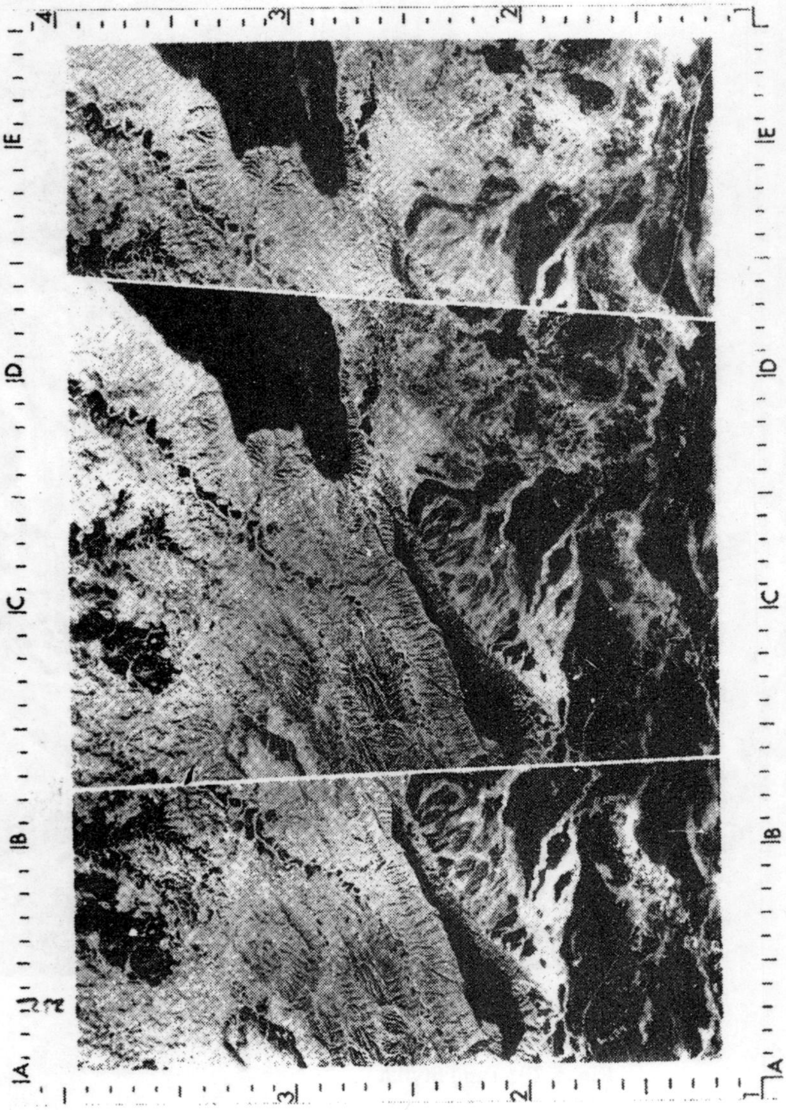

11art Mountain
Pennington County, South Dakota
September 20, 1938
RF = 1: 31, 000 H = 14,200 feet

Stereogram No. 174
Prepared from USDA-AAA
photography by the University
of Illiois Committee
on Aerial Photography.

Fig. 5.30: 11art Mountain, Pennington County, South Dakota

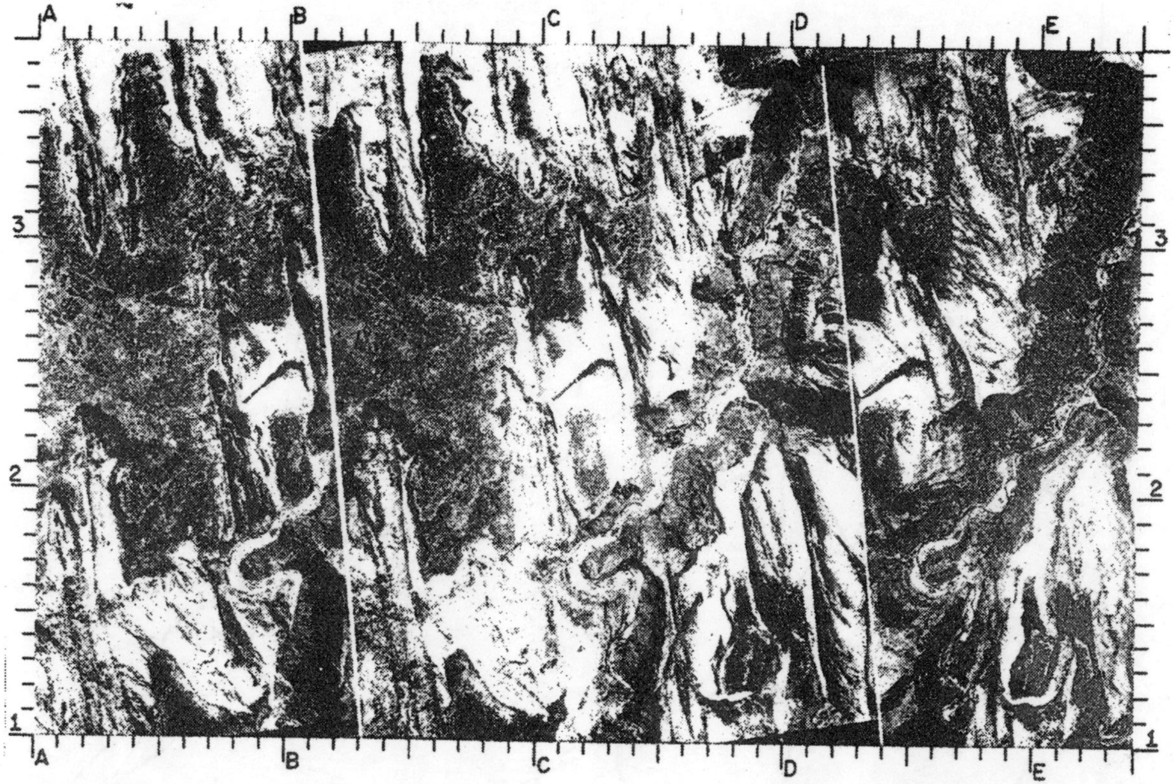

Zion Canyon
Kane and Washington Countries, Utah, USA
July 18, 1939
RF = 1: 45, 000 H = 15,000 feet .

Stereogram No. 147
Prepared from USGS-SCS
photography by the University
of Illiois Committee
on Aerial Photography.

Fig. 5.31: Zion Canyon, Kane and Washington Counties, Utah, U.S.A.

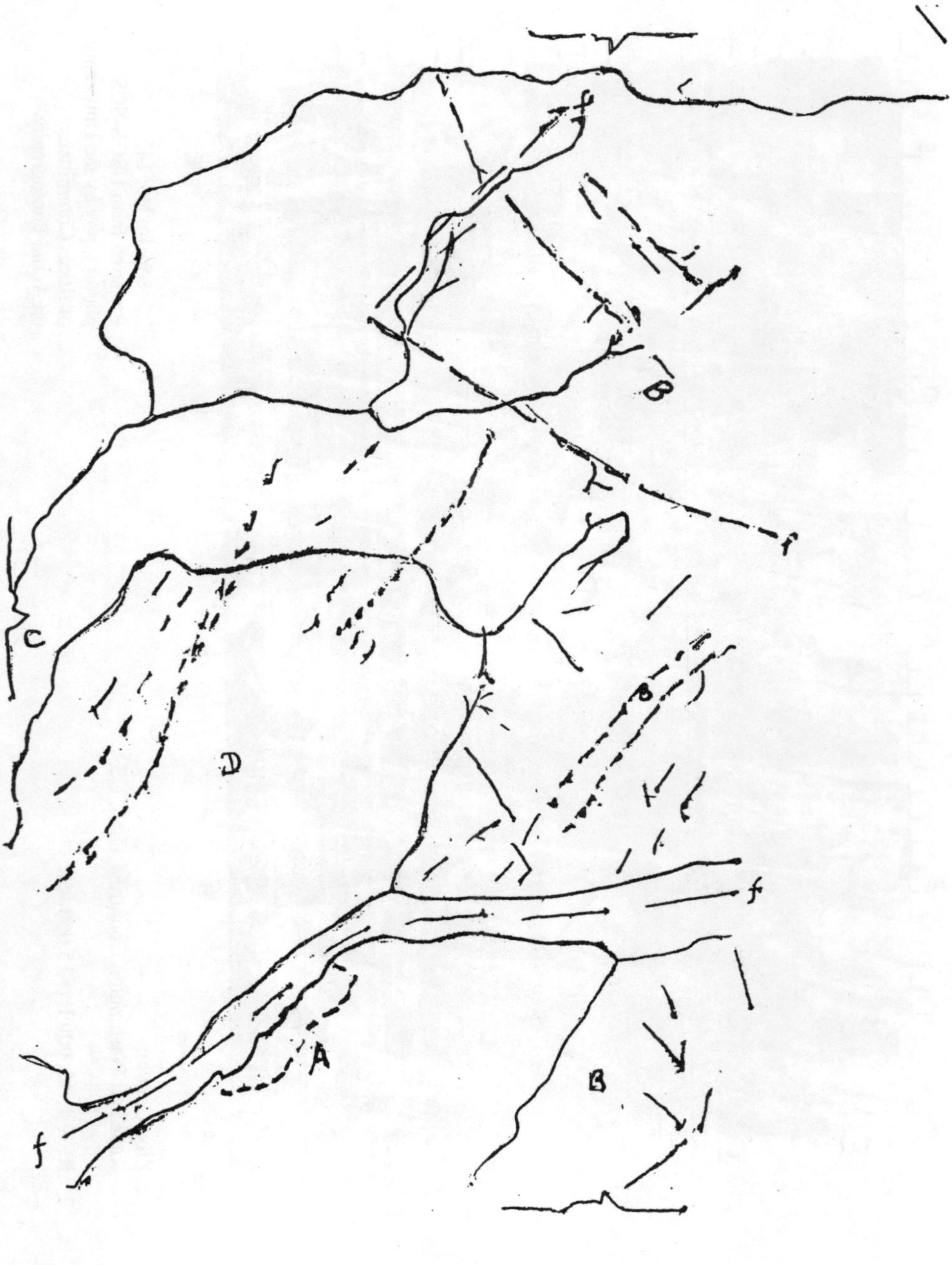

Fig. 5.32 : Overlays

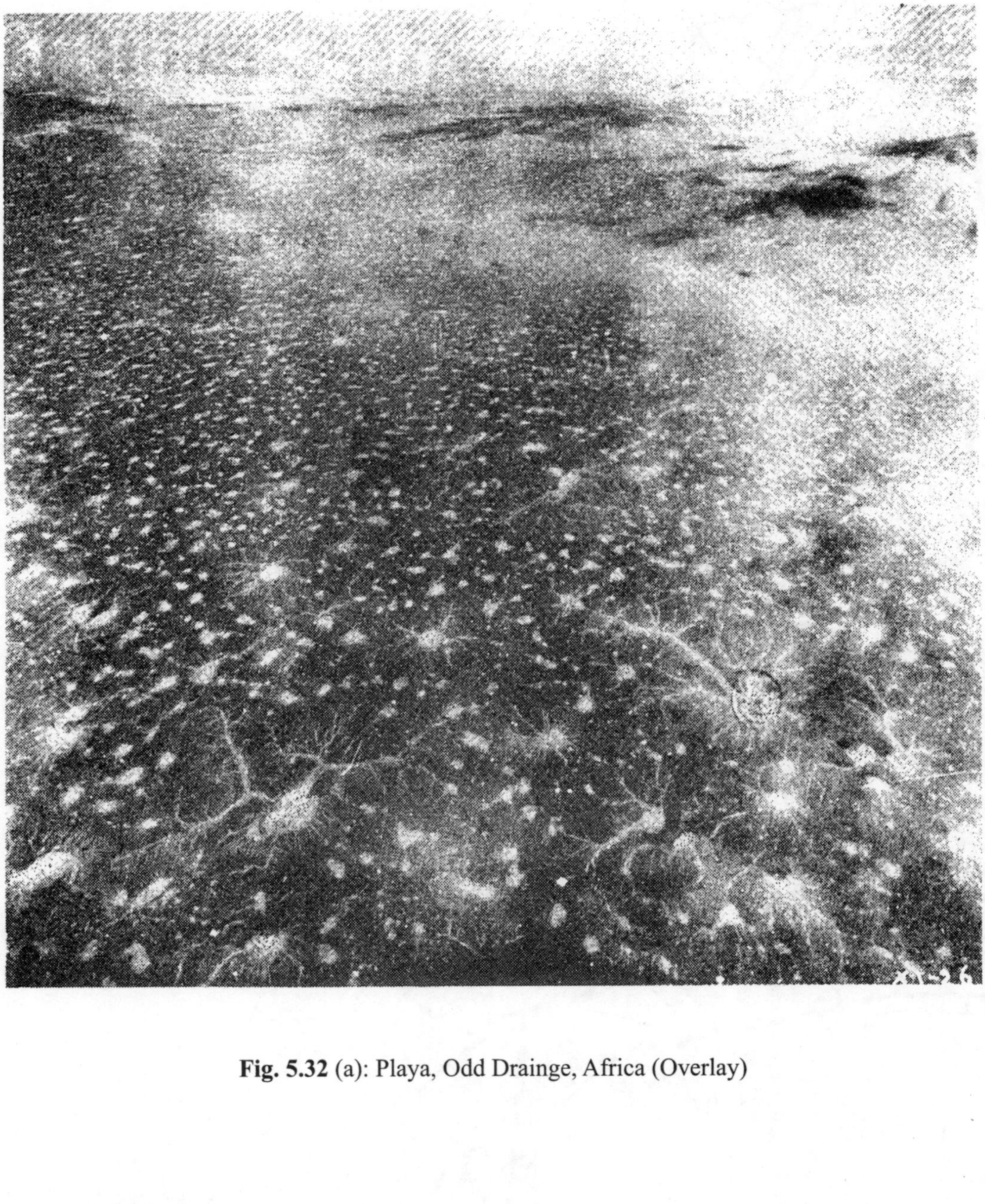

Fig. 5.32 (a): Playa, Odd Drainge, Africa (Overlay)

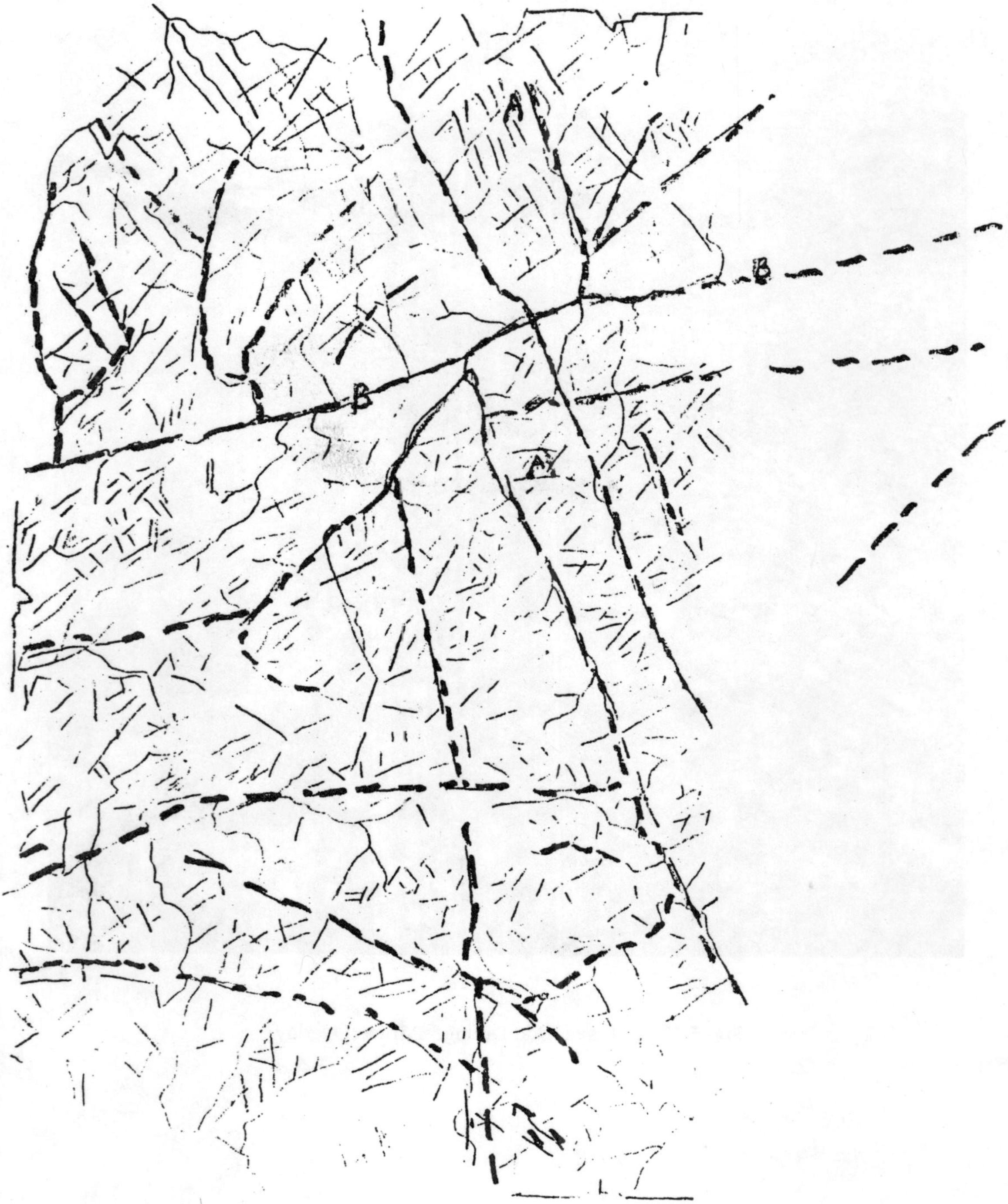

Fig. 5.33 : Crystalline Rocks

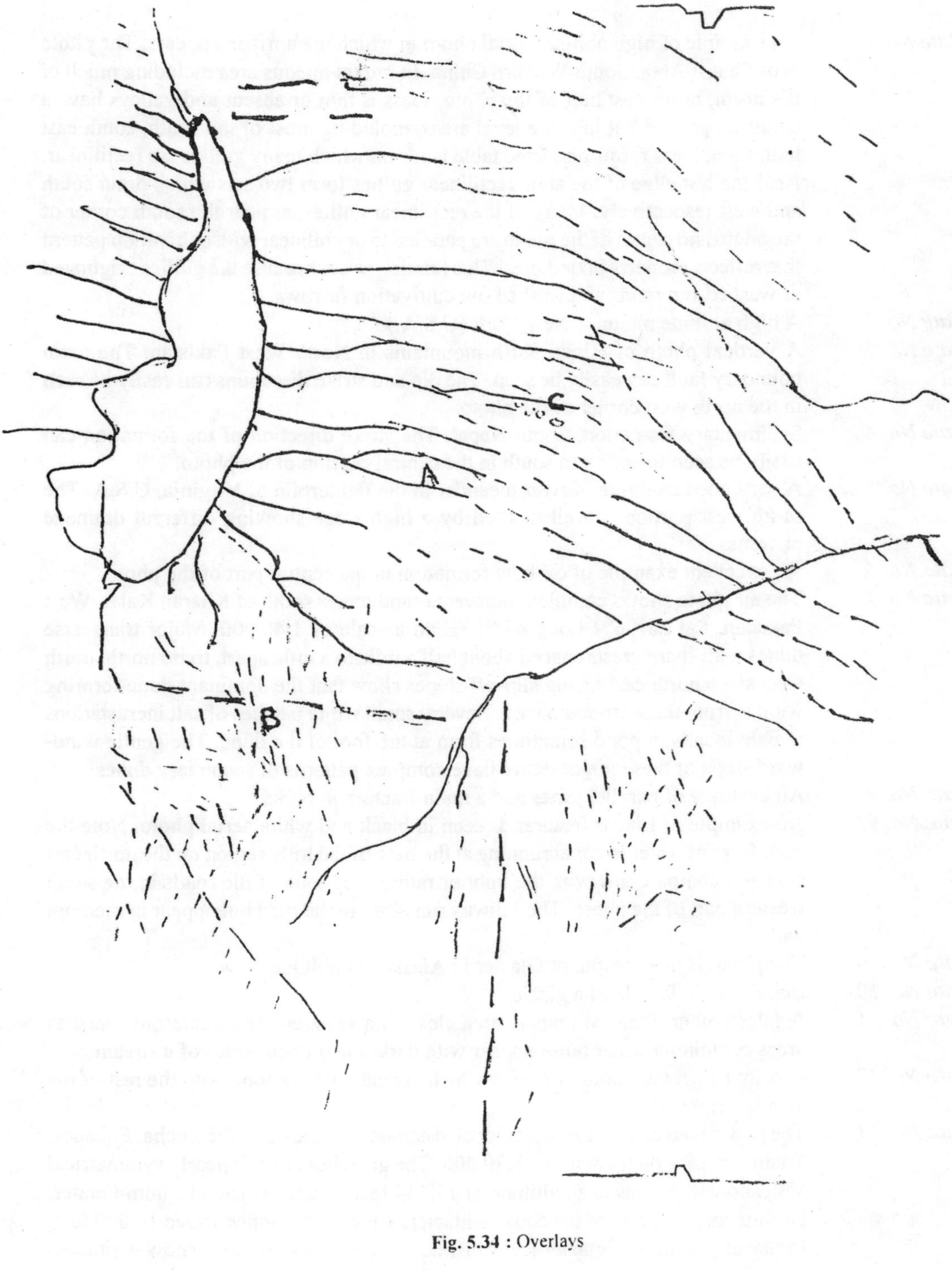

Fig. 5.34 : Overlays

DESCRIPTION OF PLATES

Plate No. 1. An example of high oblique aerial photo in which the horizon appears. The photo is of Shansi Area, South Western China. In mountaineous area including much of the north, north-east half of the photo, loess is thin or absent and valleys have a dendritic pattern but in more level areas, including most of the south, south east half, thick loess forms dissected table lands on which many gullies are rectilinear. Near the last edge of the area, rectilinear gullies form two sets which drain south and west respectively. Many of the rectilinear gullies, as near the south corner of the photo and centre of the photo are paralled to or collinear with cultivation pattern that reflects property boundaries. This relation arises because the gullies originated as washed-out roads and washed out cultivation furrows.

Plate No. 2. A high altitude photo of New York (U.S.A.)

Plate No. 3. A vertical photo of Hindu Kush mountains in North West Pakistan. The main boundary fault can easily be seen. The dip and strike directions can easily be seen in the north west corner of the photo.

Plate No. 4. Sedimentary formation, South Nepal. The strike direction of the formation can easily be seen for north to south in the central portion of the photo.

Plate No. 5. A very good example of river meander in the flat terrain of Virginia, U.S.A. The south-west portion is well marked by a high ridge showing different drainage patterns.

Plate No. 6. An excellent example of ox-bow formation in the central part of the photo.

Plate No. 7. The air photo shows complex transverse sand dunes south of Kharan Kalat, West Pakistan, Lat 28°06'N Long 65° 15'E on a scale of 1:40,000. Major transverse dunes with sharp crests spaced about half a mile to a mile apart, trend north, north west steep north east facing slip-off slopes show that the dominant dune forming wind is from the west-south west. Several small white patches of salt incrustations radiate locally, a pond sometimes form at the foot of the dune. The gentle wind-ward slope of these major dunes have complex patterns of secondary dunes.

Plate No. 8. An example of parallel joints and a main fracture in rocks.

Plate No. 9. An example of Linear features as seen in black and white aerial photo. Note the dark form of water in canal running at the base of the hilly region on the north east side and compare this with the light or rather grey tone of the roads in the south western part of the photo. The railway run close to the road but appear in medium dark.

Plate No. 10. The photo is an example of Glacier in Alaska, an oblique view.

Plate No. 10A. Longitudinal Profile of a glacier

Plate No. 11. A false colour photo of marshy area close to a sea area. The numerous marshes areas containing water holes appear with dark line on both sides of a stream.

Plate No. 12. A colour Infrared photo of a river which appears in dark tone with the rest of the area in bright colour.

Plate No. 13. The photo is an example of a glacier clad equatorial volcarp in Pichincha, Equador, South America on the scale of 1:30,000. The great bulk of this nearly symmetrical Volcano which rises to an altitude of 19,344 feet, dwarfs its round summit crater. Despite its proximity to the equator glaciers cover most slopes above 16,000 feet. In places the limit of glacier ice is difficult to determine because snow whiteness ground to well below glacier limit. Snow melts on day time due to tropical sun freezes again in the night. Snow on the rim of an inner crater is apparantly thick, suggesting that the volcano is not continuously active. Below snow line drainage is radial.

Plate No. 14. Photographs showing proposed relocation of transmission line marked by circle and dot. Old line is shown by arrows.

Plate No. 15. Photograph of a dense jungle area.

Plate No. 16. A constructed mosaic; the airport is shown on upper left portion.

Plate No. 17. An Aerial photograph of a typical built up (Urban) area.

Plate No. 18. Anticlinal nose in gently *Folded Sediments*

State Uttah : C = 6" Scale 1:37,000

Four Units A,B,C and D can be distinguished. Unit A has a dark photo-tone, it is well stratified, some of the beds forming good dip slopes.

The drainage pattern is mainly dendritic. Unit B is very similar to unit A, it has a finer drainage texture and the beds seem less resistant.

Field Evidence : Beds A and B consist of red coloured sandstone, mudstone and shale, in their lowest part occur some interbedded limestones. Unit B might be predominantly shaly.

Unit C has a light photo-tone, more resistant interbeds having a medium grey tone. The fine texture drainage shows trellis and dendritic pattern or combination of both.

Field Evidence : Beds C are weakly cemented, massive bedded sand stone. However, the dense drainage system may indicate a certain admixture or argilaceous material.

Unit D has a dark photo/tone, it is well bedded. The drainage shows combinations of dendritic and trellis patterns.

Field Evidence: Beds D are red and brown silty sandstone and shale.

The dark toned resistant rock at E is known to be a basalt dyke.

It is Interesting to note the curvature of the major stream around the gentle anticlinal nose, some minor faults have been indicated and angular forms in some of the streams may indicate fracturing or jointing.

Plate No. 19. A LANDSAT photo indicating two distinct areas of drainage. The area to the upper left is well developed with dendritic type of drainage and the area to the east with poor drainage. The drainage divide is right through the area.

Plate 1: An example of high oblique aerial photo in which the horizen appears. The photo is of Shansi Area, South Western China

Plate 2: High-altitude photograph of New York harbor provides a complete record of harbor traffic at time of exposure (Photograph *Courtesy* of Aero Service Corp.)

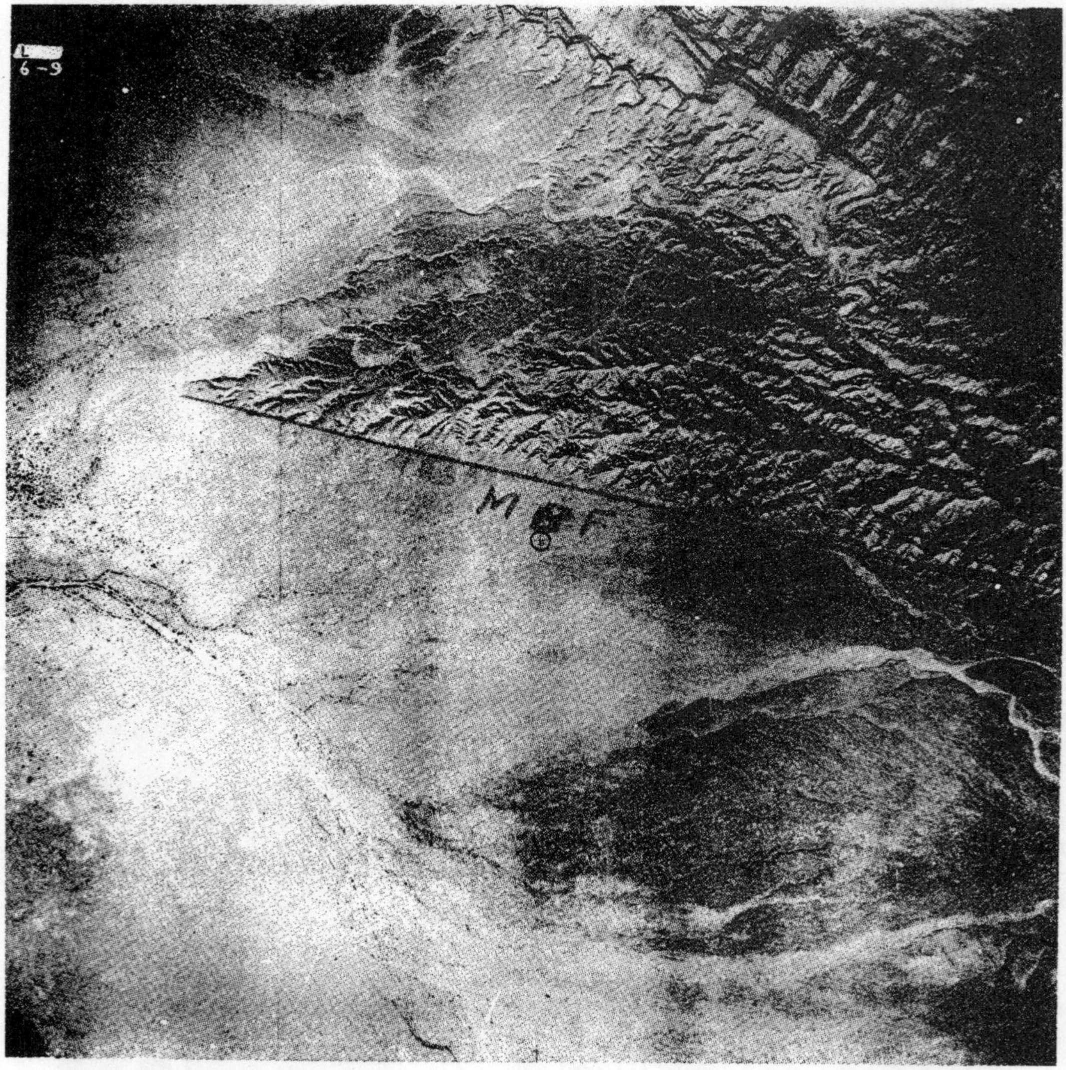

Plate 3: A vertical photo of Hindukush mountains in North-West Pakistan

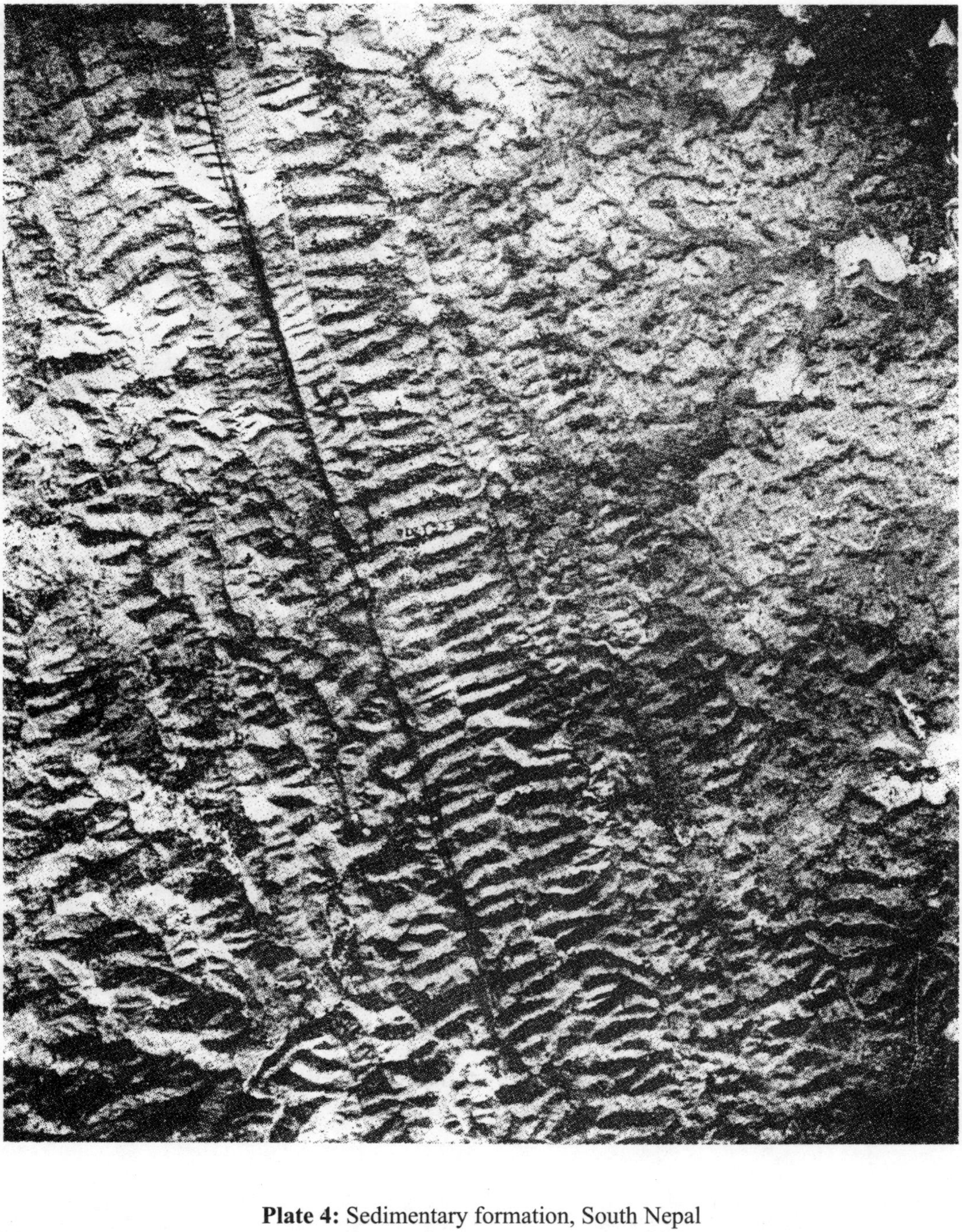

Plate 4: Sedimentary formation, South Nepal

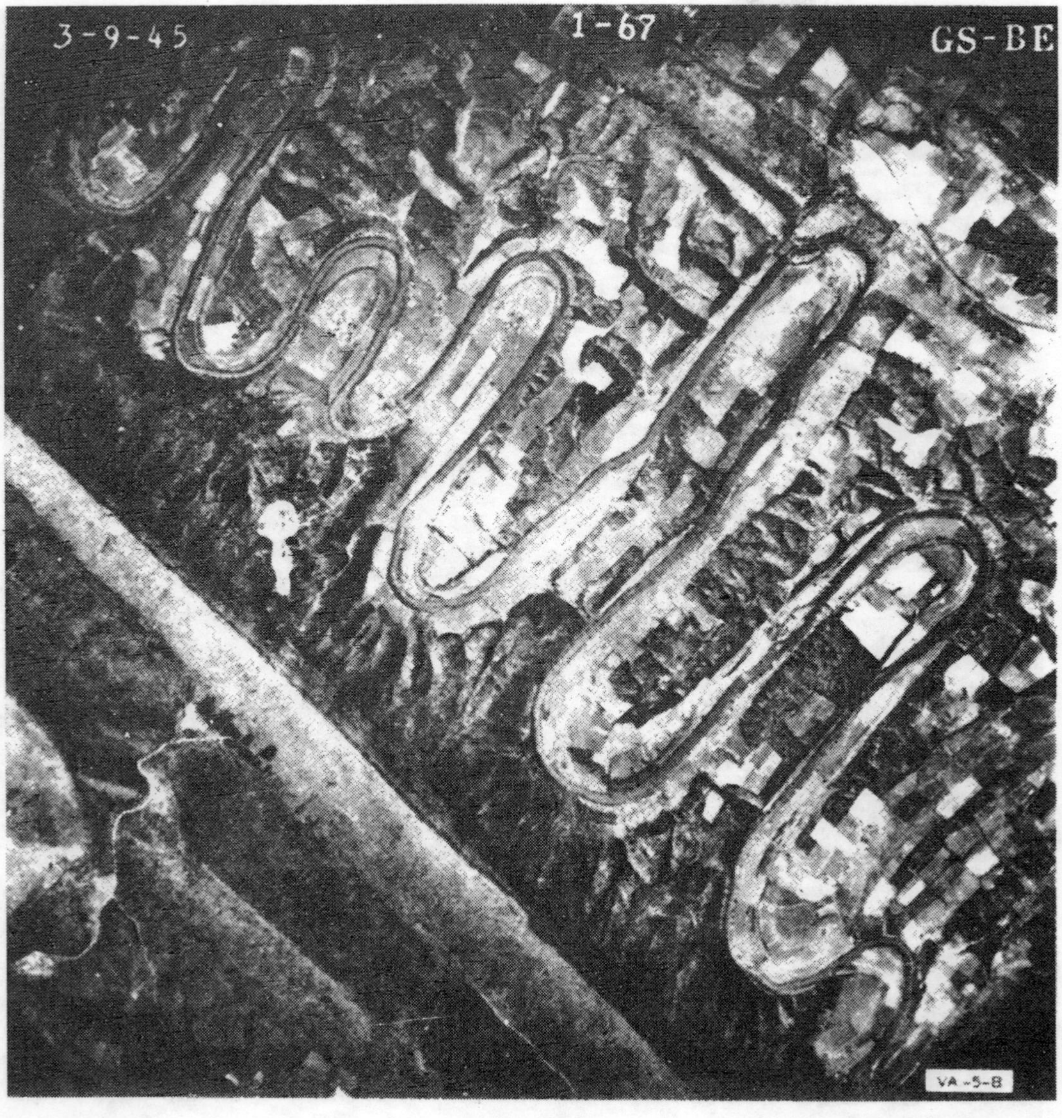

Plate 5: A very good example of River Meander in the flat terrain of Virginia, U.S.A.

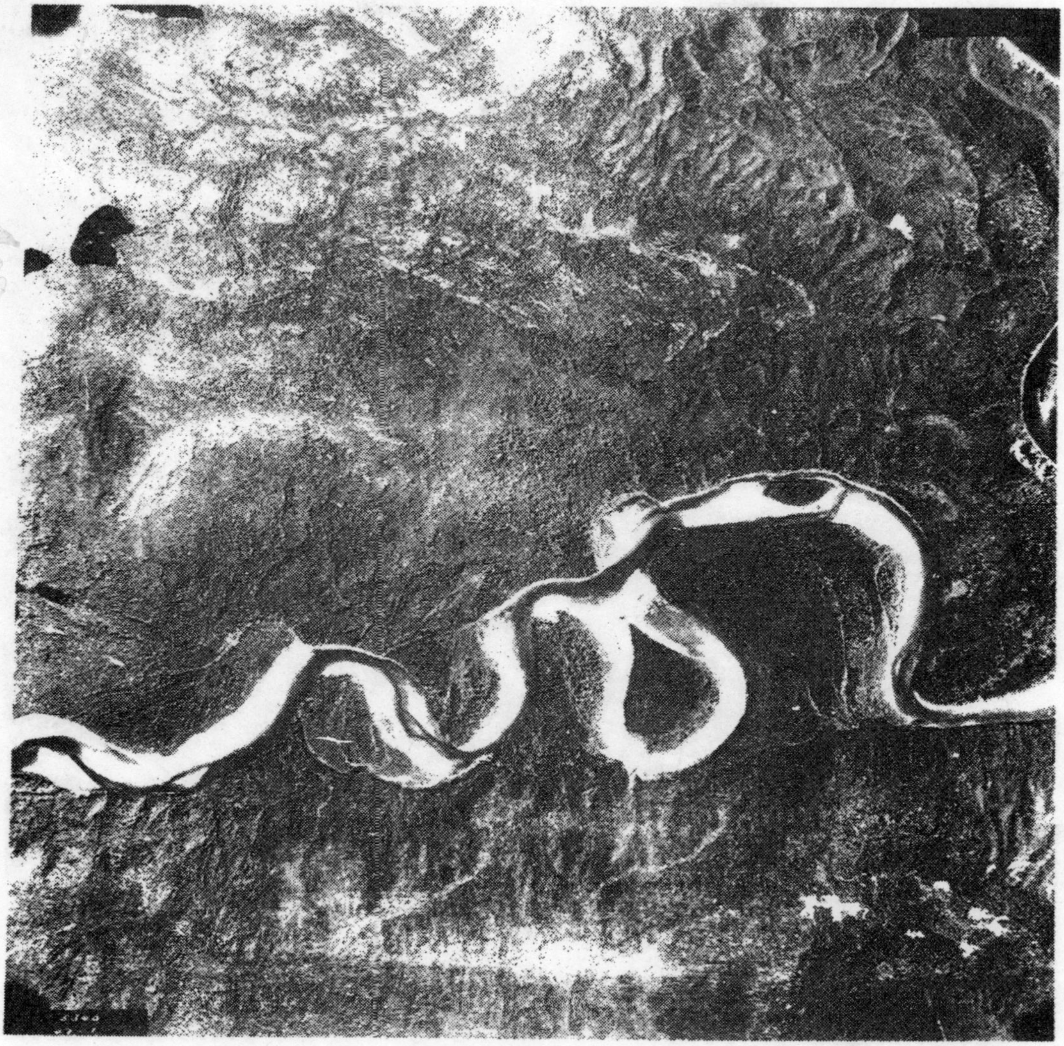

Plate 6: A excellant example of Ox-Bow formations in the central part of the photo

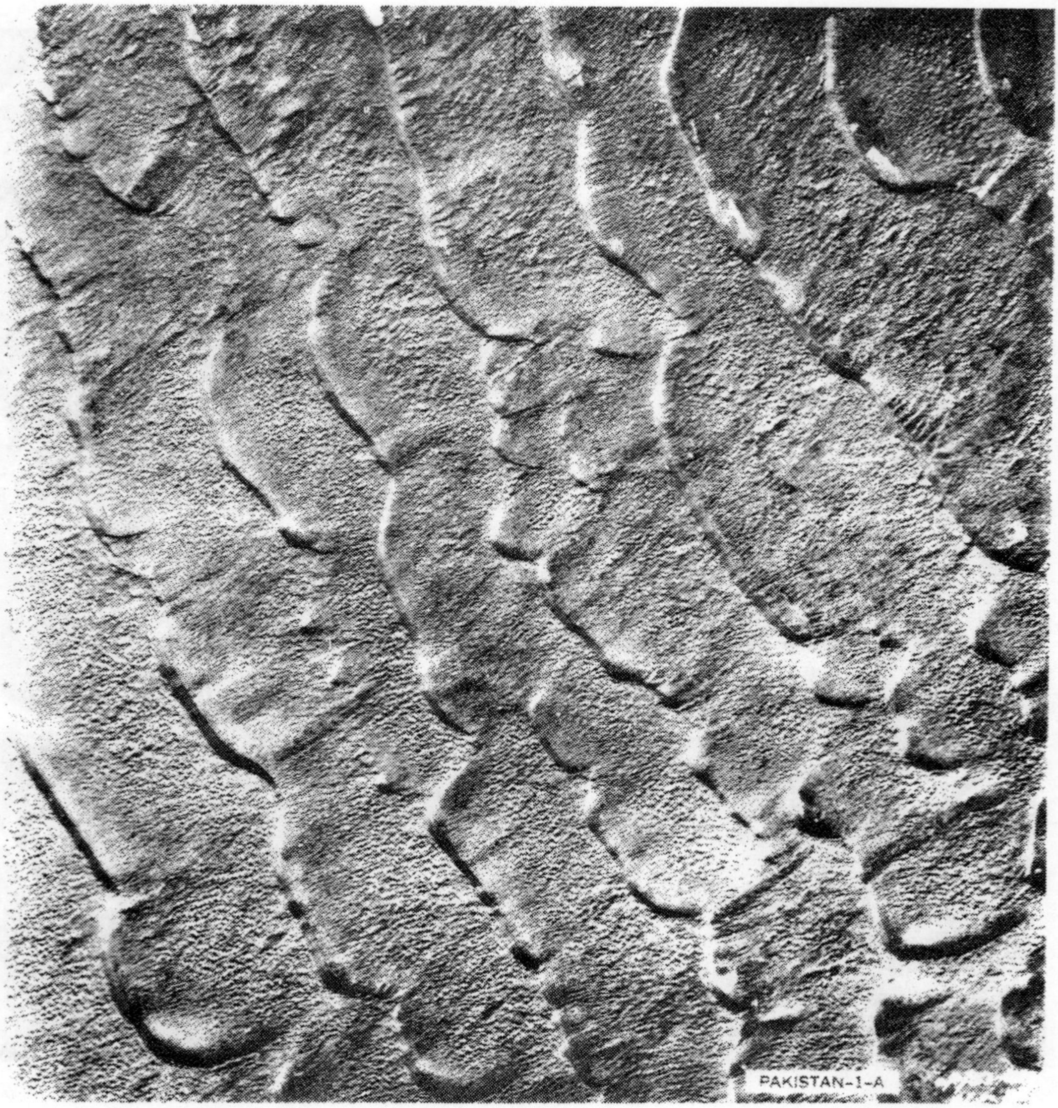

Plate 7: The Air photo shows complex transverse sand dunes, south of Kharan Kalat, West Pakistan

Plate 8: An example of parallel joins and a main fracture in rocks

Plate 9: An example of Linear features as seen in black and white aerial photo

Plate 10: Oblique aerial photograph of Klutina Glacier, Alaska (Photograph by Bradford Washburn)

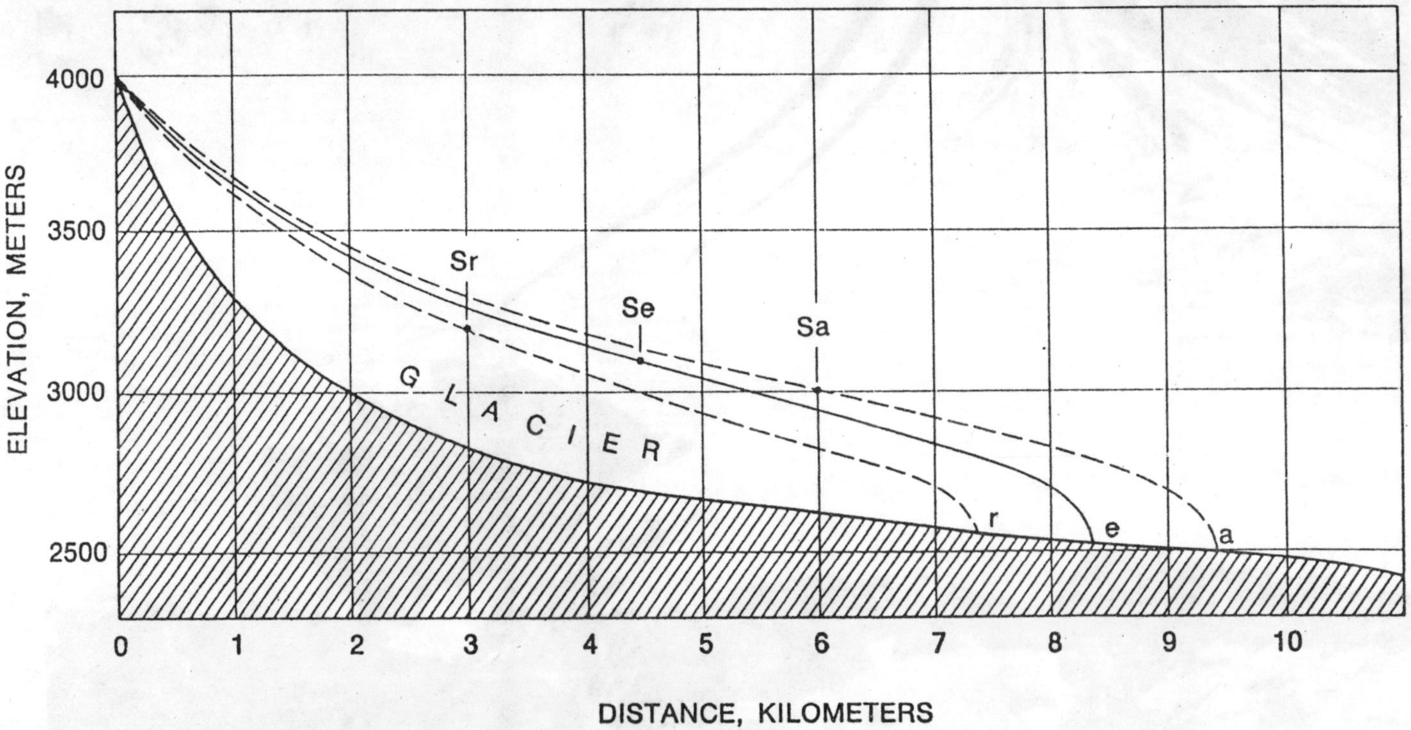

PLATE 10A : Hypothetical longitudinal profile of a valley glacier during three different stages of its history. S_e is the position of snowline where the terminus is at *e*, and *Sa* and *Sr* are the snowlines when the terminus is at *a* and *r*, respectively, Mote the increasing elevation of snowline and reduction in thickness as the terminus retreats (vertical scale is exaggerated)

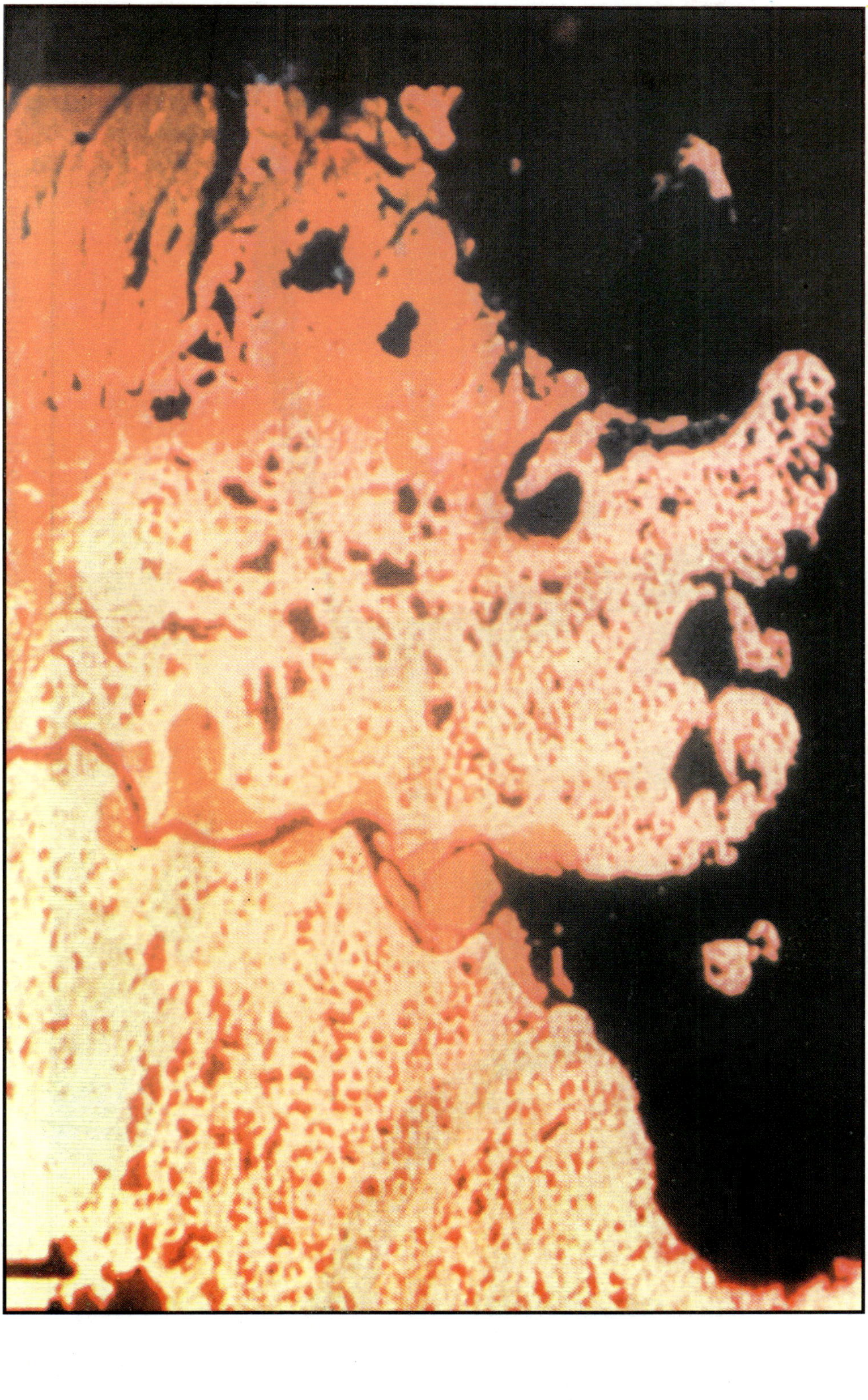

Plate 11: A false colour photo of Marshy area close to a sea area

Plate 12: A colour Infra red photo of a river which appear in dark tone with the rest of the area in bright colour

Plate 13: The photo is an example of a glacier clad equitorial Volcorp in Pichincha, Equedor, South America

Plate 14: Pair of photographs showing proposed relocation of transmission line. Placing the new line as marked by the circles would shorten the existing line 9.4 per cent and would use four fewer towers. (*Courtesy* of Failchild Aerial Surveys, Inc.)

Plate 15: Photograph of a dense Jungle area. (*Coutesy* of Fairchild Aerial Surveys, Inc.)

Plate 16: A control Mosaic. The matching of individual photographs is not readily apparent. except along the river (*Courtesy* of Jack Ammann Photogrametric Engineers. Inc.)

Plate 17: Aerial photograph of area in Nebraska
(U.S. Dept. of Agriculture Photo No. (UI-IFF-139, exposed on October 10, 1965)

PLATE 18 : Anticlinal nose in gently Folded Sediments

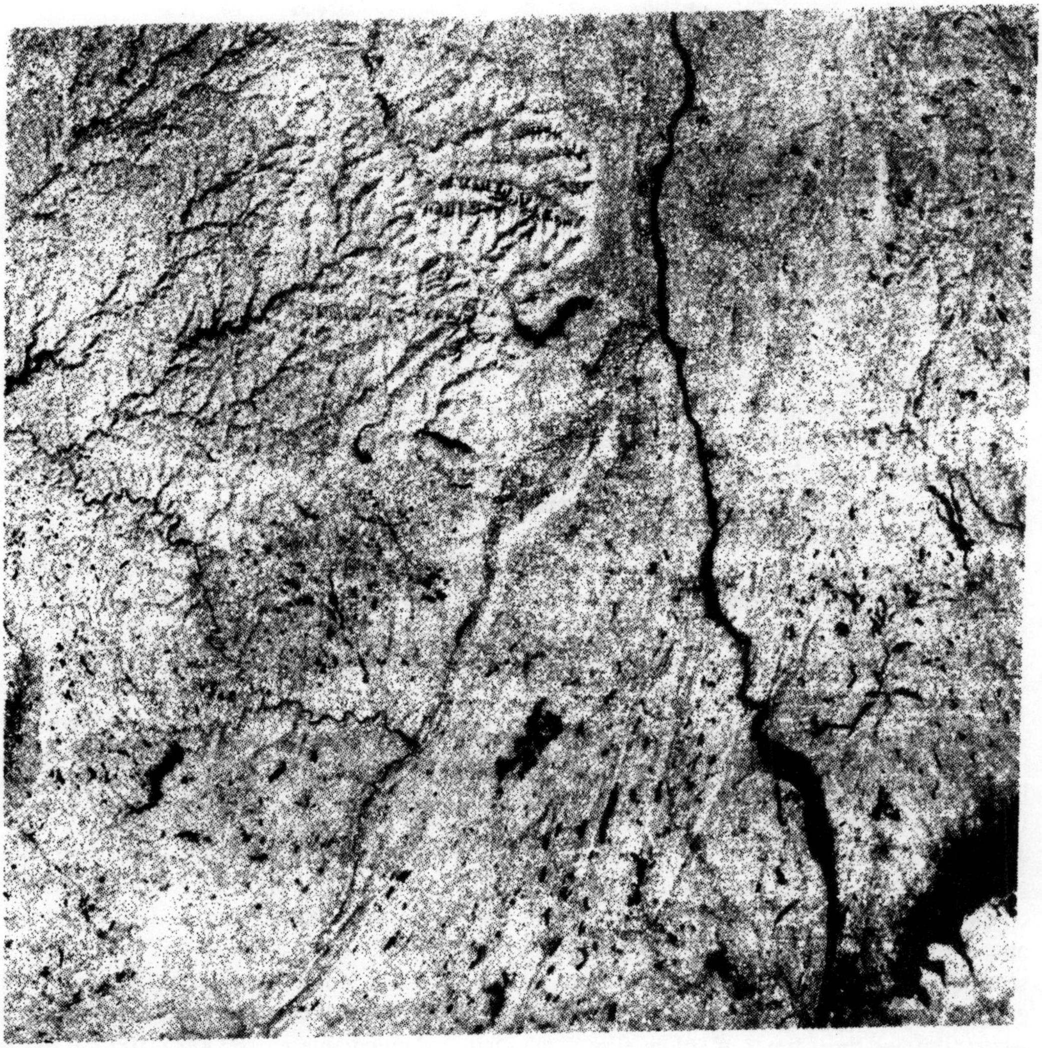

Plate 19: A LANDSAT photo indicating two distinct areas of drainage

6

SATELLITE IMAGERY

6.1. Introduction

The decade of 1950's may truly be called the beginning of era of space exploration. From high altitude rocket tests to space vehicles culminated in the landing of man, for the first time in the history of mankind, on the surface of moon. Along with this development came new techniques for photography and for the first time man was able to see his own Earth floating in space. The marvellous pictures taken by astronauts of various parts of earth during Gemini Missions and finally those of complete earth in Apollo Missions are true examples of space photography. (See Figs. 6.1, 6.2, 6.3).

Just as conventional aerial photographs were found to be extremely useful in the preparation of large scale maps, the space photographs were explored for the possibility of preparation of very small scale maps. This was done with the help of computers to store data and carry out lengthy calculations for the corrections of tilts and other factors involved.

The launching of first earth satellite, called Earth Resources Technology Satellite (ERTS) in July 1972 by U.S.A. marked the beginning of a new space development. Although the recording of observations of the earth's surface from an orbiting space-craft began in 1960 with the first U.S. meteorological satellite TIROS-I the photographs taken by astronauts in the Gemini and Apollo flights established the increased significance and usefulness of photographs from space for mapping and other purposes. Another important space vehicle which took photographs with a coverage on global basis was the Skylab satellite launched in 1973 and 1974 . The experimental sensor packages on Skylab which orbited the earth at 425 kilometres (235 miles) altitude consisted of conventional photography, near infrared photography, a 13-channel multispectral scanner and microwave sensors. Of particular interest was an Earth Terrain Camera that took photographs with an estimated ground resolution ranging from 17 to 30 metres (55 to 100 feet), using high definition black and white film and three types of colour film. Each picture showed an area 109 km x 109 km (59 x 59 miles). The resulting photos gave striking evidence of the effectiveness of space photography for cartography and landuse inventory.

6.2. LANDSAT Series

LANDSAT I circles the earth in about 103 minutes making 14 orbits a day at an average altitude of 917 kilometres (570 miles) above the earth in near circular orbit inclined at 81° to equator repeating every 18 days the coverage of any given area. The orbit is sun-synchronous, that is, it crosses any given area with the same sun inclination as in its previous orbit. The 14 strips of earth surface (see Fig. 6.4) covered each day are successively 2800 kilometres apart on the equator. One each satellite from the area scanned by its sensors is185 × 185 kilometres (115 × 115 miles). The satellite is

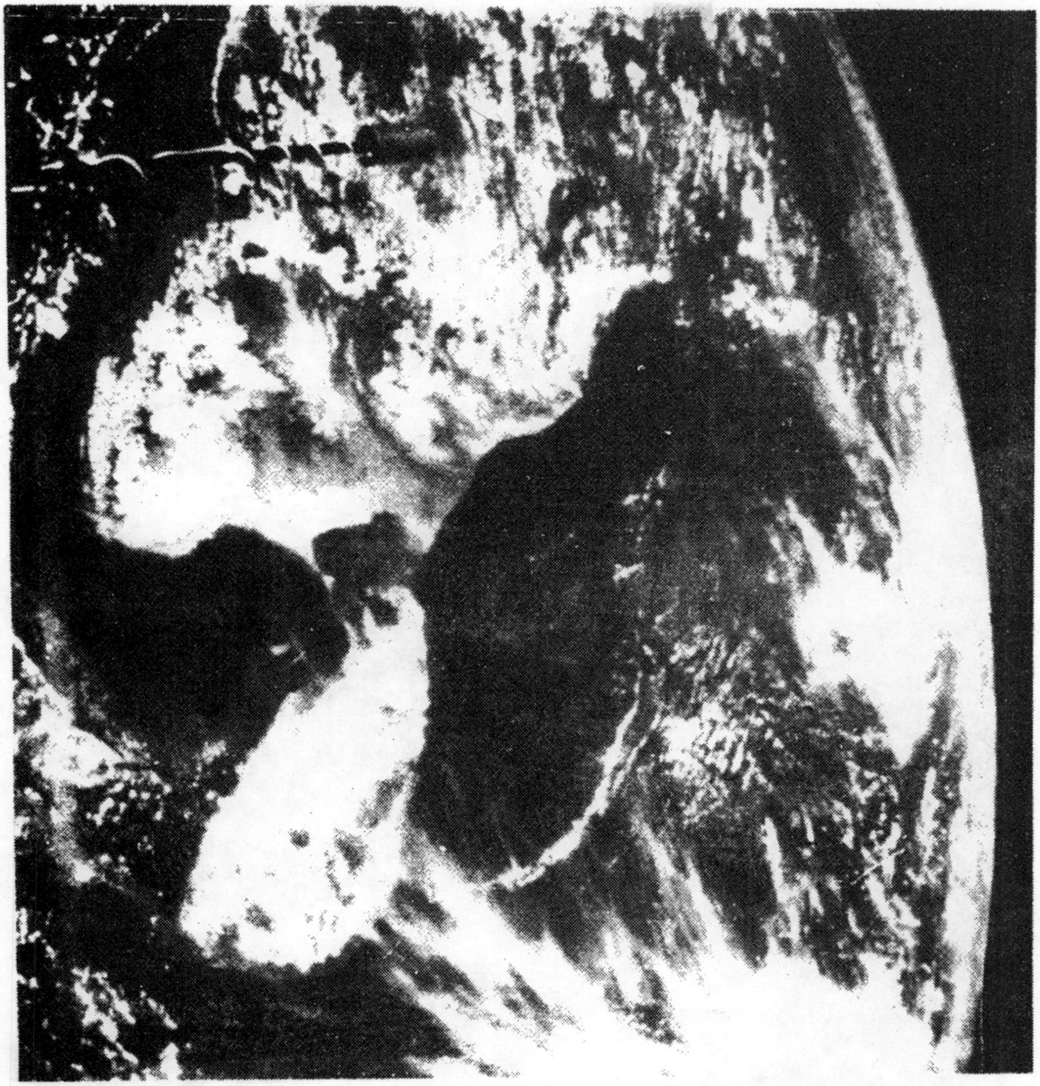

Fig. 6.1: Satellite Picture of South India and Ceylon by Space Probe Gemini
(*Courtesy* NASA, U.S.A.

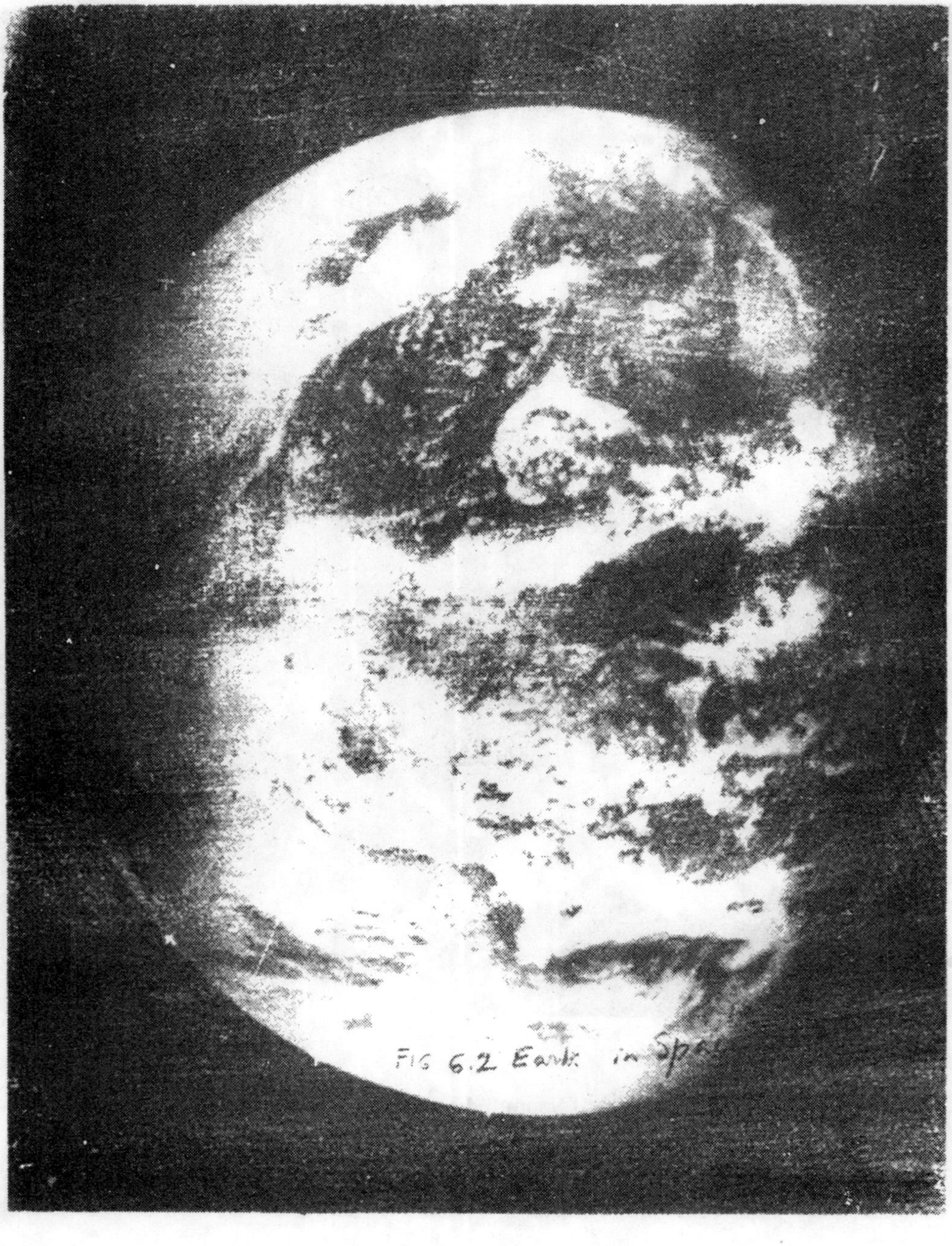

Fig. 6.2: Earth in Space (*Courtesy*, NASA, U.S.A.)

Fig. 6.3: Gemini V-Photo Over West Pakistan (*Courtesy:* American Society of Photogrammetry, U.S.A.)

butterfly shaped (see Fig. 6.5) and weighs 950 kilograms and is 3 metres high and 4 metres wide with its two solar panels. the solar panels provide electrical energy for transmission of signals to earth. When the satellite is on the dark side of the earth, batteries provide the necessary power.

The sensors in the LANDSAT consist of a Multi Spectral Scanner (MSS) and a Return Beam Vidicon (RBV) tubes. The MSS is a four-channel sensor collecting electromagnetic radiation in four bands in the visible and near infrared portion of the spectrum. This is a radiometer which scans the surface of the earth and records the intensity of the energy reflected by objects on the surface. The RBV is like a TV Camera to sense and record the image of the earth's surface in 3 different bands. At a later stage the three RBV failed to operate and only MSS data is now available. MSS scanning is done with a mirror tilted at 45° to the earth (see Fig. 6.6) and rotating about 2.9 degrees. It scans the earth's surface from east to west within 185 kilometres while the satellite moves north to south. With each sweep of the mirror the satellite advances about 474 metres.

The continuous signal received from the earth's surface is converted into electrical energy proportional to the intensity of reflection. Each scanned line is divided into 3246 separate signals and is called a 'pixel'. A pixel is equivalent of about 79 × 79 metres on the ground. This then is the ground resolution of the LANDSAT. Any ground feature or length less than 80 metres (259 feet) will not be detected. This is very important from cartographic application of LANDSAT pictures. The data from the LANDSAT is emitted by radio signals in a coded form. It is picked up by ground stations in U.S.A where the information rectified and restored in magnetic tapes, known as Computer Compatible Tapes (CCTs) for digital use by computers. Pictures are reproduced after applying the following type of corrections :

(a) Geometric corrections within each band and scene due to satellite motion, satellite altitude variations, velocity changes (due to elliptical orbit), earth rotation and other projection errors.
(b) radiometric corrections for the detectors,
(c) registration corrections for the different bands.

The video tape of the satellite data can record 64 levels of intensity with values ranging from 0 to 255 and for each scene of 185 × 185 km there are 3246 pixels with 2286 scan lines. The increasing number of pixels is due to a common overlapping from pixel to pixel in a scan line.

LANDSAT has four bands as Band 4, Band 5, Band 6, and Band 7 recording radiation in the wave bands as follows :

Band 4 0.5 to 0.6 micrometer of wavelength
Band 5 0.6 to 0.7 micrometer of wavelength
Band 6 0.7 to 0.8 micrometer of wavelength
Band 7 0.8 to 0.9 micrometer of wavelength

Band 1 to 3 lie in the ultra-violet region. The choice of these bands was originally based on the reflectance of vegetation, rock and water. Healthy green vegetation gives a reflectance in Band 4 (green colour) and Band 6 (infrared reflected by chlorophyll) and less reflectance in Band 5. Water absorbs band 7 (infrared) and thus gives no reflectance in this band. LANDSAT data, therefore, give information about vegetation water and structural geology. The following gives a brief account of MSS Bands for interpretation work :

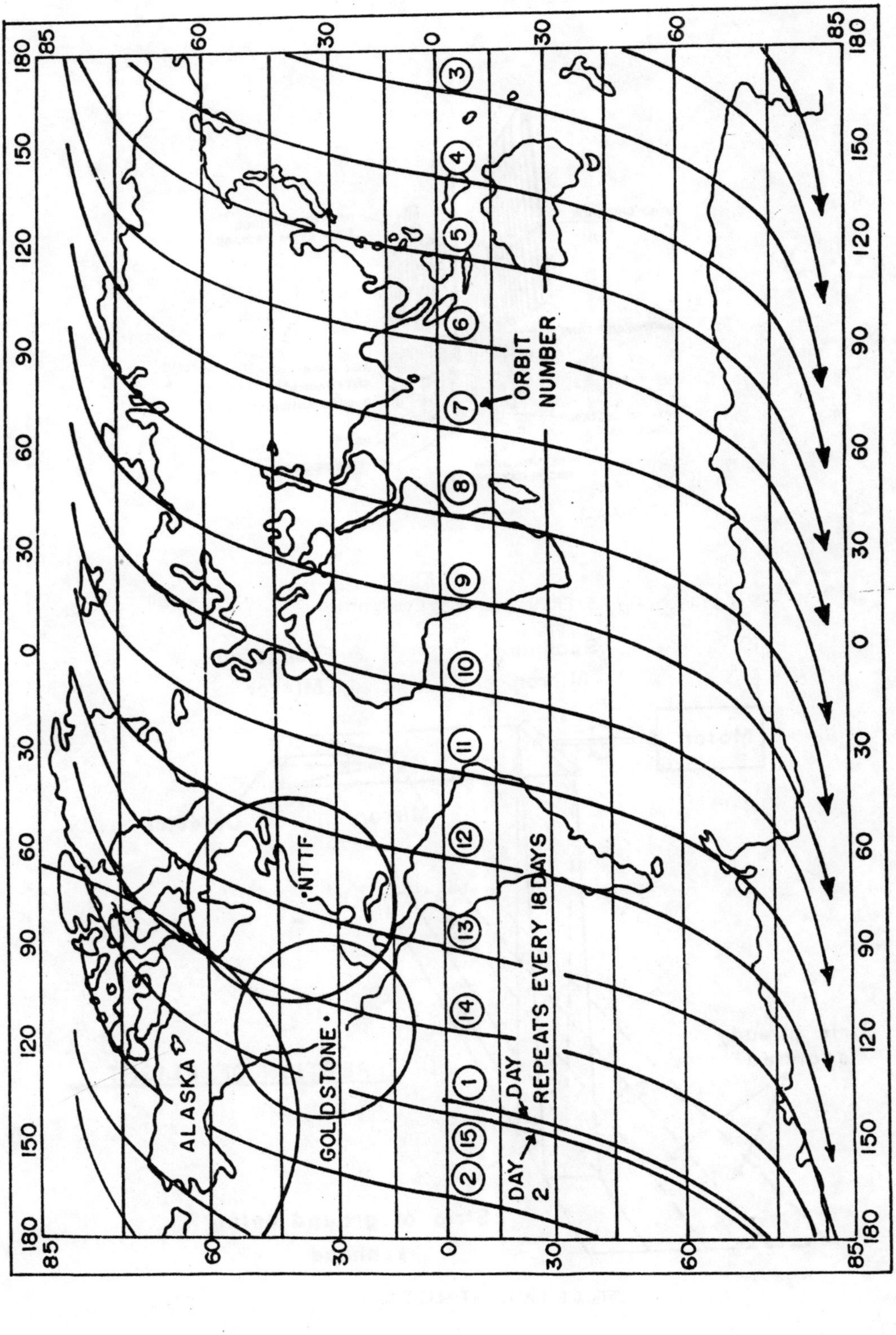

Fig. 6.4: LANDSAT Coverage of Earth by Orbital Path

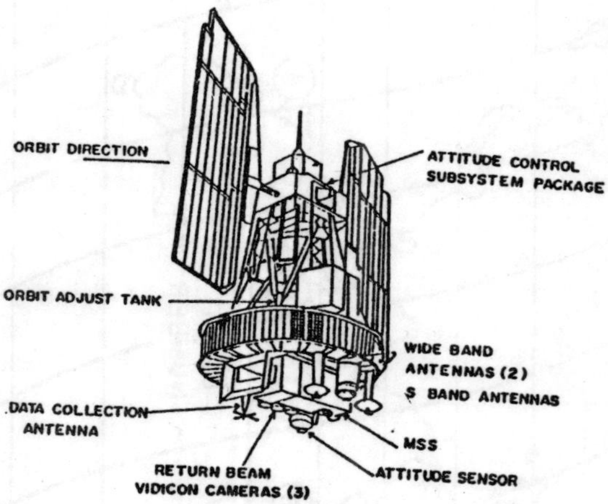

Fig. 6.5: ERTS Observatory Configuration

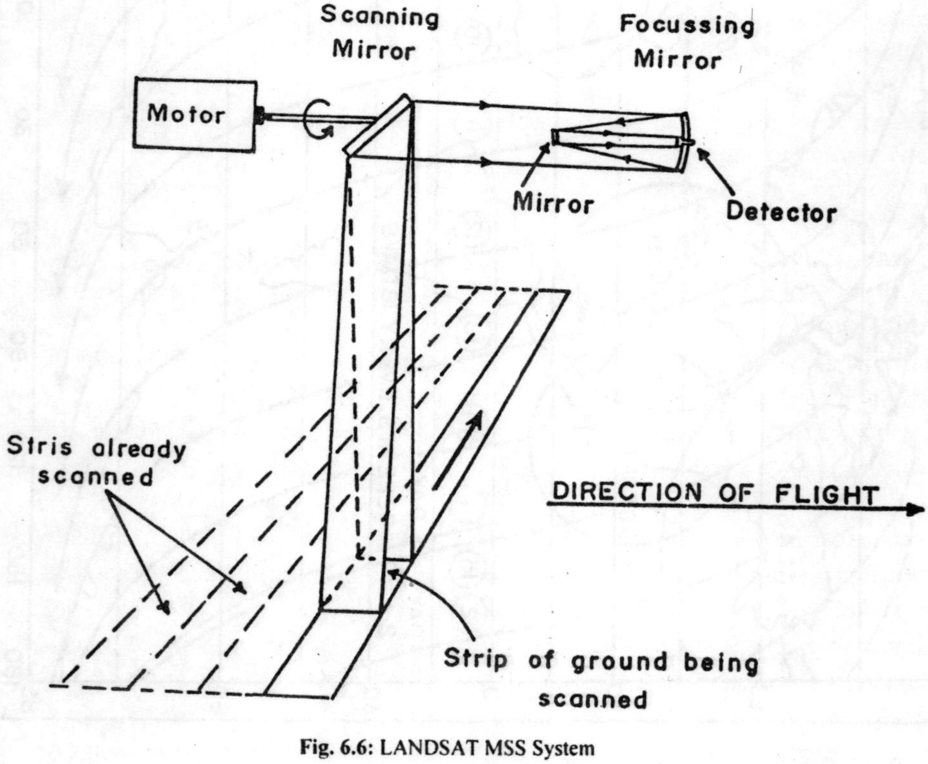

Fig. 6.6: LANDSAT MSS System

Sl. No.	*Band No.*		*Remarks*
1	4	(i)	has the best capability to penetrate water
		(ii)	can be used for study of turbidity in water bodies
		(iii)	distinguishes green vegetation from other surface covers
		(iv)	helps in identifying geologic structures
2	5	(i)	useful for defining cultural (built up), urban and topographic features
		(ii)	useful for classifying different types of green vegetation with full ground cover.
3	6	(i)	particularly helpful in landuse studies
		(ii)	useful in detecting green biomass in vegetation
4	7	(i)	extremely useful for mapping water bodies (surface)
		(ii)	very effective in delineating land-water boundary and soil-crop contrast.

Cartographic Applications : Two types of satellite imagery are available for small scale mapping; 55.8 x 55.8 mm negative and positive transparencies of each spectral band at a scale of 1:3,369,000 and film and print enlargements of 185 x 185 mm at 1:1 Million scale. Colour composites and 'False' colour composites are also available on scale 1:1 million.

The imagery of 1:1 million has been extensively used for studies in various and diverse fields. Although there was little hesitancy in the beginning for applications to cartographic compilation, later studies show that MSS satellite imagery as obtained from Landsat series is an excellant map for small scale purposes. In particular it has been found that this imagery has distinct advantages because of the following reasons:

(i) It has a uniformity of view over a wide area and does not suffer from shadow zones as in conventional aerial photography.

(ii) It has almost an orthogonal view of the earth's surface unlike perspective view in aerial photography.

(iii) It has much geometric qualities i.e. the nature of distortions are far less.

(iv) Certain objects, like water bodies in band 7, show in far superior contrast and thus help in interpretation.

(v) It can be turned into a real map at much less cost and time compared to any other imagery for small-scale mapping.

(vi) It has practically very little or rather negligible height distortion because of the altitude (920 km) at which the satellite imagery is taken.

Bacause of geometric and orthogonal qualities (extremely negligible height relief and perpendicular projection) a satellite photo on 1:1 million scale will show very little deviation from a map of the same scale.

Another big advantage in satellite imagery is in revision and updating of maps. Since the satellite imagery is repeated for any given area every 18 days the changes and updating becomes much simpler. (Figs. 6.7 and 6.8 show the changes detected in a LANDSAT frame of an area covering districts of Lucknow, Kanpur with River Ganga and Yamuna on the scale 1:1 million.

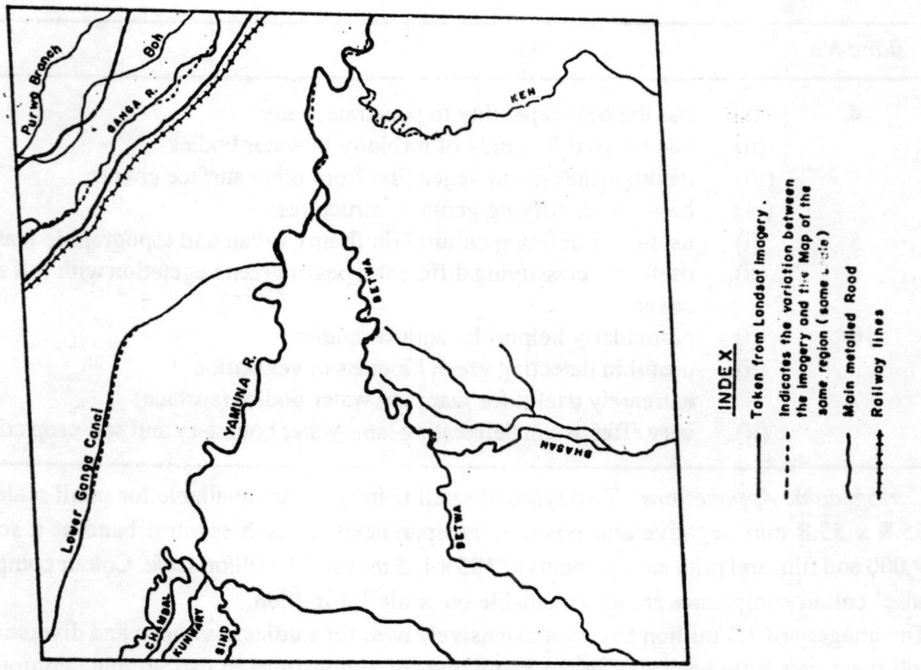

Fig. 6.8: LANDSAT (Band 6) Imagery Change Detection

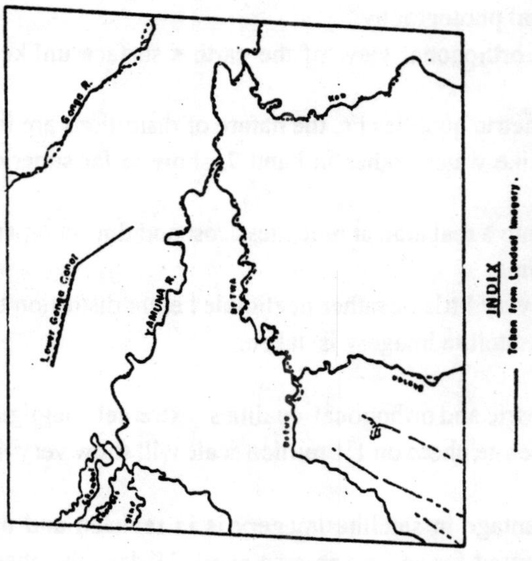

Fig. 6.7: LANDSAT Imagery Changes Detected from Ground Maps

Procedure

To map from satellite imagery such as that of LANDSAT on a small scale (1:500, 000 or 1:1000,000) the method consists of the following steps:

(a) selection of imagery
(b) selection and marking of ground control points
(c) transference of control points and aerial triangulation
(d) interpretation of detail
(e) map compilation
(f) accuracy check.

The imagery for the area on 1:1000,000 or 1:3,369,000 is selected which is cloud free. This may require examination of available imagery of several passes i.e. several repetitions. For selection of ground control points detail like intersection of road ends of airfield runways and water features are selected. These points are identified on the existing 1:250,000 or other maps for ground coordinates. If no maps exist, ground survery may be done to obtain the coordinates, This may involve regular triangulation, traversing or trilateration.

Since the LANDSAT imagery do have 14 to 20 per cent overlap, the points are selected both in the forward and lateral overlap regions for good fit. The imagery (on glass or film) are put into a stereopiotter and an Independent Model Aerotriangulation is carried out for coordinate computation of tie points. This will require a scale change azimuth rotation and translation of model points. A least square adjustment will give adjusted ground coordinates corresponding to image coordinates of the block so formed.

For interpretation of detail use is made of the various bands. As pointed above identification of certain objects is much better on MSS imagery because of the selective absorption or reflectance properties. For example even the smallest water body will be identified on Band 7 because of the complete absorption of infrared in the band 7 and hence appearance of complete darkness in the positive transparency. Similarly for vegetation and other geological features use is made of the properties of bands 4, 5 and 6 as mentioned above. The only restriction is the ground resolution limited by pixel size.

If a quick map is needed, a direct tracing from the imagery adjusted to ground control serves the purpose. For an accurate map the computer and a Digitizer will be needed. For this the procedure is as follows:

(a) Select the detail which is to be depicted on the final map.
(b) Digitize the detail on the tape.
(c) Process the data for corrections of scale due to distortion of the film or the transparency. This may require a simple two dimentional general transformation of the kind :

$$x' = ax + by + c$$
$$y' = dx + ey + f$$

This information involves six unknowns *a, b, c, d, e, f*. Here *x', y'* are the transformed coordinates and *x, y* the image coordinates. The parameters or unknowns can be determined using ground control points and then point by point transformation can be carried for each image point (*x, y*) in terms of corrected or transformed *x', y'* points. The transformation can be done with the help of a computer and the computer data stored on a tape. At a later stage this data can be replotted to prepare a small scale map.

LANDSAT 2 was launched in January 1975 and deactivated in November 1979. It was reactivated in June 1980 but finally retired in Feb. 1982. It carried MSS and RBV sensors. The RBV sensor caused many problems during operational stage. However, the picture quality was excellent. Fig. 6.9 shows LANDSAT 2 photo of area showing Yamuna and Ganga. Delhi and New Delhi are seen on the lower left corner. The picture is from MSS Band 6 and show water features in black. The Western Ganga Canal is seen very clearly starting from Haridwar. Ganga is seen in the middle of the picture. The resolution of imagery is about 80 metres. LANDSAT 3 with MSS and RBV sensors was launched in March 1978 but the RBV sensor failed in cotober 1981. It was finally retired from operation in Sept. 1983. Fig. 9.6 (a) shows the set up of the LANDSAT sensor.

LANDSAT 4 was launched with MSS and TM (Thematic Mapper) Sensors in July 1982 but TM Transmission failed in February 1983.

LANDSAT 4 provided near global coverage from its position in near polar orbit. It's orbit was sun-synchronous but in addition had its orbit adjusted periodically to maintain fixed orbital paths. There were 233 fixed orbital paths spaced equally around the Earth. Each path was covered once in 16 days. The orbital period was 98.3 minutes and the altitude (circular) was 796 km. (438 miles) above the surface of earth. Like LANDSAT 2 it crossed the Equator at 9.45. a.m. (Local Time) and the two orbits differed longitudinally by 811 km. or 24.7°. and covered area of 185 x185 km^2. Figures 6.10 & 6.11 show more details of LANDSAT 4.

LANDSAT 5 with MSS and TM Sensors was launched in March 1984 and is still in operation. Fig. 6.12 shows the LANDSAT 2 and Fig. 6.13 shows the same area photographed by LANDSAT 5. Table 6.1 below gives the comparative characteristics of the two scenes and Table 6.2 gives wave bands of TM sensor and Table 6.3 gives gives comparison between MSS and TM sensors.

TABLE 6.1 : Comparision of LANDSAT-2 and LANDSAT-5

	LANDSAT - 2	LANDSAT - 5
Area covered	185 × 185 km^2	185 × 185 km^2
Scale (approximately) (original)	1:1 Million	1:1 Million
Orbit Number & Path Number	155/42	144/42
Scanning Day	24th March 1977	6th June 1986
Band No.	6	4(TM)
Altitude of Satellite Orbit	919 kms	705 kms
Latitude of centre of scene	25°57' N	26° 1'N
Longitude of centre of scene	79° 47' E	80° 4'E

TABLE 6.2 : Showing wave Bands of TM Sensor

Band Number	Band Name	Band width (micrometres)	Points
1	Blue/Green	0.45-0.52	Good water penetration. strong vegetation absorbance
2	Green	0.52-0.60	Strong vegetation reflectance
3	Red	0.63-0.69	Very strong vegetation absorbance
4	Near infrared	0.76-0.90	High land/water contrasts very strong vegetation reflectance
5	Near middle infrared	1.55-1.75	very moisture sensitive
6	Thermal infrared	10.4-12.5	very sensitive to soil moisture and vegetation
7	Middle infrared	2.08-2.35	Good geological discrimination

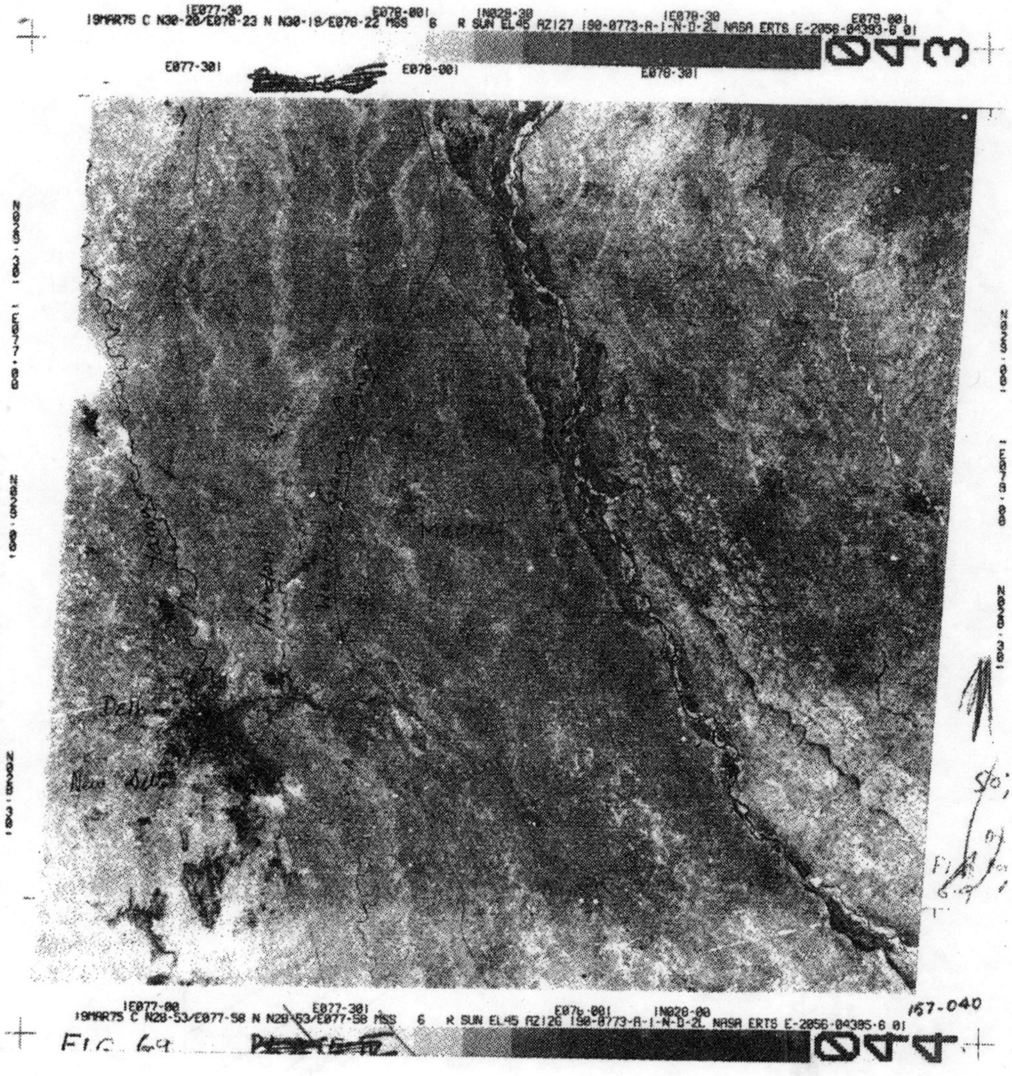

Fig. 6.9: LANDSAT - 2 Photo Area

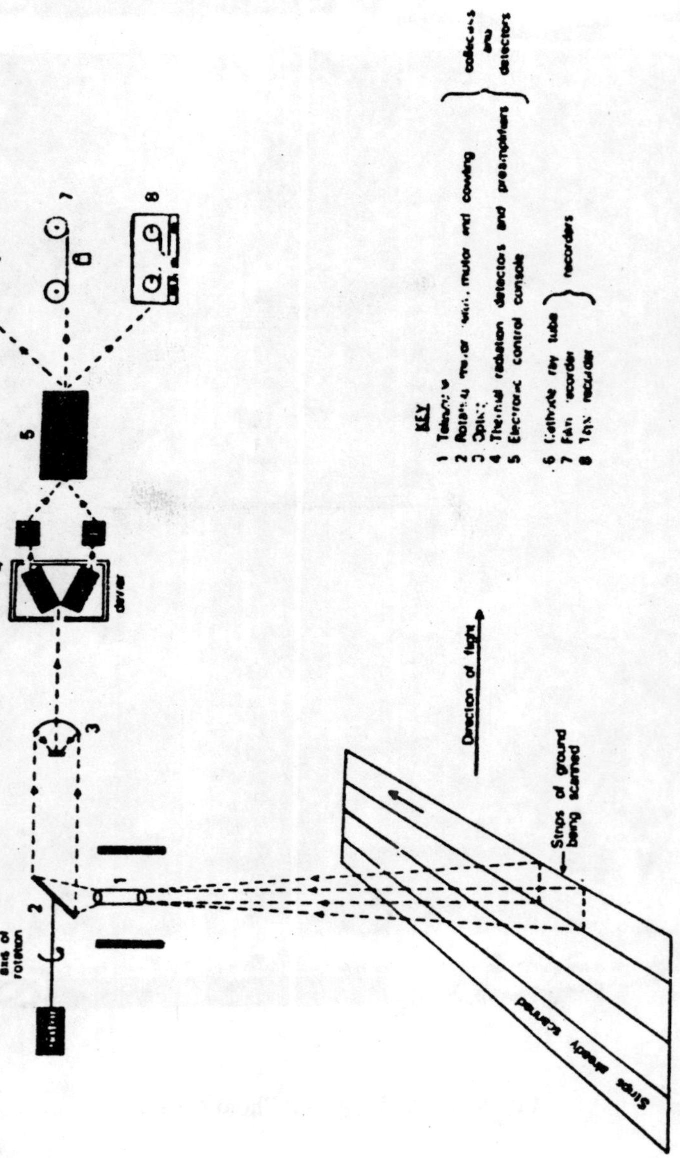

Fig. 6.9 (a) : Set up of LANDSAT-2

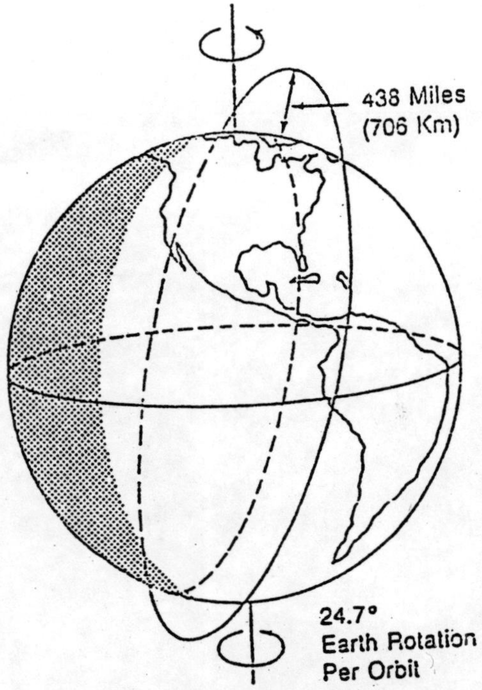

Fig. 6.10 : LANDSAT-4 Orbit

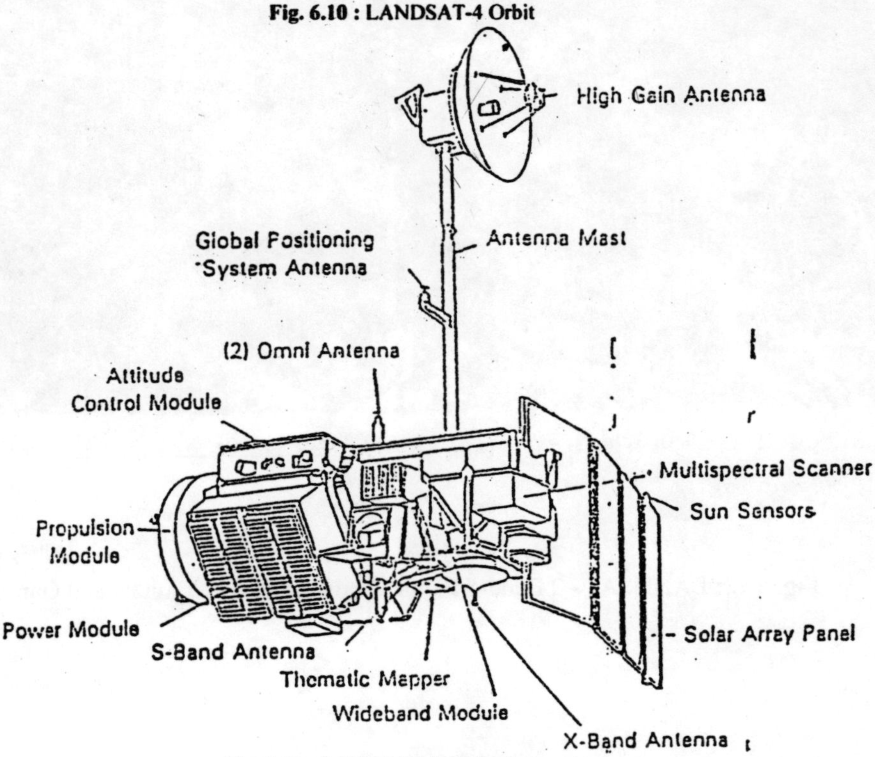

Fig. 6.11 : LANDSAT-4 Flight Segment

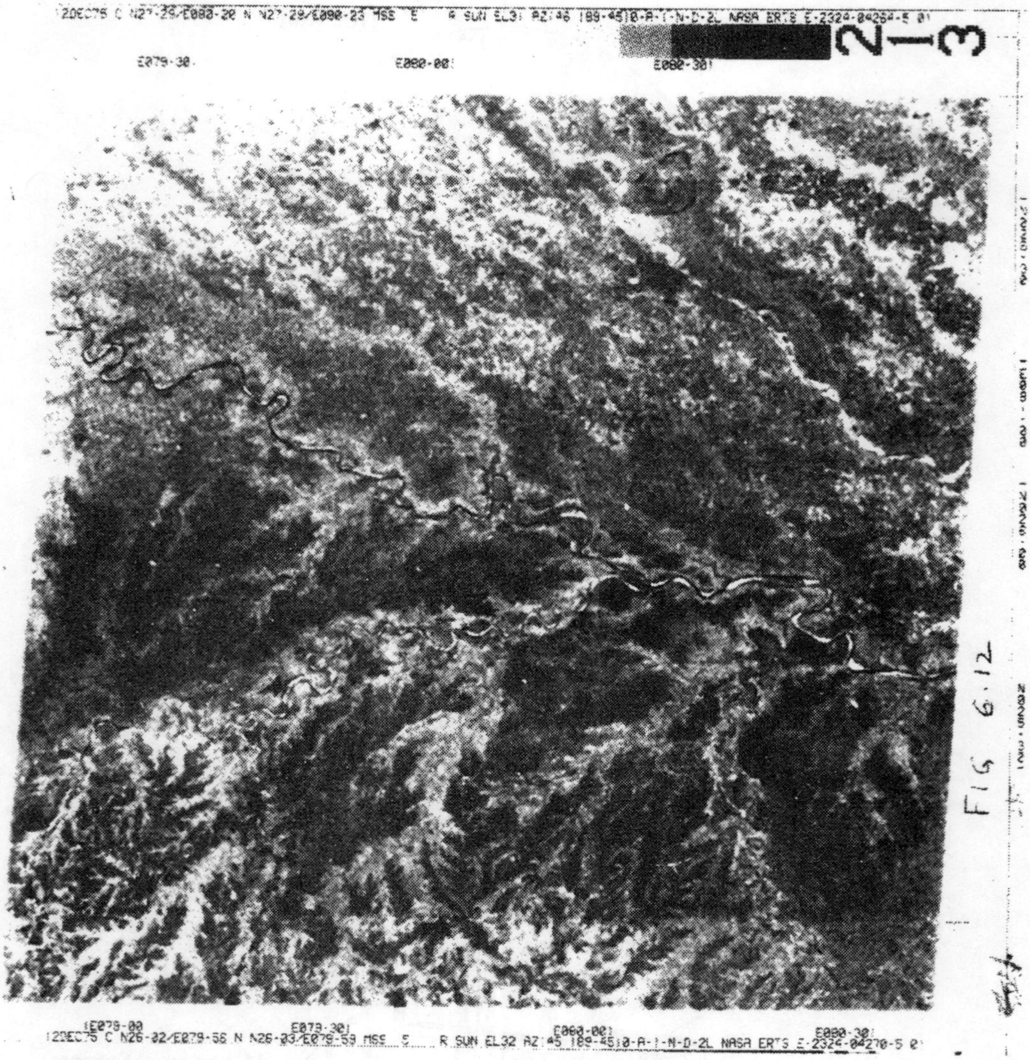

Fig. 6.12: LANDSAT - 2 Band-5 Picture Showing Rivers Yamuna and Ganga

Fig. 6.13: LANDSAT - 5 with Some areas as in Fig 6.12

TABLE 6.3 : Showing Comparison Between MSS and TM Sensor

Unmanned Earth Resources Satellites

	Multispectral Scanning System (MSS)	Thematic Mapper (TM)	Comment on (TM) details
Wavebands	4	7	See table 6.2
Spatial resolution (IFOV) metres	79	30 metres in bands 1-5 and7 120 metres in band 6	High spatial resolution provides greater detail but lower classification accuracy
Pixel size on standard computer compatible tape (metres)	56 ×79	30×30 (all bands)	Data are resampled
Field of view (FOV) in degrees	11	17	Off-vertical view angle effects are evident
Grey levels	64	256	Possible due to improved radiometric accuracy
Number of detectors	6	16	Evidence of 16 line banding
Mirror recording mode	Forwards	Forwards and backwards	Reduces mirror speed and increases dwell time but causes processing problems
Computer compatible tapes per scene (1,600 bpi)	1	7	Awkward to handle

6.3 SPOT Satellite Series

The second generation of satellites for higher resolution (30 m or less) were launched during 1985 and later periods. The first one was the French Satellite SPOT (Systeme Probatoire de l' Observation de la Terre) which literally means the Earth Observation Test System. It was launched by French Centre National d Etudies Spatials (CNES) : Two launches have been made, namely SPOT 1 in 1985 and SOPT 2 in 1986. SPOT 1 is a near polar sun synchronous satellite at an altitude of 832 km and the orbit repeats the same area every 26 day. The Scanning is done by a new system, called the 'Push Broom' system, two of them with two tape recorders and telemetry equipment for transmision of data to earth. Unlike the moving/rotating mirror for scanning in LANDSAT, the Push Broom is actually a Linear Array with charged coupled devices and record each scan line at one go by means of a line of detectors, one detector for each area sampled on the ground.

The detectors are each controlled by micro chip and are so small that each of the 8 cm. long linear arrays carried by SPOT sensors contain 1728 detectors. There are, therefore, no moving parts. SPOT 1 records data in two modes, namely Panchromatic mode (wave length 0.51 to 0.73 μm) the ground resolution is 10 meters and in Multispectral mode, (green, red and near infrared) the resolution is 30 metres. The most important feature of SPOT series is the capacity to give stereoscopic view from its imagery. This is possible due to inclusion of a mirror in the optical path of the High Resolution Visible (HRV) Scanner which points to 27° either side of the ground track (See Fig. 6.14). This also enables a greater frequency of repetition than the normal 26 days.

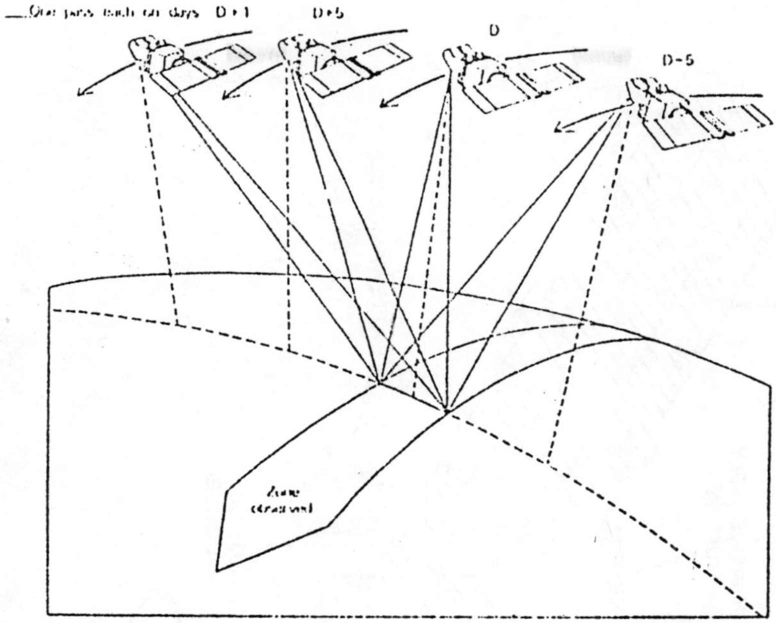

Fig. 6.14 : SPOT Stereo Coverage

Figure 6.15 gives the actual set up of the SPOT 1 & 2 system. Fig. 6.16 is an imagery obtained from SPOT 1 of New Delhi. The details like India Gate, Rashtrapati Bhavan and Connaught Place etc. are very clearly recognizable.

6.4 Indian Satellite Series

The Indian Remote Sensing Satellite IRS - 1A was launched in 1988 and successfully completed two years of successful operation on March 17, 1990. This satellite has covered the entire India more than 32 times and has provided with more than 200,000 imageries. IRS-1A has become a vital component in the national level projects like wasteland mapping, landuse mapping, forest mapping, agricultural crop acreage and yield estimation, integrated drought management, water resources management including ground water targetting, flood mapping and management, mineral resources exploration, ocean development including coastal monitoring and mapping of marine and inland fisheries potential.

The space craft (Fig. 6.17) Control Centre, located at Bangalore, alongwith ground station at Lucknow and Mauritius regularly track, monitor and control the space craft. The spacecraft orbit and altitude are precisely controlled to enable imaging of pre-specified scenes. IRS-1A carries two advanced imaging sensors, namely Linear Imaging Self Scanner (LISS-1 and LISS-II) and has sophisticated systems for high bit rate image transmission, autometic payload operation, driven deployable sun-tracking solar panels, three axis body stabilization employing dry tuned gyros, reaction wheels, scanning sensors and reaction control systems.

The data reception station of the National Remote Sensing Agency (NRSA) of India at Shadnagar

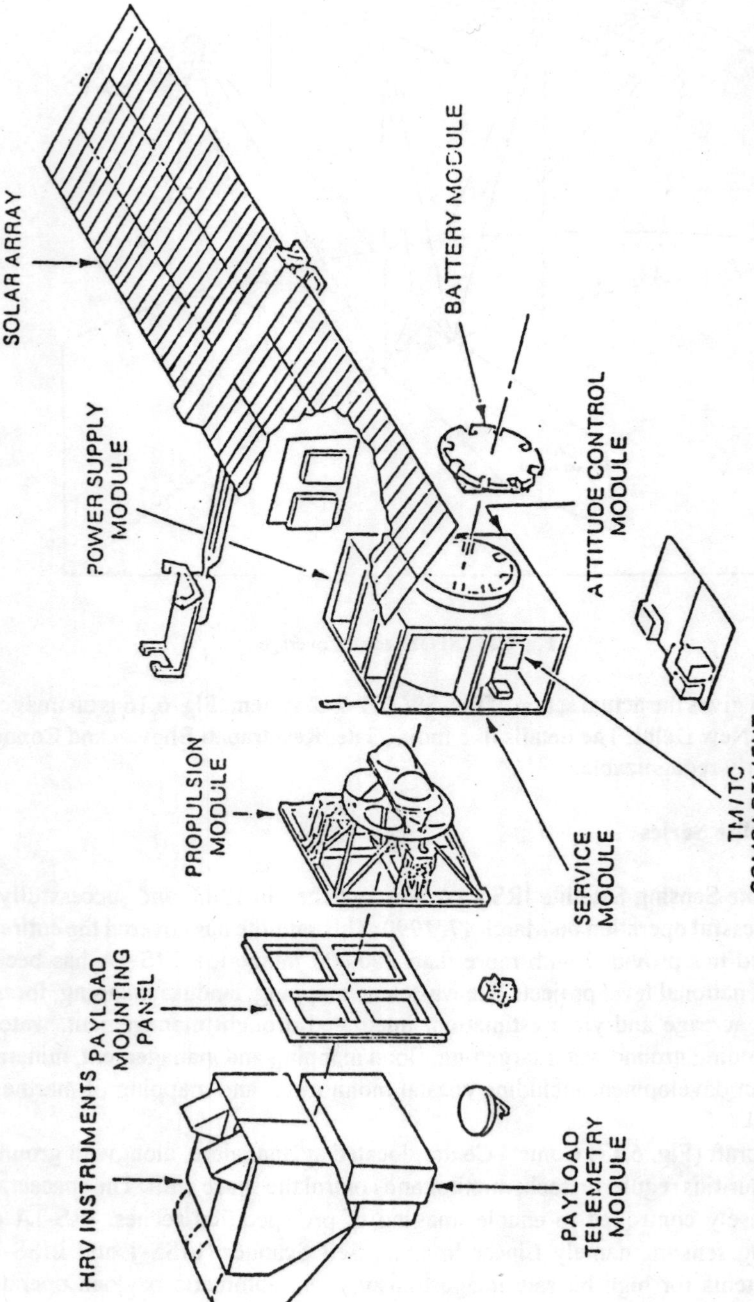

Fig. 6.15 : Set up of SPOT 1 and 2.

Fig. 6.16: SPOT Picture of New Delhi (*Courtesy* : French Embassy, New Delhi)

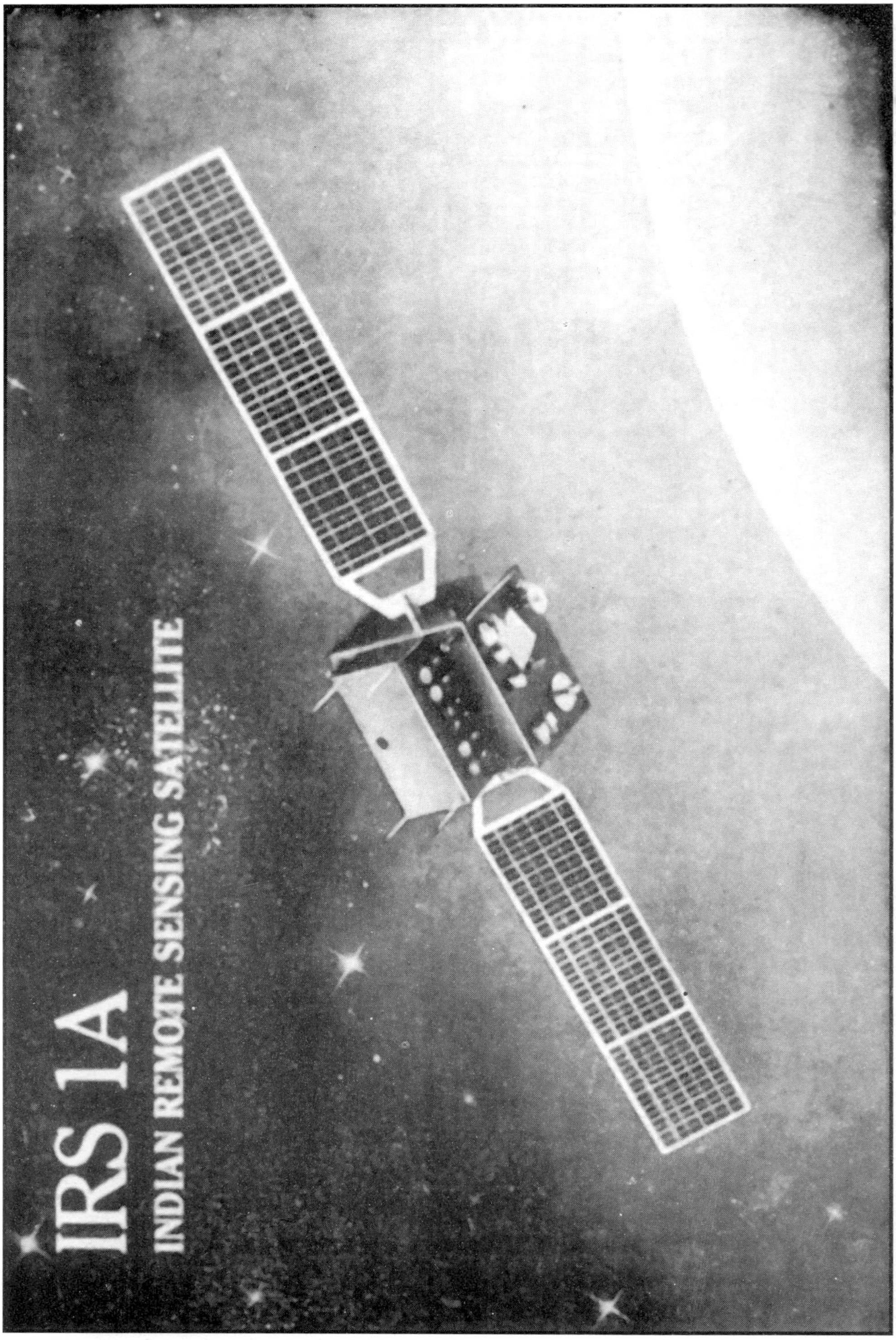

Fig. 6.17: Indian Remote Sensing Satellite IRS-1A

near Hyderabad receives the data from IRS -1A in S-Band and X Band. Data products generation is carried out at NRSA, Balanagar and at Space Application Centre (SAC) Ahmedabad.

The second satellite IRS-1B was successfully launched on Aug. 29, 1991 on board the Vostok launcher from Baikonur Cosmodrome in USSR and the satellite after testing started sending picutres on Sept 16, 1991. Some of the salient features of the satellite IRS-1B are:

Orbit Altitude	904 km (circular polar & sun-synchronous)
Repetition	22 days
Equator Crossing	10.30 am (Local Time)
Platform Control	3 axis body stabilised using reaction wheels, magnetic torque and reaction control system.
Spatial Resolution	72.5 m with LISS-1 and 36.25m with LISS-II
Swath	148 km with LISS-I and 74 km with LISS-II
Spectral Bands	Application
0.45-0.52 micrometer	Coastal water mapping and soil/vegetation differentiate
0.52 - 0.59 micrometer	Green reflectance of heavy vegetation
0.62-0.68 micrometer	Chlorophyll absorption of plants
0.77 - 0.86 micrometer	Biomass survey and water bodies
Radiometric Resolution	128 levels.

IRS-IC, launched on December 28th 1995, is India's second generation operational remote sensing satellite. LISS-III camera is one of the three sensors on IRS-IC.It provides multispectral data in four bands : Two in visible (0.52–0.59 and 0.62–0.68 microns), one in near infrared (NIR–0.77–0.86 microns) and one shortware infrared (SWIR 1.55–1.70 microns) region of electro magnetic spectrom. It has a spatial resolution of 23.5 m in visible and NIR region and 70.5 m in SWIR region.

A path row based full scene product covers an area of 141 × 141 km. A Shift Along Track (SAT) product is sapplied by sliding the scene in forward direction.

Fig. 6.18 and Fig. 6.19 show IRS-1A with LISS-II area of Ambala and Karnal and Dehra Dun respectively.

Several studies have been made for the utilization of LANDSAT and other satellite imagery for mapping on small scales. The general conclusion is that not only satellite imagery helps to map a given area very quickly on scales 1:1 million but also revision surveys can be carried for the existing small-scale maps. An enlargement up to four times has been possible without loss of detail for interpretation. Thus for maps on 1:250,000 scales the satellite imagery could be used without loss of accuracy especially when time is a great factor. Similarly in the region of the Great Himalayan territory with very rugged terrain, satellite imagery may be the only answer to the problem of mapping on small scale.

For the future it may not be too imaginative to say that the main data-collection machinery with small-scale and perhaps medium-scale maps will be a cartographic satellite. This satellite would be equipped to produce basic control data and at the same time produce high resolution imagery for topographic automatic mapping. The ground control would be obtained by means of ground-based Doppler masurements of satellite signals. Orthophotomaps would then be produced by automating mapping technique along with a complete digitization of the terrain in terms of X, Y and Z coordinates at closely spaced intervals which may be used for the production of slope or profile maps.

6.5 Miscellaneous Stellites

The Satellite systems described so far had one objective, namely, thematic mapping of earth's surface. There are have been and are being launched various other satellites such as for Weather and Environmental studies. Some of them are Polar and other Geostationary, that is, there orbits are such they appear stationary in space. This is possible due to the time of orbital motion being exactly equal to the earth daily rotation. They are aproximately 36000 km above the earth surface and cover practically the whole surface of the earth. Fig. 6.20 describes such system.

6.6 Weather Satellites

There are two types of weather satellites: Polar orbiting and Geostationary. Polar orbiting weather satellites provide global data. There are two now in orbit. (See Fig. 6.21)

Characteristics:
Orbit type: Near polar, sun-synchronous
Altitude (Circular): 854 km (530 mile.) morning satellite
833 km (518 mile.) afternoon satellite
Orbit Period: 100 minutes
Orbit Times (Equator.Crossing); 7:30 a.m local, morning satellite
2:30 p.m. local, afternoon satellite
Longitudinal separetion of adjacent orbits at the Equator: 821 km (510 mile) 25° longitude
Sensor Cross Track Scans:
Imager - 2800 km (1740 mile)
Sounder- 2347 km (1458 mile)

Geostationary weather satellites provide continuous viewing of the United States and adjacent coastal waters. Two in orbit.

Characteristics:
Altitude: 35,000 km (22, 300 mile)
Orbit Period: 24 hours
GOES East: 75° W covers ± 50° latitude and longitude around subsatellite point.
GOES West: 135°W covers ± 50° latitude and longitude around subsatellite point.

6.7 Tiros Polar–Orbiting Environmental Satellite

The TIROS satellites, which are labelled NOAA–A, –B, etc. before launch and NOAA–1, –2, etc. after successful launch, provide operational coverage of the entire Earth four times per day. They are a principal source of environmental data for the 80 per cent of the globe that is not covered by conventional data. The purpose of these satellites is to make measurements of temperature and humidity in the Earth's atmosphere, surface temperature, cloud cover, water-ice boundaries, and proton and electron flux near the Earth. They have a capability of receiving, processing and retransmitting data

Fig. 6.18: IRS–1A LISS 2 Image of Ambala and Karnal Area.
With Compliments from: Publications and Public Relations Unit, Indian Space Research Organisation, Department of Space, Bangalore.

Fig. 6.19: IRS–1A LISS-2 Image of Dehradun Area.
With Compliments from: Publications and Public Relations Unit, Indian Space Research Organisation, Department of Space, Bangalore.

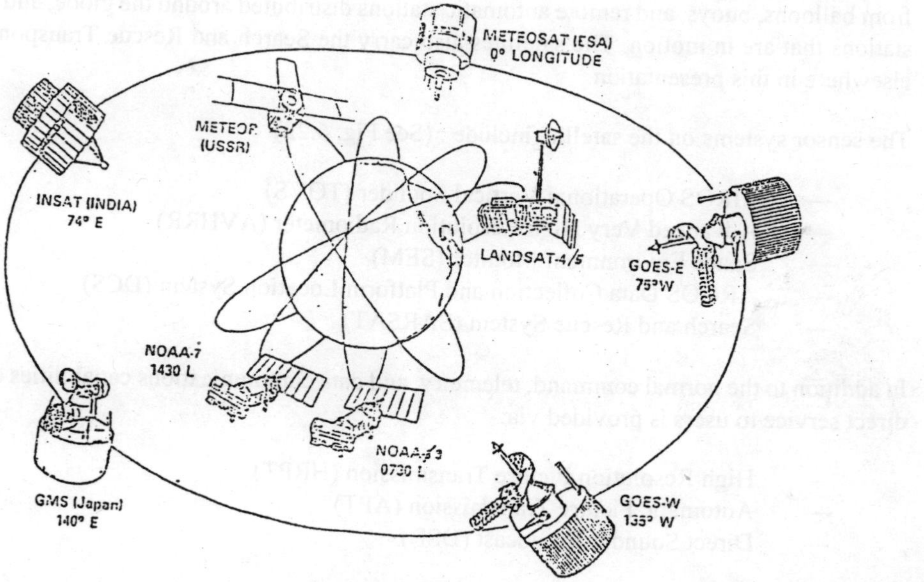

Fig. 6.20 : Operational Earth Observation Satellite

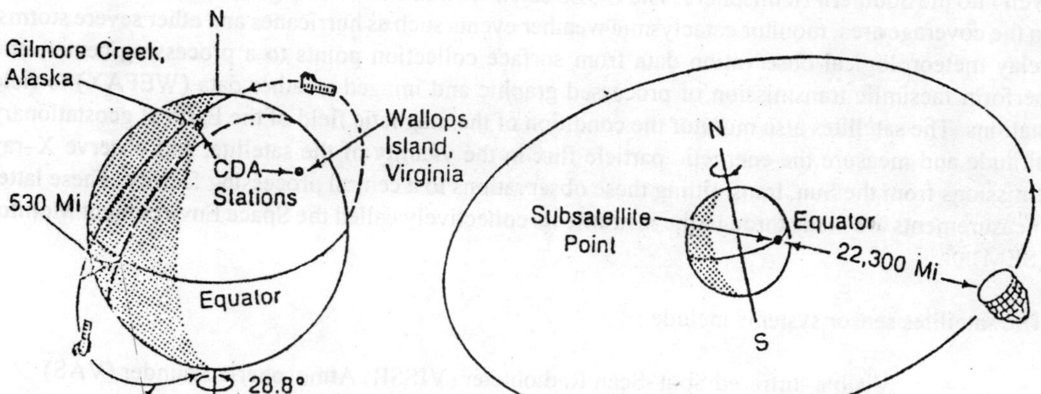

Fig. 6.21 : Polar Orbiting Satellite and Geostationary Satellites

from balloons, buoys, and remote automatic stations distributed around the globe, and can also track stations that are in motion. The satellites also carry the Search and Rescue Transponder described elsewhere in this presentation.

The sensor systems on the satellite include : (See Fig. 6.22)

- — TIROS Operational Vertical Sounder (TOVS)
- — Advanced Very High Resolution Radiometer (AVHRR)
- — Space Environment Monitor (SEM)
- — ARGOS Data Collection and Platform Location System (DCS)
- — Search and Rescue System (SARSAT)

In addition to the normal command, telemetry, and data communications capabilities of the satellite, direct service to users is provided via:

- — High Resolution Picture Transmission (HRPT)
- — Automatic Picture Transmission (APT)
- — Direct Sounder Broadcast (DSB)

6.8 Geostationary Operational Environmental Satellite (GOES)

Two GOES satellites (See Fig. 6.23) observe the Eastern and Western United States and the adjacent ocean areas from their vantage points over the Equator, but also have coverage zones which extend well into the Southern Hemisphere. The GOES satellites make day and night observations of weather in the coverage area, monitor cataclysmic weather events such as hurricanes and other severe storms, relay meteorological observation data from surface collection points to a processing center, and perform facsimile transmission of processed graphic and imaged weather data (WEFAX) to field stations. The satellites also monitor the condition of the magnetic field of the Earth at geostationary altitude and measure the energetic particle flux in the vicinity of the satellite, and observe X–ray emissions from the Sun, transmitting these observations to a central processing facility. These latter measurements are made through the instruments collectively called the Space Environment Monitor (SEM).

The satellites sensor systems include :

- — Visible–Infrared Spin–Scan Radiometer (VISSR) Atmospheric Sounder (VAS)
- — Space Environment Monitor (SEM)
- — Data Collection System (DCM)

The VISSR sensor provides operational day-night imaging of the Earth. When it operates in the VAS mode, it is providing experimental sounding measurements.
In addition to the normal communications functions, users can receive data directly from the satellite via:

- — VAS Direct Broadcast
- — Weather Facsimile service (WEFAX)
- — Search and Rescue Transponder (Beginning on GOES–G)

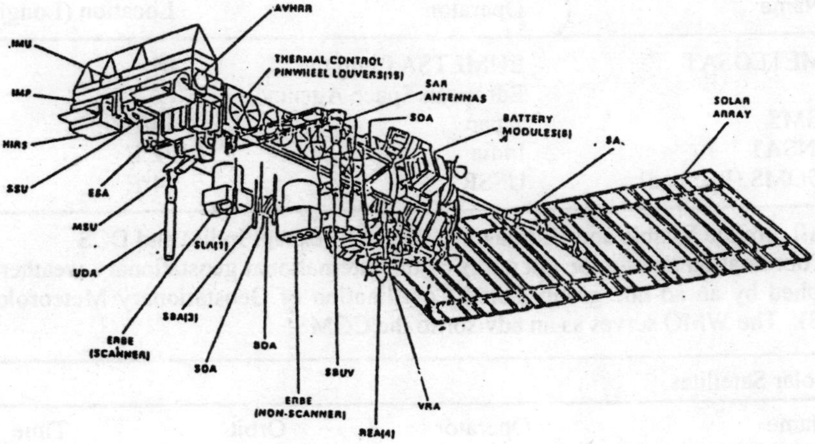

Fig. 6.22 : Advanced TIROS-IV Satellite Configuration

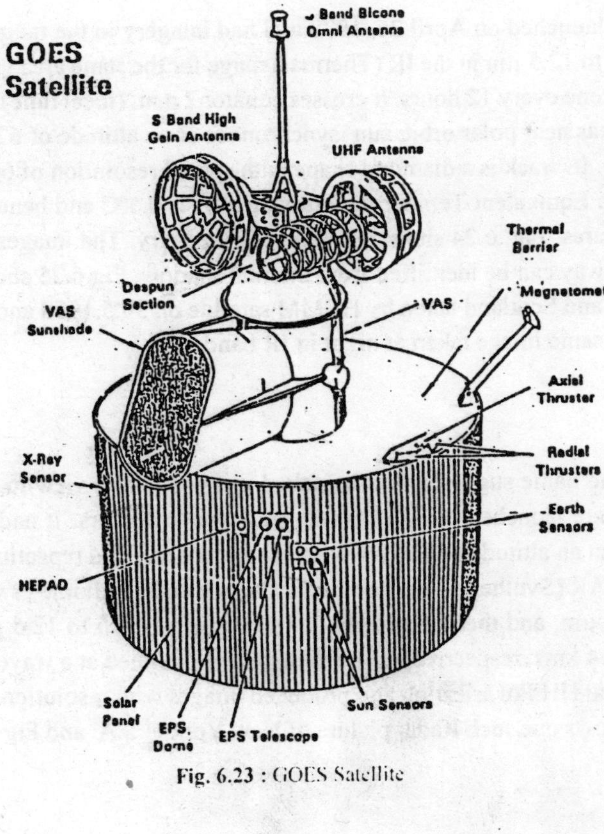

Fig. 6.23 : GOES Satellite

6.9 International Weather Satellites

Geostationary Satellites

Name	Operator	Location (Longitude)
METEOSAT	EUMETSAT and the European Space Agency	0°
GMS	Japan	140°E
INSAT	India	72°E
GOMS (Planned)	USSR	74°E

All provide Visible and IR Imagery, WEFAX (except India) and DCS

Coordination among the operators of the international geostationary weather satellites is accomplished by an ad-hoc group called Coordination of Geostationary Meteorological Satellites (CGMS). The WMO serves as an advisor to the CGMS.

Polar Satellites

Name	Operator	Orbit	Time
METEOR	USSR	900 km	1500 Local

6.10 Heat Capacity Mapping Mission (HCMM) Satellite

This satellite was launched on April 26, 1978 and had imagery in the range of 0.5 to 1.1 μm in the day time and 10.5 to 12.5 μm in the IR (Thermal) range for the same area in the night time. Hence it covers the same scene every 12 hours. It crosses equator 2 p.m. (local time) with its ascending mode south to north. It has near polar orbit, sun synchronous at an altitude of 620 km (385 miles) above the earth's surface. Its track is a diamond shape with spatial resolution of 600 m and scene width of 715 km. It's Noise Equivalent Temperature (sensitivity) is 0.3°C and hence can map out scenes at different temperatures. Fig. 6.24 shows one Thermal Imagery. The images of aircrafts which have left the airport runway can be identified from thermal shadow. Fig 6.25 shows day time imagery of Northern England and Scotland taken by HCMM satellite on 30.5.1978 and in the visible range and Fig 6.25 (b) is the same image taken at night in IR band.

6.11 Seasat

This satellite, as the name suggests, was launched in 1978 with a view to map the seas. It was an experimental satellite launched by NASA with microwave sensors. It had a circular but non–sun synchronous orbit at an altitude of 800 km with 14 orbits a day and repeating same scene every 152 days. It carried a SAR (Synthetic Aperture Radar) sensor and a radiometer which recorded imagery in the 0.47 to 0.94 μm, and thermal imagery in the range of 10.5 to 12.5 μm range with a spatial resolution of 2 and 4 kms. respectively. The SAR sensor operated at a wave length of 23.5 cm (L B and) with Horizontal HH Pol arization and produced images with resolution of 25 m with 100 km as swath. Fig. 6.26 shows one such Radar picture of New York U.S.A. and Fig. 6.27 shows a picture of Kedah Malaysia.

Fig. 6.24: A Thermal Sensor Picture

A thermal image of an airport. Warmer features are light-toned, Coal ones are dark. Note the numerous "shalows" of departed aircraft; the cement apron is cooler there. (*Courtesy* of Taxas Instruments, Inc.)

Fig. 6.25: Daytime imagery of Northern England and Scotland (IRS IA Indian Remote Sensing Satellite)

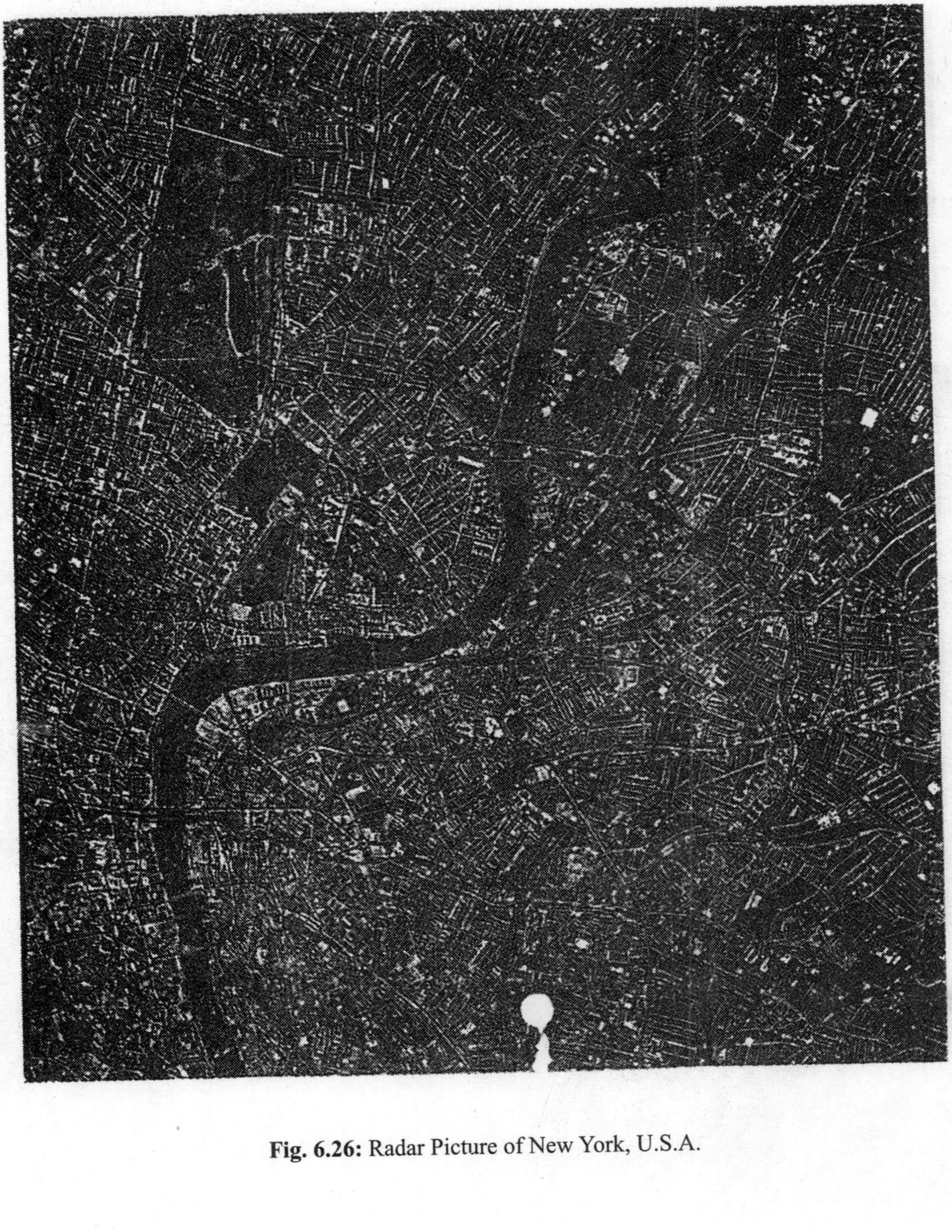

Fig. 6.26: Radar Picture of New York, U.S.A.

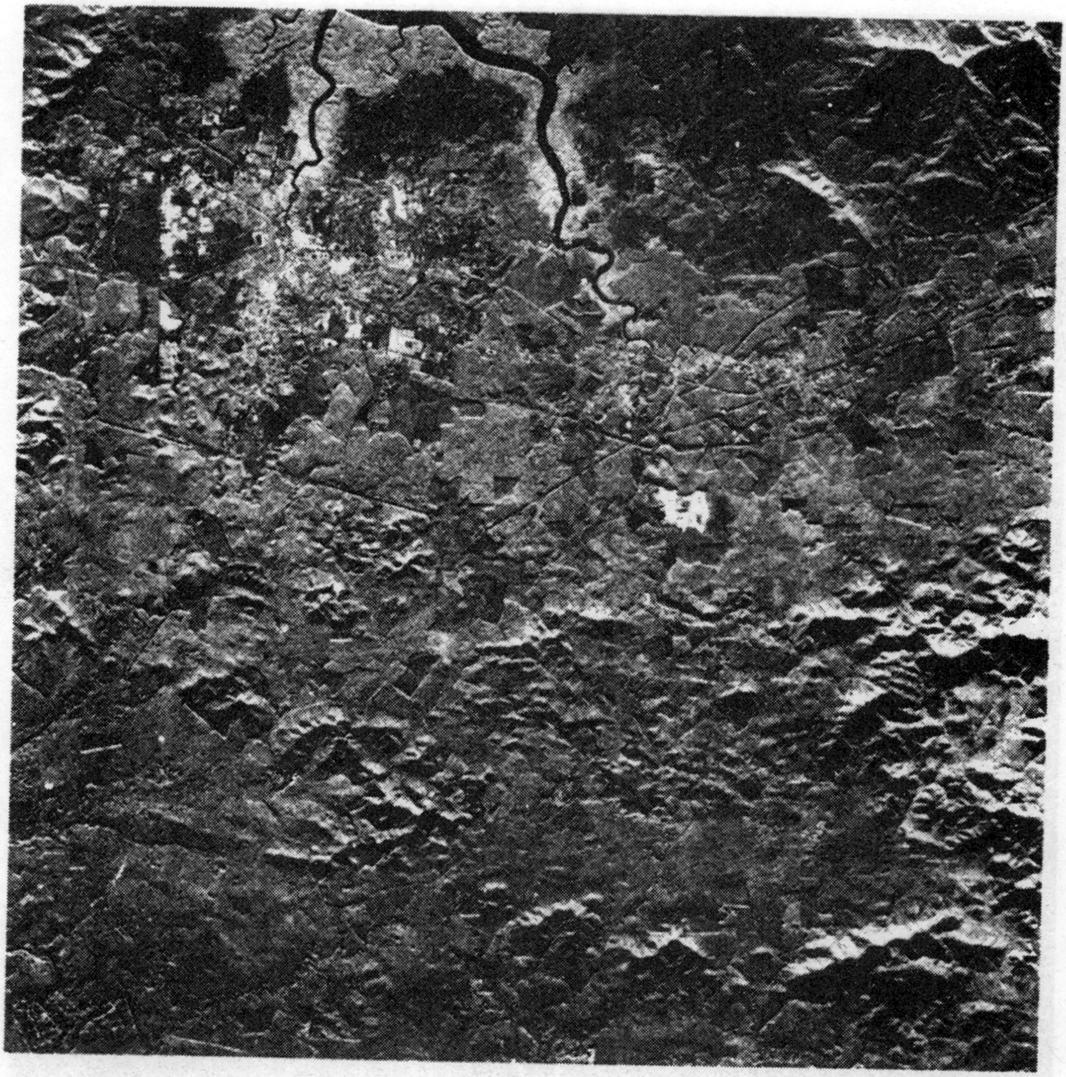

Fig. 6.27: Radar Picture of Kedah, Malaysia 1: 100, 000 Scale

BIBLIOGRAPHY

Aerial Discovery Manual, C. Strandberg Wiley, 1967.

Aerial Photo Ecology. John A. Howard, American Elsevier Publishing Co. New York 1970

Aerial Photographic Interpretation, D.R Lueder. McGraw-Hill Book Company, New York, 1959.

Aerial Photographs in Field Geology, L.H. Lattman & R. G. Ray, Holt, Rinehart & Winston, New York, 1965.

Aerial Photographs their use and Interpretation, A.J. Eardley, Harper & Brothers, New York, 1942.

Aerial Photographs and their Application, H.T.U.Smith D. Appleton Century Co., New York, 1943

Aerial Photo Interpretation in Classifying and Mapping Soils, U.S. D. A, SCS 1966.

Aerial Photo Interpretation, G. Sully Bellhaven House Ltd. 1970.

"*Aerial Photographs in Geological Interpretation and Mapping*" U.S. Geological Survey, Washington D.C Professional Paper No. 373.

Aero Geology, H.F Von Bundat, Gulf Publishing Co, Houston 1962.

Air Photo Analysis, J. Mollard, Bellhaven House Ltd. 1960

Air Photo Interpretation for Land Planning, D. Way, Harvard University Press, 1968.

Aerial Survey in Economic, Development, R. Hammond, American Elsevier Publishing Co. 1967.

An Introduction to Aerial Photography for Natural Resource Management. Oregon State University, 1975.

Assessment of Land Resources, M. Brunt, Directorate of Overseas Surveys, London, 1967.

Aerial Stereo Photographs, H. Warlen Hubbard Scientific Co. 1965.

Element of Photogrammetry, R.R. Wolf McGraw Hill, New York, 1974.

Interpretation of Aerial Photographs, T.E. Avery & G. L. Berlin, fourth edition, Burgess Publishing Co., 1985.

Interpretation of Aerial Photographs. 2nd Edition, Burgess Publishing Co. Minneapolis, 1968.

"Mannual of Photographic Interpretation " American Society of Photogrammetry and Remote Sensing, Falls Church Virginia U.S.A.

Multispectral Photography for Earth Resources. S.E. Wenderoth, E. Yost, West Hill Printing Co. 1972.

Optical and Photographic Reconnaissance Systems, N. N. Jensen, Wiley, New York, 1968.

Planning and Aerial Information, M. Branch, Harvard University Press, 1971

Photogrammetry and Photo Interpretation, S. Spurt Ronald Press, 1960.

Photo Geology and Regional Mapping, J.A.E.Allum Pergamon Press, New York, 1966.

Photo - Geology, V.C. Miller Mc-graw Hill Co., New York, 1961.

Remote Sensing in Geomorphology. H. Th. Verstappen, Elsevier Scientific Publishing Co. Netherlands, 1977.

Remote Sensing and Image Interpretation, Thomas M. Lillesand & Ralph W.Kiefer, John Wiley & Sons, 2nd edition 1989.

"Selected Aerial Photographs of Geological Features" U.S. Geological Survey, Professional paper No. 590.

The Physical Aspects of Aerial Photography, G.L. Brock, Dover Publications Inc. U.S.A. 1967.

A Short History of Photo Geology, J.F.M Mekel ITC Enschede, Netherlands, 1974.

Terrain Analysis: A Guide to Site Selection Using Aerial Photographic Interpretation. D. Way Dowden Hutchinson and Ron 1973.

The Use of Aerial Photographs in Geological Mapping. J.F.M Mekel I.T.C Enschede Netherlands, 1970.

Remote Sensing in Civil Engineering. edited, by I.J.M. Kennie & M.C Matheus, Surey University Press, Johny Wiley 1985.

INDEX

Index